**Tasty Jesus**

# Tasty Jesus

Liberating Christ from the Power of Our Predilections

Bryan F. Hurlbutt

Foreword by
J. P. MORELAND

RESOURCE *Publications* • Eugene, Oregon

TASTY JESUS
Liberating Christ from the Power of Our Predilections

Copyright © 2013 Bryan F. Hurlbutt. All rights reserved. Except for brief quotations in critical publications or reviews, no part of this book may be reproduced in any manner without prior written permission from the publisher. Write: Permissions, Wipf and Stock Publishers, 199 W. 8th Ave., Suite 3, Eugene, OR 97401.

Resource Publications
An Imprint of Wipf and Stock Publishers
199 W. 8th Ave., Suite 3
Eugene, OR 97401

www.wipfandstock.com

ISBN 13: 978-1-62032-915-3

Manufactured in the U.S.A.

For Jennifer

I am inexorably drawn to you. I feel the love of the Father in your hands, see the grace of Christ in your eyes, and hear the peace of the Spirit in your voice. You are my treasure who points me to the Great Treasure. I cannot thank you enough for the joy you bring to my life. This book is as much yours as it is mine.

# Contents

*Foreword* | ix

*Preface* | xi

Introduction | 1
1. Cream Puff Jesus: The Christ of Liberalism | 12
2. Deconstructing a Cream Puff | 37
3. No Carb Jesus: The Christ of Fundamentalism | 67
4. Enjoying the Fruitfulness of a Carbohydrated Christ | 91
5. Smorgasbord Jesus: The Christ of Postmodernism | 119
6. Giving Jesus the Freedom to Form His Own Menu | 146
7. Gourmet Jesus: The Christ of Prosperity Theology | 186
8. Feasting on the Rations of a Simple Savior | 214
9. Homogenized Jesus: The Christ of Evangelical Pop Culture | 239
10. Resting in the Relevance of a Disparate Christ | 261

Epilogue | 288

*Bibliography* | 291

# Foreword

JESUS OF NAZARETH STANDS at the center of history and current world culture. If you take a moment to reflect on this fact, it is actually quite bizarre. Nazareth, which I have seen, and out-of-the-way Galilee were far from the centers of influence in Jesus' day. Yet he spent thirty-some-odd years in the former and virtually his entire three-and-a-half year ministry in the latter. And, then, he was executed in Jerusalem in the same manner that a large number of other Jewish men were. Yet Jesus predicted that he would stand at the center of history, and it's hard to understand how it happened, especially compared to Plato, Einstein, Galileo, and Darwin. Hard, that is, unless he actually did miracles and rose from the dead! Still, Jesus would not make Time magazine's top one hundred list either of the smartest or most influential people of history. But facts are facts, in spite of what our cultural elite is willing to certify. As much as I pray for the "New Atheist" Richard Dawkins, unfortunately, he just doesn't get the right to state the actual facts of Western history.

Today, our culture is overrun with a variety of portraits of Jesus tailored to suit the personal preferences of different ideological tastes. Bible-believing academics have addressed these portraits, but their efforts have largely been limited to the scholarly world. But Bryan Hurlbutt's *Tasty Jesus* changes things. I have known Bryan for several years. I trust him. And I have great confidence in his insights about culture and ministry. He is an example of the scholar-pastor, having achieved solid academic degrees and a track record in pastoral ministry for sixteen years. Over my four decades of knowing Jesus, one thing had become evident to me: Academics are incredibly overrated. With rare and (thankfully) notable exceptions, as a group, they have little wisdom and almost nothing to say to the average person. If that is true, the natural question arises as to whom, exactly, can speak helpfully to us? I think the answer is obvious, even if it is not acknowledged at Harvard or on the latest version of the national news: pastors. Yes, pastors!! It doesn't take a rocket scientist to recognize that, for millennia, it has been Christian leaders—specifically, pastors—who have fulfilled this role.

That is why I am moved and strengthened by this book. To be sure, it is an excellent and timely presentation of the real Jesus against the backdrop of rival, contemporary versions. But, besides that, it is written by a pastor. Consequently, this book demands to be read not only because of its content—which is considerable—but also because of the role-modeling of its author. Read and think very carefully about the pages to follow.

J. P. Moreland
Yorba Linda, California
August 2013

# Preface

THIS BOOK IS BIRTHED out of my passion for Christ and his Bride. I love them both. And my hope is that reading this causes others to find a greater desire for Jesus and a greater dedication to the church. I firmly believe that the local church is the hub of God's kingdom. So if theology is to be preserved and God is to be honored and people are to be loved, it will be the local church that leads the way. In order to do that, some culturally appealing portraits of Jesus need to be exposed and torn down. The goal of this book is to help equip the reader to do just that.

This book exists because I pastor a church of people at Lifeline Community who don't want to rot their teeth on Tasty Jesus. It exists because my love for them stirs me to teach and disciple them to be aware of his various forms and flavors. It exists because they have loved me well as their shepherd and permitted me the opportunity to write and share these thoughts with others. I am very thankful for my Lifeline family. It is a joy serve and be served by them.

A special thanks to John Smith who, after enduring a motorcycle accident, poured hours into editing and formatting this manuscript. I thank God for you brother. Also, much thanks to Tom Stroman for taking the time to perform a conscientious proofread of the manuscript. Any remaining errors in the text are all mine. This book does not go forward without either you! Also thanks to Christian Amondson and the staff at Wipf and Stock for moving this project forward.

I want to thank my fellow elders and pastoral staff at Lifeline. Your support and prayers through this process have meant the world to me. Laboring with you in compassion for the church has been a privilege. Our camaraderie is a special grace to me. Brad, Darren, Bill, Eric, and Myke: Thanks for guarding the Bride. Also special thanks to my administrative assistant Mary Ann. Your faithfulness and competence are a real blessing.

Much thanks to J. P. Moreland for his input into my life and ministry. His model of a first-rate scholar with an irrepressible love for the local church has been a great encouragement to me. Thanks for being God's instrument to remind me that the Spirit is alive and well.

Several close pastor friends have provided encouragement and fellowship along the way. Jeff Bucknam (a real life mega-church pastor) and Kyle "the Dawdler" Meeker walked with me through doctoral studies and made the journey an absolute blast. God has used you both to sharpen me. Cory Anderson, my confidant and accountability partner, your investment in my life and loyal friendship have kept my hands to the plow even when I thought they might slip. "Thank you" is insufficient.

Thanks to my mother who has never wavered. Her relentless pursuit of the One who purchased her has left me thirsty for the same. Thank you for showing me that the race of faith is well worth the run. Thanks to my father for staying on the anvil even when the hammer has hit rather hard. May Christ's grace carry you.

I am blessed to be the father of three amazing girls. My life is an ocean of estrogen, and I love every minute of it! My prayer is that they grow rooted in a love for the Christ of Scripture and possess a deep affection for the local church. Brynne, may God take your passionate spirit and let it soar in his kingdom. Reghan, may God take your sensitive heart and let it yearn to know him above all else. Tierney, may your boundless energy be poured out for the One who loves you above all.

My wife literally made this book a reality. Without her commitment to create time for me to write and her dedication as a mom and ministry partner I could not have finished it. If anyone's fire to get this written burned hotter than my own it has been hers. Jennifer, you are my best friend. Your love for me, with all of my failings, gives me hope that maybe the church can love its flawless Groom with similar virtue.

Lastly, to God who found me on a dead-end road in a sleepy, upstate-New York town, who has lifted my head more times than I can remember, whose grace has never been impotent to see me through, may your name be praised and may your character never be misrepresented by our personal predilections.

Bryan Hurlbutt
West Jordan, Utah
August, 2013

# Introduction

*I love the Church, O God! Her walls before Thee stand,*
*Dear as the apple of Thine eye and graven on Thy hand.*
*For her my tears shall fall, for her my prayers ascend;*
*To her my cares and toils be given till toils and cares shall end.*

TIMOTHY DWIGHT

A FRIEND OF MINE is a commercial airline pilot. I asked him to work out some aviation figures for me. I wanted to see if I started a trip on an airplane and was one degree off-course at the outset of my trip from the target point of my destination how far away from it would I land. Here is what he calculated for me. If I were going from Los Angeles International Airport (LAX) to John F. Kennedy International (JFK) in New York City I would miss the airport by forty-three miles. If I were going instead from LAX to London, I would miss London by ninety-five miles. If I were making a trip around the circumference of the world back to the place I started (LAX), I would miss it by five hundred miles. And if I were traveling to the moon (depending on my precise starting point) I would miss the moon by approximately 4,800 miles! Getting off course early on clearly can really screw things up, especially if you think it has little-to-no impact on your destination. My pilot friend added in his response to me the following statement: "Flying without GPS is challenging." I am sure it is. While I am no aviator I can appreciate the value of staying on course. One degree makes a lot of difference and distance only multiplies error. This is true for pretty much anything, and theology is no exception. The further off-line we start, and the further away from the actual events we get, the more difficult it becomes to return to an accurate course. Before takeoff we might borrow a question from the old absurd comedy movie *Airplane* and ask: "What's our vector Victor?"

According to the Bible, getting Jesus right is quite literally a matter of life and death. In fact, in an important Pauline text and in a text from the pen of the apostle John, the importance of an accurate Christology is emphasized well beyond its cognitive impact. For Paul and John, getting the identity of Jesus correct is the difference between heresy and orthodoxy, right and wrong, heaven and hell. Just as taking off in an aircraft one degree in the wrong direction can put you in the ocean rather than on the landing strip, so starting wrong on your identification of Jesus can land you in a spiritual abyss.

The closest thing to an ongoing conversation between the early church and apostolic leadership is found in the letters to the Corinthians. There are two extant letters from Paul to the church at Corinth in our Bible. However, through careful study, we know that these two are actually letters number two and four in an interchange that had at least four letters sent from Paul to the Corinthians.[1] In his final letter to them, Paul gets to the heart of his concern about false teachers that are attempting to infiltrate the ranks. In 2 Corinthians 11:3–4 he states:

> But I am afraid that as the serpent deceived Eve by his cunning your thoughts will be led astray from a sincere and pure devotion to Christ. For if someone comes and proclaims another Jesus than the one we proclaimed, or if you accept a different gospel from the one you accepted, you put up with it readily enough.

These false teachers were preaching a "different" Jesus. For Paul this allegiance to an aberrant view of Jesus was demonic and threatened to take them away from a "sincere and pure devotion to Christ." This text teaches us something important: Sincerity of worship does not make up for false content. These teachers got the person and work of Jesus wrong, and no matter how much they claimed they were teaching and preaching the real Jesus, they weren't, because the essential attributes and the essential acts of Jesus need to be rightly understood and rightly labeled to truthfully say it is in fact the Jesus of the Gospels. Paul would not permit them to make Jesus malleable to their intentions and ideas.

1. Throughout 1 Corinthians 5:9 Paul refers to a previous letter of his. And in 2 Corinthians 2:3–4 Paul refers to a letter he wrote that was rather severe in its rebuke. The nature of this letter doesn't fit 1 Corinthians, and so it seems apparent that there were at least four correspondences two of which (the second and the fourth we have). And they are canonized as 1 and 2 Corinthians.

The Apostle John's concern and affection for the church and his fidelity to Jesus pour out in a short letter he wrote that has been included in the Bible as 2 John. It is a letter that is all about the local church. Just catch the phraseology of the first two verses:

> The elder to the elect lady and her children, whom I love in the truth, and not only I, but also all who know the truth, because the truth abides in us and will be with us forever (2 John 1–2).

There are a few vital things to note here. First, John identifies himself as a local church leader. Second, he appeals with the felt warmth of domestic metaphors. Third, he expresses his ministry motivation as rooted in two concepts: love and truth. It is this last observation that establishes the focus of John's words in this little epistle. His ethical thrust is clear. He wants them to "love one another" (2 John 5), and he understands this to be accomplished by exercising a fidelity to God in keeping his ethical commands which has love at its apex. But the occasion for the letter is a threat to his readers' fulfillment of this virtue of love, and it comes in the form of an attack on the truth. It is this intersection between disposition and doctrine, between ethos and logos that forms the crux of the issue on multiple misinterpretations of Christ. I am convinced that this problem must be practically dealt with for the church to embrace the right Jesus and exemplify that Jesus rightly.

The threat for John's audience was an adherence to a deviant Christology that saw Jesus as not really being a man. It was a seminal or incipient gnostic idea called "docetism" which taught that Jesus was divine but did not really take on the trappings of human flesh. So John is warning the church against falling prey to a christological error that redefines the essence of Jesus because he is convinced that to do so—or even to welcome those who do so—would be to lose ground. That is why in 2 John 8 he says, "Watch yourselves, so that you may not lose what we have worked for, but may win a full reward."

"Watch yourselves!" That is what this book is about. It is about corporate introspection. I am trying to meddle in the ideological hallways of local churches, in pastors' studies, in elder board meetings, in youth department discussions, in children's ministry planning meetings and in denominational leadership venues. "Watch yourselves!" I want us to get all of Jesus right and let the church fly its course without turning to the right or to the left. "Watch yourselves!" I want teachers to think twice and thrice before they describe Jesus to the church and tell the church what Jesus wants them to do.

"Watch yourselves, so that you may not lose what we have worked for." John's concern is mine. We—meaning him and his fellow apostles and today I might add countless individuals throughout the history of the church—have worked toward holding fast to an orthodox vision of Jesus, his life and doctrine, and the church as his Bride. If we, today, do not pay attention we stand to "lose what we have worked for." So it is our job as Christians whether we are church leaders, vocational ministers or lay people to make sure that we "abide in the teaching of Christ" (2 John 9). Scholars wrestle with whether this phrase means the teachings of Jesus or the teachings about Jesus. While I am inclined, because of context, to see it as the latter, it is of relatively small importance because Jesus taught us about who he is. So whether we are thinking in terms of Jesus' teachings or apostolic teachings about him we will arrive at the same point, which is basically: "Get Jesus right."

Aberrant views of Jesus do not come down to us on storks. They emerge out of theological and philosophical confusion and are fueled by cultural reactions. In this milieu of philosophy, theology, and culture there are spiritual forces at work that accentuate and exacerbate the ideas and the tensions. All of this makes for creeds and conjectures that are what they are because a past story of information and individuals formed ideas the way they did. So the history of ideas and the preferences of varied cultures meld to produce, in this case, christological cameos that end up dictating enormous aspects of Christian faith and practice. In fact, it is safe to say the historical Jesus, while suffering no personal identity crisis, has been refabricated so much that a snapshot of western culture today could drive us into a spiritual seizure at all of the images posting at random before the mind.

This affectation for different visions of Jesus, coupled with the individualism of western intellectual history, has immersed us in a quandary of literally biblical proportions. Jesus now comes in so many shapes, styles, and flavors—and carries with him all sorts of political agendas, doctrinal creeds, and humanitarian perspectives—that it seems he (whoever "he" is) cannot be found. Is Jesus liberal or conservative? Is he hippie-minded? Is he hipster cool? Is he loaded with money or poor and needy? Is he communal or a maverick? Is he manly or effeminate? Is he a warrior or a peacekeeper? Is he consumed with right doctrine or right living? Is he defined by justice or mercy? Is he angered more by corporate evil or personal evil? Is he concerned with cultural relevance or historical fidelity? Is he God, providing redemption—or man, providing a role model?

On the face of it these are questions about Jesus' identity, but the process in getting to that identification is fraught with its own queries. What type of hermeneutic is necessary? How does history unfold? What role does culture play in looking at ideas and people? Who gets to say who Jesus is? Are the differences of interpretation substantively a matter of emphasis or are they emphatically a matter of substance? What role does Christology play in theology? What role does an orthodox Christ play in replicating an orthoprax Jesus? In other words, it is simply not enough to know what is off course, but we must also be able to determine where and why we went off course.

## Who Holds the Compass?

Unfortunately most Christians in the west today possess gross overconfidence in their own mental capacities and hold serious suspicion of other minds. They envision themselves as spiritual Eagle Scouts with biblical compass in hand ready to pick their way through the forest of fallen ideas and arrive at the shores of enlightenment. In this regard our present intellectual culture shows us to be the ideological children of Cartesian rationalism, filled with the personal subjectivism of Hume, possessing the prophetic cynicism of Nietzsche. We are sure of ourselves and skeptical of everyone else. We are desperate for relationship but despise accountability. We long for God but wish he would leave us alone. In truth, we are lost, and, while the reasons for it may take on a different rhyme, our disorientation has been present since the garden.

So who holds the compass that can lead us back? If we are wayfarers what has God provided to show the way? The answer to that is three-fold. First, he has given us the *Scripture*. However to stop there (as many do today) is to fail to account for the other resources God has distributed liberally for our direction. Additionally he has given us the *Holy Spirit*. We are told in John 16:13a that "When the Spirit of truth comes, he will guide you into all truth." So is it enough to say that a human who has the Spirit and the Scripture can navigate the world with precision? I think there is yet a third element to providing a holistic answer to the question of the compass for right thinking and right living and that is the *church*.

For some, whom I would call protestant-Protestants (Protestants injected with the steroids of individualism and either modernism or postmodernism, pick your poison), this smacks of Roman Catholic or Eastern Orthodox baggage. It elicits images of a tightly wound ecclesiastical system with top-down controls and privatized knowledge that keeps people under its corporate thumb. However, the look of pioneer Protestantism with its independent spirit and anti-authoritarian bent is a long way from the vision of the Reformers themselves who responded to the parochial machine of the late medieval period.

John Calvin, the most defining theologian of the Reformation, reflected on the Apostle Paul's words to a young pastor about the role of the church in 1 Timothy 3:15. Calvin wrote:

> It is of no small importance that it is called "the pillar and ground of the truth" and "the house of God." By these words Paul means that the church is the faithful keeper of God's truth in order that it may not perish in the world. For by its ministry and labor God willed to have the preaching of his Word kept pure and to show himself the Father of a family, while he feeds us with spiritual food and provides everything that makes for our salvation.[2]

Notice that for Calvin the church is the guardian of the purity of Scripture. It is the "faithful keeper of God's truth." And so the church serves as the institution that God chose to minister and labor on his behalf in order to guide his people to a right understanding of his word. It absolutely is "the pillar and ground of the truth" (KJV).

It is therefore my strong conviction that God instituted the church in general and the local church in particular to be the flag bearer of his kingdom agenda. Since Christology stands at the center of any belief system that tries to take on the moniker "Christian" then it is incumbent that the church gets Jesus right. If Christ is to be correctly perceived then his Bride must be prepared to propositionally and personally know him. But here is the rub: Christ is not and can never be understood in a narrative vacuum. He is always viewed from a place riddled with ideas, apparitions, folklores, customs, traditions, social structures and mores, collective attitudes, and communicative conventions. In other words, Jesus always bumps into culture.

Much has been made of how the church relates to culture. The defining work, written over sixty years ago, was *Christ and Culture* by

---

2. Calvin, *Institutes of the Christian Religion*, 4.1.10.

H. Richard Neibuhr. Books written on the subject subsequent to it are largely geared toward interacting with Neibuhr's five descriptive models for how culture and Christ collide. My intent is not to add to this body of literature but instead to specify five cultural Jesuses that have come to us through the sluice pipe of history, assess them, and give some thoughts as to what the local church can do to stem their tide in the marketplace of ideas. Ultimately this is a book about the fact that the church can be an agent of cultural transformation, but it will take christological and ecclesiological acumen coupled with cultural awareness to do it.

## Summary of Chapters

This book breaks down into five couplets that survey five of the most significant christological malformations present in the western world. As an American pastor, I am uniquely attuned to the issues faced in the United States when it comes to our present church's propensity for shallow pragmatism. As a theologian and student of the history of ideas I also understand that these fallacious pictures of Jesus are polyphyletic in nature. That is to say, they come to us through a line of different ideas and stories down through our western intellectual heritage. It is absolutely crucial on several fronts that we understand what these "Christs" look like, and how they got here. First, we won't know how to really deal with them if we can't pinpoint where they went wrong. Second, we won't take the differences seriously if we don't realize the danger that each Jesus represents. Third, we won't take our role in the kingdom seriously if we don't realize that it is in our hands as stewards of God's kingdom to think and act in ways that reflect the truth about his Son. And fourth, we simply need to stop being so superficial when it comes to knowing Jesus and seek to both know and know why we know.

The first couplet looks at the Christ of theological liberalism. Chapter 1 looks at how a Jesus bereft of deity and supernatural capacity came to be the standard for many religious people. The chapter is also concerned with what forms the subtext of this perspective. The second chapter articulates what the local church needs to do about this Jesus. It is a chapter about re-deifying Jesus and not giving into the pseudo-intellectualism of largely naturalistic thinkers.

The second couplet looks at the Christ of Christian fundamentalism. I personally have some warm-hearted forbears in this community, and so I find a special interest in its assessment and a heightened awareness to its subtle but insidious dangers. In the third chapter I trace its developments and look at some of its key ambassadors. We will also note some of its problems and come to see that its doctrinal interest and zeal for truth have a way of blinding it to the real purpose of doctrine and the actual point of truth altogether. In the response chapter to this assessment of fundamentalism (Chapter 4) I chart a course for the local church to rectify the rigidity of this Jesus and suggest some practical tools for doing so.

In chapter 5 and chapter 6 a rather elusive Jesus is discussed: the Christ of postmodernism. Specifically of interest is the Jesus adopted by the emergent church movement. The inconspicuous relativism amidst the genuine and biblical concern for authentic community informs this vision of Jesus that has, over the last twenty years, been recalibrating North American and European church life. Similar to the other couplets, chapter 5 is intended to recount the influences credited with the formation of this portrait and show some of its dangerously appealing properties. Chapter 6 articulates how we can respond carefully, critically, and kindly to this vision. This chapter is especially concerned with the concept of "community" and provides a response to the appeals of emergent thought.

The fourth couplet feels a little odd on the face of it. In chapter 7 and chapter 8 I look at the Christ of prosperity theology. At the intellectual level this Jesus seems as though he could be dismissed. However, millions of people have thrown themselves before this Christ with little to no thought of the implications of such whimsy. In the assessment portion I show the ideological connections from modern day practitioners all the way back to seminal beliefs cropping up in the second and third centuries. How we deal with this Jesus is deeply a matter of Christian discipleship, and in chapter 8 I propose a direction for the church to take this area of discipleship.

The final Jesus is a challenging one to deal with because it feels like we have to extract him from the epicenter of our cultural motifs. He is at once so obvious that he can be clearly seen, but so entrenched that it is difficult to uproot him even when we know he is present. He is the Christ of evangelical pop-culture. His devotees go on K-Love music cruises, eat Bible Bars and Scripture Cookies, and hand out Testamints. Their kids play with Bible Man, Bibleopoly, and Bible Pictionary. They wear Jesus jewelry and Jesus junk, and their boss is a Jewish Carpenter.

So what's the problem? In chapter 9 I show that you can be so consumed with being relevant that you miss the very heart of your target. And in chapter 10 we look at how Christology can be rescued from being trite and cliché and how the church can take the reins in not accommodating a shallow and spurious Jesus.

Some readers may come to the end and wonder where the real Jesus is. They may wonder why I haven't taken a couple of chapters to develop a fuller Christology (although I do clearly develop one). The short answer is that my intent is to form what one might call an antithetical theology of Jesus and a practical theology of his church. My hope is that by describing who Jesus is not and what his church ought and ought not be, we can get a more clear sense of both the real Christ and the real church. My desire is that in the prescriptive details of each response chapter we will see what a community with a robust Christology is supposed to look and act like. Because we are a community of Christians, Christology and ecclesiology are indelibly linked. To be the people of Christ is to live communally in the *personal* knowledge of him rooted in the right *propositional* knowledge about him. This is the end for which I write.

## A Word about the Motif

There is a quote that gets variously attributed to Pascal or Mark Twain that goes something like "God created man in his own image and man returned the favor." This is a favorite quote of atheists because they import it into Freud's Projection Theory[3] (that God is a projection of humans longing for a fatherly connection) even though it does not fit. The problem is not that the existence of God is a creation of man, but that the nature of the God we worship is often defined by what we would like him to be. In fact C. S. Lewis pointed out that one of the great evidences for the reality of the God of the Bible is that he is not at all the kind of deity that we would fashion for ourselves. I think this is particularly true of God the Son as well.

---

3. Freud's theory was actually borrowed from Ludwig Feuerbach. It taught that the idea of God was a "projection" of individual psychological longings for an ideal father figure. Freud had no controlled data or psychoanalytic observations for his theory. Rather it served as a means for him to use his platform to advance an untested idea. Needless to say, it was decisively turned on its head in a book by NYU scholar Paul Vitz called *Faith of the Fatherless*.

Jesus has taken on so many cultural facelifts that one of the great dilemmas we face is getting back to who he really is. Is he a guru Jesus who speaks in mysterious antinomies? Is he a mountain adventure Jesus that would like us all to quit our jobs, follow our passions, and come alive to what we were made for? Is he a hipster Jesus with black-rimmed glasses and skinny jeans who reads on his six-hundred-dollar tablet, drinks a five-dollar latte, and tells everyone through his blog that they should feed the homeless? Does he look like Rob Bell, Mark Driscoll, John Piper, Dallas Willard, John Shelby Spong, Cornel West, or (God forbid) Bryan Hurlbutt? The truth is no one is permitted to make him in their (or anyone's) image because he just is. However, we subsist as people with deep proclivities, one of which is to make Jesus suit our tastes. This is true when it comes to the most trivial aspects of pop culture, and when it comes to the most treasured aspects of our personal worldview. It is out of this enormous problem that Tasty Jesus comes to life. We can now join the '80s electronic music group Depeche Mode and have our own "Personal Jesus."

I chose "Tasty" Jesus because in addition to the conundrum of Christology being held hostage by our preferences, I really like food and thought it would be an apt metaphor to utilize in creatively exposing the issue. Similar to cuisine, Jesus gets sampled, like cheese and crackers from a kind old lady running a booth at Sam's Club or Costco. He gets cut up and served out in disparate parts. As a result people make him out to be entirely like the part they tasted. Jesus then gets an overhaul and ends up looking like the people who picked him up off the shelf. This is our problem at present. Both Jesus and the church, as perceived in the West, are subjected to the individual tastes of present ideological palates.

## Who Is This Book For?

I am writing for the church. I am writing for people in the body that care about the direction that their local church goes. I am writing for people who have seen that ideas indeed have consequences, and who realize that discourse at the ideological level is crucial to the formation of our attitudes and our actions. I am writing for church leadership, for those individuals whose role it is to guard the faith once entrusted to the saints (Jude 3). My hope is that out of the descriptions of these false Christs and my proposed prescriptions for dealing with them we can keep the Bride of Christ on course. Where Jesus goes his Bride will follow. So getting him right is definitive for our lives as participants in his church. As you read I hope that you take care to consider both from whence these Jesuses have come and where they are going. I hope you prayerfully process how God might want you to stand in holy love championing a correct portrait of Christ and his Bride.

# 1

## Cream Puff Jesus

### The Christ of Liberalism

*The Bible is both inspired and covered with human fingerprints—but the Bible is not what we worship. The God to which the Bible points us is what we worship, and the claim of the first followers of Jesus was not that he was God, but rather that he revealed the fullness of God at work in a human being.*

ROBIN MEYERS

MY MOTHER-IN-LAW IS AN extraordinary cook. She does with a spatula what fairy godmothers do with wands. She moves it here and waves it there, tosses in a dash of this and a dab of that and—*bibbity bobbity boom!*—a delicious delight springs to life and flour lies like fairy dust all about. When I am fortunate enough to be around her I like to take part in the fruits of her labor and eat my fill. (Okay, so it's not just when I am around her, but that's not the point.) My visits to the in-laws often mean two things for my diet: first, I will be in food-heaven for a week or so; and second, my caloric intake is going to take a serious hit. Oh, make no mistake, I'll enjoy it all right. But, I'll enjoy too much of it, and I'll start seeing the margin between the two numbers on my jeans size widening. That's never good. So I've got to be careful and do what I am not predisposed to do: to eat for sustenance more than I do for pleasure. I need to be a calorie counter rather than a calorie container. My problem, like most people in the western world, is that I am more driven by the taste of the food than by the truth about the food. The last thing I want to hear as I am watching the game and downing my favorite chips or ice cream is how many calories each serving has. Truth is not exactly on my radar screen as I tickle my taste buds and satiate my momentary urges with recreational snacking that ultimately pollutes my body and leaves me less satisfied and more wanting than when I started indulging. If only such self-indulging vices were limited to our physical diets! But, the hard and more dangerous fact is: *they are not.*

Unhealthy ideologies pollute the soul just like unhealthy food pollutes the body. And, tragically, just like the unhealthiest of foods are often the most savory, so are some of the most toxic of ideas that contaminate the soul the most delightful to our thoughts and feelings. They only ask of our wills that which we already desire to give. This fact rears its head and licks its chops when we come to the subject matter of the theologically liberal vision of Jesus. I would characterize this vision as a cream puff, a Jesus devoid of his deity and vacated of his supernatural power. This Christ has little to offer the church and less to offer the world.

The subject of this chapter ought to be of great concern to every thinking Christian that values their spiritual heritage and holds biblical orthodoxy with any sort of vigor. However, my fear, quite frankly, is that we are content to let the contemporary apostles of a liberal Jesus roam about preaching and proclaiming their christological cream puff and simply leave the rebuttals in the charge of seminary-level academics. While I have great regard for and have learned much at the knees of these great minds, I have grown weary of the local church's inability to stand for truth intelligently amid the poisons of our culture. The local church is the institution that God has chosen to use in advancing his kingdom. But that advancement is being halted by the ineptitude of Bible-believing local church leaders and attendees to respond to the repeated hijackings of their savior and redeemer. Enough is enough! In this particular case, the Bride of Christ must clearly and resolutely defend the honor of her groom as he is made out to be a spiritually benign social reformer more interested in rejecting political oppression under Caesar than proclaiming eternal reconciliation with God; or, a sage whose pithy guru-like wisdom serves as a sort of ancient life coach on society's tumultuous seas. This liberal cream puff may taste great, but he is high in spiritual calories and ultimately destructive to the individual soul—and to the church at large.

Our goal in this chapter is to get a handle on just how this cream puff emerged in western thought. If the church is to deal with the liberal Christ then she must clearly grasp from whence this vision came. To accomplish our goal we will take three steps: First, we will look at a brief sketch of some major contributors to this tasty Jesus. Second, we will get a crystallized picture of this contemporary cream puff. Finally, we will gain an understanding of the underlying appetite that has generated this theological craving.

## The Historical Ingredients of a Christological Cream Puff

Ideas, like babies, never come down in the mouth of a stork. They come to us through a long history of thought, dialogue, and debate. They are shaped and formed by great minds from diverse intellectual disciplines and often take years to crystallize into a moderately coherent framework of ideas. The theological liberalism of today is no different. Scholars did not wake up one morning and decide to create a particular view of Jesus. Many of them are not devilish men purposely swept up in a sinister scheme to overthrow the biblical Jesus (we will leave all bizarre historical theology conspiracies to the Dan Browns of the world). Instead these scholars are the product of a heritage of thinking that has come down to us over the past 200–250 years. I do not intend to champion their innocence—far from it. But scholars are not immune to pre-commitments. They do not come into the marketplace of ideas with a *tabula rasa*, as it were. The recipe for the creation of this christological cream puff, two centuries in the making, includes philosophical, theological, and cultural ingredients. These ingredients combine to form a tasty Jesus who is high in concentrated spiritual fat and ultimately bad for the health of any who are buying what he is selling.

## A Dash of Kant

When I attended Dallas Theological Seminary, I concentrated my studies in historical theology and had the privilege of sitting under the instruction of Dr. John Hannah. Dr. Hannah's vast knowledge of the historical development and flow of Christian doctrine was only matched by his rapier wit. One time in class, as we began our study of modern liberal theology, he shared with us that if one could, hypothetically, turn Germany upside down, the bottom would read "Made in Hell." His humorous insight was actually deeply poignant. Many of the most dangerous ideas that have impacted the western world in the last two hundred years had been given intellectual birth in German lecture halls by way of Enlightenment and Post-Enlightenment thinkers.

The Age of Enlightenment was the nineteenth-century child of two married movements. The first parent of Enlightenment thinking was a great cultural movement known as the Renaissance. The Renaissance was an artistic and scientific revolution that captivated the life of the western world from the fourteenth to the seventeenth centuries. It is no exaggeration to say that the advances in creative expression and scientific knowledge brought by this shift forever changed the way we as humans see the world. The spouse of the Renaissance was a sixteenth-century theological movement known as the Protestant Reformation. Through the Reformation, spiritual freedom was achieved as the theological tyranny of the medieval Roman Catholic Church was broken. Under the guise of men like William Tyndale and Martin Luther, laymen were liberated to read the Bible in their own vernacular tongues. No longer were the Scriptures privatized by the clergy in Latin. No longer were the common people held captive to the rule of prelates, priests, and popes. Led by theologians like Philip Melanchthon, John Calvin, and Theodore Beza, the cumbersome weight of unbiblical tradition began to be lifted, and a reformation of theology was birthed.

This marriage of the Renaissance and the Reformation created an ethos rife with a sense of spiritual liberty, personal autonomy, and intellectual independence. As this atmosphere settled in over the next two centuries, a perfect storm began to take shape for the genesis of the Age of Enlightenment under the brilliance of that age's greatest thinker: the German, Immanuel Kant (1724–1804). Kant's thought set the stage for the next two hundred years of western intellectual life. It would be almost impossible to overestimate his importance to the way that we see the world.

In short, we should understand Kant as a synthesizer of competing philosophies. In his era he stood at a point of convergence, bringing together two modes of thinking. One was called Rationalism and the other

Empiricism. The former saw that reality was apprehended accurately by the mind and is often linked with the great Catholic thinker René Descartes (1596–1650). Descartes determined that the only thing that could not be doubted in the world was the fact that he had the mental processes of thought. Thus stands his famous utterance, "I think, therefore I am."[1] He rooted his existence in the fact that he had clear and distinct thoughts. Reason, our modes of thought or rational capacities, became, for Descartes and many others, the most reliable aspect of our existence, indeed the very manner in which we could verify our existence at all.

Set opposite the mindset of the rationalists was that of the empiricists. The great empirical thinkers were men such as John Locke (1632–1704), David Hume (1711–1776), and George Berkeley (1685–1753). Empiricist philosophy understood the world to be a sense-apprehended and sense-interpreted reality. To ask, for example, if a chair exists, is in many ways a silly question to an empiricist. The question could only be answered by saying "I *see* a chair." For the empiricist, the world is sense-dependent. It can only be talked about in terms of subjective personal apprehension, not in terms of objective sense-independent existence. The empiricist's sense of the world is all they can ultimately speak about with any confidence.

On the heels of the rationalist thinkers on the one hand and the empiricist thinkers on the other comes Kant. His approach to looking at reality ended up synthesizing the two camps but left individuals without any surety of whether or not they were experiencing the world as it really was. Kant tipped his hat to the rationalists by understanding the mind as the key interpretive filter by which the world is apprehended. He tipped his hat to the empiricists by postulating that that there exist two realms: a *noumenal* one and a *phenomenological* one. The noumenal realm is what a thing actually is in and of itself. The phenomenal world is the world as we perceive it when filtered through our mental apprehension of space and time; and through the categories of perception—twelve to be exact—that color our individual minds. These two lenses or filters keep us living in the phenomenal world and don't allow us access to the noumenal world, the world as it really is. In other words, we are trapped behind our perceptions and mental grid. This entrapment and its implications for the future of western, religious thought are very important, and we should be careful not to miss it. Here the seeds of personal autonomy and postmodernism are buried in deep philosophical soil.

1. His famous Latin phrase was *cogito ergo sum*, often simply referred to as "The Cogito."

Now, with all of this said, you may be wondering what all of this Kantian chatter has to do with the price of tea in China, let alone a liberal cream puff Jesus. Well, the rubber meets the road in this: If we cannot know the world as it really is, then we cannot know what really happened in the world; we can only speak in terms of what we understand or perceive the world to be. If that is the case, then any historical record is only the interpretation or perception of the particular historian, not a statement about what actually happened. With that in mind, then what do the Gospel records of the four evangelists Matthew, Mark, Luke, and John become? You guessed it—subjective interpretations of Jesus' life rather than objective records of his life. If that is the case, then Jesus becomes an almost infinitely malleable figure who can only be spoken about in terms of a particular historian's Jesus or the Jesus of a particular community's collective perception. Theology then becomes just an opinion or an assent to other opinions postulated from a particular perspective of the world; or to use Kant's term, a view of the *phenomenal* world. From Kant's philosophy an important dichotomy of knowledge emerges. On the one hand, we can all have a common perception of scientific facts because, as humans, we share the first filter of space and time. So the realm of science is one that can be settled in knowledge, or at least as settled as anything can be. In contrast, the realm of religion, ethics, and morality is relegated to personal postulations, because our categories of perception (the second filter) may be colored differently. The disastrous effects of this dichotomy are still felt today.

**Kantian Reality**

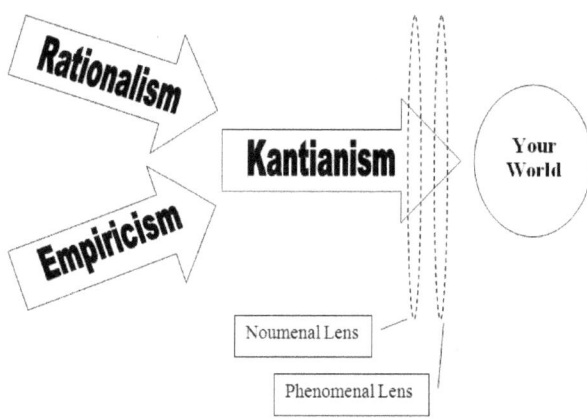

## A Smidgen of Schleiermacher

With this Kantian view of reality in hand, one of the most influential theologians in the history of the church, Friedrich Schleiermacher (1768–1834), went to work recasting the way Christian theology ought to be thought about. Kant's philosophy was in capable theological hands. The heart of Schleiermacher's theology was rooted in his idea that humans have a personal intuition or internal sense of the divine. For him theology finds its source in our personal God-consciousness. As James Livingston has noted, for Schleiermacher "God cannot possibly be known as an independent object, out there somewhere, but only in relation to our own self-consciousness."[2] One might say that theology is simply our self-conscious God-consciousness. Or, to say it another way, the heart of comprehending God is found in our personal sense or awareness of him.

To understand Schleiermacher's contribution to the liberal cream puff recipe, two important points need to be kept in view. First, as a post-Kantian theologian, Schleiermacher, like his philosophical forbear, held that we are trapped behind our perceptions as we look at what happened in the past. History is personal interpretation. This translates into Schleiermacher's understanding of Gospel Scripture as early church reflections on the significance of Jesus' person to them. What we have then in the Gospels are records or interpretations of how the early church understood Jesus in terms of their own personal, religious experience.[3] Second, Schleiermacher understood Jesus as the archetype of the purely God-conscious person, but sadly it basically ends there for him. Jesus is our savior in the sense that he models and implants in the world a sense of life lived in God-dependence. We can follow this example and experience as he did the joy of a God-dependent existence.[4]

This of course leaves us asking who exactly Schleiermacher's Jesus is. What does he actually amount to? By now you have probably guessed . . . a cream puff. By Schleiermacher's lights Christ is reduced to a God-aware and God-dependent human who gives us the gift of a living example that we too can follow and so rise above our baser proclivities.

---

2. Livingston, *Modern Christian Thought: The Enlightenment and the Nineteenth Century*, 101.

3. For Schleiermacher the Gospels are "interesting from the perspective of historical theology but are not legitimate bases from which we can begin our own theological endeavors." Wilkens and Padgett, *Faith and Reason in the 19th Century*, 57–58.

4. cf. Livingston, *Modern Christian Thought: The Enlightenment and the Nineteenth Century*, 103.

In that sense Cream Puff Jesus sits in the driver's seat of a bus filled with people who have a heightened and realized sense of God-consciousness. That bus could be labeled "Christianity." He isn't saving people from their sins but is leading them by example to a lifestyle that moves them beyond themselves toward God-dependence.

## A Pinch of Hegelian History

Liberal scholars speak about the Jesus of history and the Christ of faith as two different people. What they mean by this is that the Jesus who actually walked on the soil of first-century Palestine, and the Christ who was remembered by the early church becoming the object of worship throughout the centuries of Christian history, are not the same. They do not share a point-for-point identity. The Christ of faith is a creation of religious devotion, and the Jesus of history is a being who lies beneath layers of early Christian writings known as the Gospels. At the very least these layers are seen as grossly exaggerated distortions of a historic figure. At most they are mythical narratives never intended to grant us insight into historical reality.

To clearly and accurately grasp how the Jesus of history gets fully divorced from the Christ of faith, it is necessary to look at the impact of a man named Georg Wilhelm Friedrich Hegel (1770–1831). At this point it is probably hard to believe, but he too was German. Whatever we make of his conclusions, Hegel's brilliance, like that of Kant, cannot really be overstated. At the height of his influence, Hegel served as the chair of philosophy at the University of Berlin. His thought is complicated, but for the purposes of understanding his influence on the matter at hand, we need simply note a couple of important points.

To begin with, Hegel saw history as an unfolding ideological drama that operated in what is called a *dialectic*. In the sense that the term is used here, it refers to the interface between conflicting ideas or paths of reason. Hegel's dialectic consisted of one idea (a thesis) interacting with another idea (an antithesis) to produce a new idea (a synthesis). For Hegel the history of ideas developed along these lines: One idea would emerge in history and a competing idea would emerge, and the result of that ideological conflict over time would be the development of another idea that bears traits of both previous concepts. The dialectical engine of ideas then pushes the narrative of history forward.

This dialectical approach to history has an important result. No longer is history an issue primarily of facts, but rather a stage where a philosophical drama is played out. Ideas emerge from other ideas and bump up against other ideas and create yet new ideas. This is the story of history. History then becomes not the relating of what happened in space and time in the past, but the forward movement of ideas. For Hegel, a panentheist who understood God to be a divine entity permeating the world, history is Mind (or his understanding of God) taking shape in events. Now at this point the natural thing to wonder is what this Hegelian dialectic has to do with the development of a liberal Jesus. And to this we turn to David Friedrich Strauss.

Strauss (1808–1874) was a product of Schleiermacher's theology and Hegel's philosophy. He is most noted for his controversial work *Life of Jesus*, originally published in 1835. Strauss's understanding of Jesus was born from dissatisfaction with both supernatural explanations for Gospel miracles and rationalist approaches that tried to redefine them in natural terms. For example, Strauss could see the account of Jesus walking on the water as recounting neither an actual supernatural event nor an event explained by rocks that held the Savior up just underneath the surface of the water but were somehow out of the disciples' sight. Such events were neither miracle nor divine "sleight of hand."

Then what precisely were these miraculous narratives in Strauss's view? Well, in a word, they are "myth." That is to say, such stories like Jesus walking on the water are sacred legends written by early Christians to communicate their ideas about Christ. Hegel would have been pleased that his view of history as the outworking of the divine Mind found expression in Strauss. With the introduction of the mythological explanation for the miraculous phenomena described in the Gospels, Strauss establishes a path that liberal scholars today are still on. While he was not received well in his own day, Strauss's work has had a deep impact on Jesus studies throughout the last two centuries.[5] His indelible mark on the way the scholarly world after him has approached the Bible in general and the person of Jesus in particular is likely without equal.

---

5. "While the response to Strauss was swift and overwhelmingly negative—with some more conservative voices going so far as to say that he was the 'anti-Christ'—the impact of Strauss's work is felt to this day, and he continues to function as something of a patron saint for those who aspire to hard-nosed criticism of the Gospels." Beilby and Eddy, "The Quest for the Historical Jesus," 16.

## A Dusting of Liberal and Social Theology

A great cream puff usually gets dusted with sugar, adding to its sweetness and making it even more delectable. The tasty liberal Cream Puff Jesus is no exception. Everyone loves a historical figure that lights the way for us by means of moral example, social involvement, and love for others. This in a nutshell is the creation of Jesus in the fuller expressions of theological liberalism found in the latter part of nineteenth-century Protestant thought and the twentieth-century mainline, liberal church tradition.

The master chef for this dusting of the cream puff was yet another German, Albrecht Ritschl (1822–1889). Three important points need to be made concerning his contributions to liberal Christology. First, in Ritschl's view, the Gospel writers were primarily concerned with giving pictures of Jesus that would speak to the world of their day. They were not seeking to represent Jesus specifically as he existed in space and time, but attempting to craft a portrait of him conducive to the realm of Greek thought in which they lived. But today, as in Ritschl's day, we do not live in a Greco-Roman culture and are not immersed in the world of Greek thought, so by his understanding we need to recast Jesus for our world. In fact, the task of theology all along has been to take what one of Ritschl's pupils, Adolf von Harnack, would refer to as the "kernel" of Jesus teaching and put a new husk on it. It is Ritschl who introduces us to what has become typical of liberal theology's cultural re-envisioning of Christ. Liberal church historian Christopher Evans has noted that this is what sets this era of theology apart:

> If one had to categorize what separated the growth of nineteenth-century liberal theology from earlier forms of Christian theology that emerged out of the sixteenth-century Protestant Reformation heritage, it would be the ways liberalism engaged in a sustained reinterpretation of the nature of Jesus Christ.[6]

I would add, as Evans clearly notes throughout his work, this "reinterpretation" continues on as a hallmark of liberal theology.

Second, and very crucial to the development of the post-Ritschlian, liberal Christ, was his focus on Jesus' gospel as the proclamation of the kingdom of God . . . so far so good. However, a problem emerges in the realization that for Ritschl the kingdom is merely the human community that Jesus founded. There is no future realization of God's kingdom, only

---

6. Evans, *Liberalism Without Illusions*, 40.

its ethical representation in the life of Jesus' people. It is his people, the church, who operate as God's kingdom in their morality and their love for others. The salvation that Cream Puff Jesus brings as the community's founder is his footprints of love and good deeds that his community is to step in as well. Jesus as savior and redeemer is a moral exemplar who shows the way of salvation via a life of goodness.

Third, Ritschl brought Kant to a boiling point in one aspect of his theology. Following Kant's dichotomy between scientific and moral or religious knowledge, he made a distinction between fact and value. It was a fact that Jesus lived and served as the progenitor of a moral human community, but it was a value judgment that he was deity in the sense intended by the traditional creeds.[7] Ritschl rejected this value judgment, seeing Jesus as exuding the divine presence by his ethical life rather than encompassing deity in his person.

Ritschl's influence has been deeply felt in the liberal Protestant tradition. The three observations made concerning Ritschl's Christology set trajectories for the future development of liberalism throughout the twentieth century. The nineteenth century winds itself down with a liberal portrait of Christ who needs to be updated for the contemporary world, who kicked off an ethical community, and whose essence was lost in the theological distortions of the Christian creeds and church history. Jesus is now an official tasty cream puff—a really loving, nice man who was conscious of God in his life and went about creating a following to carry on this wonderful ethical legacy. It sounds more like Gandhi than God. He is not deity. He is not a savior from sins that violate God's law and threaten to slate us for an eternity alienated from God's presence. All that is left of Jesus are inspirational moral remnants that can only be seen when we finally sift through the clouded lens of tainted, inscripturated references to this Christ that have been remembered and misremembered, represented and misrepresented by his historic community.

---

7. This is specifically seen in the creed formulated at the council of Chalcedon in AD 451. The first portion of the creed states: *Following, then, the holy fathers, we unite in teaching all men to confess the one and only Son, our Lord Jesus Christ. This selfsame one is perfect [teleion] both in deity [theotēti] and also in humanness [anthrōpotēti]; this selfsame one is also actually [alēthōs] God and actually man, with a rational soul [psychēs logikēs] and a body. He is of the same reality as God [homoousion tōpatri] as far as his deity is concerned and of the same reality as we are ourselves [homoousion hēmin] as far as his humanness is concerned; thus like us in all respects, sin only excepted.* Leith, *Creeds of the Churches*, 35–36.

This morally-aware Jesus found expression in the early portion of the twentieth century in the rise of the Social Gospel movement. Liberal theologians and pastors picked up the Ritschlian, moral Christ and ran with him. Under the guise of theologians like Walter Rauschenbusch and pastors like Harry Emerson Fosdick, "Social Jesus" came to life. Rauschenbusch built on Ritschl's view of the kingdom of God and saw that the goal of ministry was not to point people toward heaven, but to remedy their plight in the here and now. Their present need for relief from suffering and poverty needed to take a center focus in the work of the church. We must acknowledge that such a vision, while flawed in its de-emphasis of eternity, indeed reflected a proper, biblical concern for the poor and marginalized,[8] a concern not shared adequately by the later fundamentalist reaction to liberalism. But for all of its social reform, such a vision of the church and its divine forbear remained theologically inadequate.

## Nineteenth Century Theology

|  | KANT | SCHLEIER-MACHER | HEGEL | RITSCHL |
|---|---|---|---|---|
| *Major contribution to liberal theology is . . .* | Dichotomy of Knowledge | Subjective Spirituality | Ideological Dialectic | Fact/Value Distinction |
| *Theology is a matter of . . .* | Personal Opinion | Personal Intuition | Historical Location | Cultural Reinterpretation |

## The Nineteenth Century Jesus

| SCHLEIERMACHER | STRAUSS | RITSCHL |
|---|---|---|
| Jesus = The Ideal Man | Jesus = Mythologized Figure | Jesus = Moral Reformer |

---

8. Helpful Scripture is found in Prov. 14:31; 17:5; 19:17; 21:13; 28:27; Gal. 2:10.

## A Recipe Modification: The Quest for the Historical Jesus

As liberal theology has taken form over the last two centuries, an important christological development has been an essential component of it. We need to recall that Kant's division of knowledge into two spheres and Ritschl's role in cementing that idea fashioned and fueled a perceived dichotomy between the Jesus who actually lived and the Christ who grew to be worshipped by the church. As this dichotomy emerged, scholars began to ask the question: Who is the real historical Jesus? The question itself was a good one, but it came from a wrong presupposition, namely, that the Christ who plainly jumps off the pages of the New Testament and the one who is revered as God through creedal confessions and affirmed to be full deity through church history is different than the Jesus who walked in first-century Palestine and breathed earthly air in space and time. Who the Jesus of history is matters greatly. If we don't get that right, then we will be worshipping a non-reality, and our devotion to Christ will have been tragically misplaced. For if the Christian is nothing else they are a follower of Jesus, and they must know from whence this Christ came and where this Christ would have them go.

The quest for the historical Jesus is really three quests. We should be careful not to see these quests as merely stages of one large quest, for while they are interrelated, each has its own driving assumptions and distinct methodologies. They cannot be exhaustively surveyed here, but a brief sketch is needed, if for no other reason than that it will provide a clearer picture of our present-day cream puff.

The first quest is typically dated from after the work of Hermann Reimarus (1694–1768) to Albert Schweitzer's writing of the classic *The Quest of the Historical Jesus* in 1906. If Reimarus gave birth to the quest, Schweitzer wrote its death certificate in his monumental publication. The first quest operated on the premise that the Jesus of history, the one who walked the earth, was distinct from the Christ created by the theological history of the church. So the Christ of the Bible was the Christ of early church theology, not of first-century history. These "questers" saw a discontinuity between the historical Jesus and the Christ of faith. Of course the leading light on this quest was the aforementioned David Strauss, and its guide book was his *Life of Jesus*. But with such a leading light and such a magisterial guidebook, we must ask, "Where did it all lead?" It seems that Schweitzer saw the answer to this clearly when he wrote:

> There was a danger that modern theology, for the sake of peace, would deny the world-negation in the sayings of Jesus, with which Protestantism was out of sympathy, and thus unstring the bow and make Protestantism a mere sociological instead of a religious force.[9]

His words were both keenly perceptive of the present situation in the early twentieth century and modestly prophetic of the rise of the Social Gospel movement that owned the church in pre-World War II America.

Additionally, while Schweitzer signed the quest's death certificate, he set the stage for the future by writing that such a quest for the historical Jesus was superfluous:

> But the truth is, it is not Jesus as historically known, but Jesus as spiritually arisen within men, who is significant for our time and can help it. Not the historical Jesus but the spirit which goes forth from Him and in the spirits of men strives for new influence and rule, is that which overcomes the world.[10]

For Schweitzer, Jesus' historicity is a distraction from the religious impact of his spirit for the modern world. In light of this, there was, immediately following Schweitzer, an extended time of over sixty years where the quests were seen as unnecessary—even counter-productive.

The second quest is usually understood to be served on the heels of theologian Rudolph Bultmann (1884–1976) by the hands of one of his pupils, Ernst Kasemann (1906–1998). Bultmann thought the Gospels were myth and needed to be "demythologized" in order to find out what was really being said from God to man. But Kasemann was more concerned than his mentor with determining some continuity between the historical Jesus and the Christ of faith. If the first quest was characterized by discontinuity between the two, the second (or "new") quest was marked by continuity. This does not mean that those in this quest saw the Christ of faith as parallel to the Jesus of history as articulated in the Gospels, but they did bring more optimism to the Gospels with the expectation that something could be learned concerning the historical Jesus from the words of the evangelists. It wasn't all myth. There was some history to be had. Kasemann was partly motivated by a theological concern that Jesus' humanity not be utterly rejected in the fashion of the ancient docetic heresy which saw a divine Jesus *appearing* as human but

---

9. Schweitzer, *The Quest of the Historical Jesus*, 400–401.
10. Ibid., 399.

not actually possessing human form. It must be emphasized that those in the new quest did not see Jesus plainly articulated by the Gospel writers, but they did sense that some historical facts regarding the events and actions of Jesus could be gleaned from the portrayals.

The third quest is what we are in the midst of now. Its starting point is the early- to mid-1980s. This quest is characterized by a variety of theological bents and approaches as well as a wide discussion regarding methodology for analyzing the historical Christ. Perhaps in the future we will be able to look back at this period and get a clearer sense of how it all plays out. At this point the quest is probably best understood as one that has put the issue of historical method in the driver's seat. Various approaches to historical method account for some of the vignettes of Jesus that are emerging in the present discourse. In addition to historical method, the quest is characterized by an interdisciplinary approach that draws in scholars from the fields of history, New Testament studies, theology, anthropology, sociology, and philosophy. Finally, this quest, like the others before it, reflects the theological pre-commitments of its "questers." One of the places this is most apparent is in the work of the Jesus Seminar.

## The Contemporary Cream Puff

### The Jesus Seminar

The quintessential example of the creation of a Jesus that is as soft and fragile as a cream puff has to be the scholars that comprise the Jesus Seminar. These men are the ideological heirs of Kant, Schleiermacher, Hegel, Strauss, and Ritschl. The Seminar consists of a group of liberal scholars who, by their own words, are "devoted to improving biblical and religious literacy by making the scholarship of religion available and accessible to the general public."[11] Let me translate: They are a group of scholars interested in feeding the masses a cream puff Jesus that diminishes the grandeur of God the Son and, under the covering of "improving biblical and religious literacy," they are reducing the theological acumen of any non-discerning enough to eat what they are preparing.

The Seminar's approach to determining the authenticity of Jesus' words in their 1993 volume *The Five Gospels* consists of a voting method

11. Funk, Hoover, and the Jesus Seminar, *The Five Gospels: What Did Jesus Really Say?*, 554.

whereby colored beads are cast in an effort to establish whether or not Jesus spoke in the manner in which the Gospel writers articulate. In short, a red bead indicates that Jesus undoubtedly said this. A pink bead indicates that Jesus probably said this. A gray bead indicates that Jesus did not say this, but the ideas are like his. A black bead indicates that Jesus did not say this and the ideas are from a later or distinct tradition. Each scholar casts an individual vote using one of these four beads on each saying of Christ. In addition to *The Five Gospels*, they produced a similar volume in 1998 dealing with the works of Jesus, called *The Acts of Jesus*. As already stated, these scholars have their own particular bents. Should we really be surprised with their findings? Probably not. It seems that the Jesus they found was already determined by each before they ever voted.

So who exactly are these scholars? In 1995, conservative scholar Craig Blomberg gave an excellent assessment of the academics that at that time made up the Seminar:

> Of the seventy-four 'Fellows' of the Seminar, as they are called, about fourteen of them are among the leading names in the field of historical Jesus scholarship today (e.g., John Dominic Crossan of DePaul University and Marcus Borg of Oregon State University). Roughly another twenty names are recognizable to New Testament scholars who keep abreast of their field, even if they are not as widely published . . . The remaining forty, or more than half of the entire seminar are relative unknowns. Most have published at best two or three journal articles, while several are recent Ph.D.'s whose dissertations were on some theme of the Gospels. For a full eighteen of the Fellows, a computer search of two comprehensive data bases of published books and articles turned up no entries relevant to the New Testament at all! Thirty-six of the group, almost half, have a degree from or currently teach at one of three schools—Harvard, Claremont and Vanderbilt, universities with some of the most liberal departments of New Testament studies anywhere. Almost all are American; European scholarship is barely represented. In short, the Jesus Seminar does not come anywhere close to reflecting an adequate cross section of contemporary New Testament scholars.[12]

Contrast this with the Jesus Seminar's own portrayal of their scholarship found in their 1999 work, *The Gospel of Jesus*:

---

12. Blomberg, "Where Do We Start Studying Jesus," 19–20.

> The Jesus Seminar is composed of gospel scholars dedicated to the advancement of the quest of the historical Jesus. The members of the Seminar, called Fellows, are professional biblical scholars, most of whom teach in colleges, universities or theological seminaries. The Seminar is not sponsored, supervised, endorsed or funded by any academic or religious organization. Anyone with appropriate academic credentials can become a Fellow regardless of religious commitments or point of view... We welcomed *the broadest spectrum of opinion* we could enlist in order to make our membership genuinely ecumenical.[13]

The Seminar would like us to believe that they speak to the masses because they represent the masses. In reality this is manipulative speak. They actually consist of a far-left brand of Jesus studies scholarship that has an agenda to deconstruct the Gospel narratives and reconstruct their own[14] due to their philosophical pre-commitments.

Possibly the best means of getting a sense of where the Jesus Seminar is coming from is, oddly, from the dedication written in their aforementioned seminal work, *The Five Gospels*. It reads as follows:

> This report is dedicated to
> GALILEO GALILEI
> who altered our view of the heavens forever
>
> THOMAS JEFFERSON
> who took scissors and paste to the gospels
>
> DAVID FRIEDRICH STRAUSS
> who pioneered the quest of the historical Jesus[15]

Galileo (1564–1642) is, of course, best known for his monumental work in astronomy as he furthered the Copernican heliocentric theory of the solar system. The reason that the authors have chosen Galileo is not because they want to laud him posthumously for his scientific achievements. No, instead they see him as the prime example of a man whose quest for knowledge led him into conflict with a myopic ecclesiastical

---

13. Funk and the Jesus Seminar, *The Gospel of Jesus: According to the Jesus Seminar*, 107; emphasis added.

14. The proof is in the pudding with their publication of *The Gospel of Jesus*.

15. The dedication found at the front of Funk, Hoover, and the Jesus Seminar, *The Five Gospels: What Did Jesus Really Say?* The writers mention Galileo, Jefferson and Strauss in their introduction insinuating that they are part of the "tragic and heroic story of those who endeavored to break the church's stranglehold over learning...", 3.

big brother more interested in control than learning. Because of his astronomical views, Galileo was pressured by the Roman Catholic Church to abandon heliocentrism. Galileo stood his ground for most of his life before, famously, and likely against his real desire, recanting in 1633. So their work is first dedicated to an intellectual martyr, a man victimized by a dark cloud of ignorance propagated by alleged servants of God. Are you beginning to get the picture of their self-perception?

Thomas Jefferson (1743–1826), the third president of the United States, was a deist. Attempts by right-wing conservatives to claim him as a founding father filled with deep Christian faith fail in the face of historical analysis. As a deist, Jefferson saw a place for a divine being but conceived of that being as largely inactive in the world. Therefore any understanding of Jesus would necessarily be one that had little room for supernatural activity. In 1820 Jefferson completed his *The Life and Morals of Jesus of Nazareth*. It became known as "The Jefferson Bible." As the Jesus Seminar dedication states, he literally took scissors and paste to the Gospels. In a letter dated October 13, 1813, to John Adams, Jefferson discusses his first attempt at establishing Jesus' words from the four Gospels in a work entitled *The Philosophy of Jesus of Nazareth*. Of his efforts in collating Jesus' words he tells Adams, "I have performed this operation for my own use, by cutting verse by verse out of the printed book, and by arranging the matter which is evidently his, and which is as distinguishable as diamonds in a dunghill."[16] Similarly he wrote of Jesus' words in an 1820 letter to Francis Adrian van der Kemp: "I separate, therefore, the gold from the dross: restore to Him the former, and leave the latter to the stupidity of some and roguery of others of his disciples."[17] Jefferson's intellectual elitism in his letters is frankly hard to stomach. They read like, well . . . a Jesus Seminar manifesto. Perhaps Forrest Church's words concerning the former president's project is an apt description of the Jesus Seminar's attempts as well:

> In 1820, at seventy-seven years of age, Thomas Jefferson removed the six testaments from his shelf, where they had been sitting for a decade and a half, and carved out a Gospel for himself, one whose witness he could respect and whose message he could understand. . . . Jefferson's was a search not so much for the historical as for the intelligible Jesus.[18]

16. Church, "The Gospel According to Thomas Jefferson," 17.
17. Ibid., 28.
18. Ibid., 30–31.

For Jefferson, as for the Jesus Seminar, the Christ looms as a moralistic sage who gives us a life of deep wisdom and pristine virtue, one they can respect and one they understand.

David Strauss has already been mentioned, but his role in pioneering the quest and introducing the idea that the Gospels should be read as myth absolutely defined much of subsequent Gospel study. The idea of the Gospels as mythological narratives is a starting point for the Seminar's scholars. Their deconstruction and reconstruction take place because of this presupposition. Since we can't know the historical Jesus behind the layers of myth, let's vote and gain a consensus on what he said, what he did, and what he was like! As James Edwards notes, "The Jesus Seminar has turned the wine of myth into the cold water of reality."[19]

While the Seminar stands on the liberal left of the third quest, it has engineered a serious attempt at swaying public opinion. The popular works of the two leading lights of the Jesus Seminar, John Dominic Crossan and Marcus Borg, and their many appearances on network and cable news and information television, show that the agenda is being realized. The church needs to equip its people to not be swept away by the History or Discovery channels. We live amid a media blitz where the people in our local fellowships will take in cream puff portrayals of a de-deified Jesus. How will church leaders help them beyond quoting Bible verses and regurgitating theological clichés? This, in part, is the focus of the next chapter.

## Ambassadors of Cream Puff Jesus

In a similar vein to the Jesus Seminar, others have taken up the task of serving as ambassadors of a liberal Christ to the masses. Over the last two hundred fifty years this Jesus has found representation in both academia and the church. But in the last twenty-five years, a concerted effort has been made to make this Jesus widely known and commonplace in everyday theological discussion. An example of the academic attempt to reach into the understanding of everyday people is University of North Carolina professor Bart Ehrman. Ehrman's self-described journey took him from Moody Bible Institute to Wheaton College to Princeton University. Along the way he went from having a "bona-fide born-again experience"[20] to his

---

19. Edwards, *Is Jesus the Only Savior?*, 27.
20. Ehrman, *Misquoting Jesus*, 3.

present agnosticism. He credits an epiphany that came to him as he read a comment from one of his Princeton professors for the beginning of his journey away from faith. Ehrman had written a paper which entailed explaining away particular discrepancies in the Gospel of Mark. At the end of the graded paper, the professor had responded to his student's attempt to deal with Mark's alleged errors by responding, "Maybe Mark just made a mistake." Here is Ehrman's response in his own words:

> I started thinking about it, considering all the work I had put into the paper, realizing that I had to do some pretty fancy exegetical footwork to get around the problem, and that my solution was in fact a bit of a stretch. I finally concluded, "Hmm . . . maybe Mark *did* make a mistake." Once I made that admission the floodgates opened.[21]

Sounds simple, right? Mark made mistakes, and the floodgates of seeing a Bible filled with errors open, and the shackles of religious ideology that kept the young scholar in intellectual bondage are loosed. Ehrman writes as one who has escaped Plato's Cave and now sees that what he thought was a religious and historical reality was only shadows on the wall fooling him all along. But he merely drank in the wine of modern liberal scholarship squeezed from the grapes of naturalism. Does Ehrman now, in his liberal posture, have no "fancy exegetical footwork" to do? Of course he does! No credible scholar assumes that Jesus studies are problem free, but answers that don't sacrifice the integrity of the text are available.

Ehrman is presently an agnostic regarding the existence of God, but he does believe that Jesus existed as a real person. His own view of Jesus follows Schweitzer in seeing him as a Jewish apocalyptic prophet. While he credits "other reasons" for his move to agnosticism, there should be little question that Ehrman is a living example that a de-deified Jesus is of little value to human life. There are enough moral examples of selfless living in the history of the world, there are enough men who took on the mantle of social reformation, and there are enough inspiring "spirits" to spur us on to human achievement. This does not mean that Jesus was not a moral, social reformer who provides inspiration through his life, but it does mean that, if this is all he was or is, "we are to be pitied more than all men" (1 Cor. 15:19b).

21. Ibid., 9.

Probably the most vocal churchman representing a Cream Puff Jesus is John Shelby Spong. Before his retirement Spong was the Bishop for the Episcopal Diocese of Newark, New Jersey. He himself is a member of the Jesus Seminar but, because of his role as a churchman, it merits highlighting him separately. Spong has written voluminously advocating a new approach to Christianity. He sees the Gospels as "first-century narrations based on first-century interpretations."[22] Spong's Jesus is basically a serving of recycled Ritschl with a side of Schleiermacher dressed on plate of postmodernism. He writes concerning the evangelists' depiction of Jesus:

> What these writers were trying to say, within their limited concepts, was that in the particular life of the spirit person Jesus, they saw not only God, but also a picture of what each of us might look like in our fulfilled spirit state. They were suggesting that Jesus was the portrait of the destiny available to all who are recipients of the Holy Spirit. They were hinting that the spirit person Jesus could be discovered over and over in each of us as we open ourselves daily to new human heights.[23]

Spong sounds like his fellow Seminar scholars. He wants to trump his Jesus up with lofty language to be a really significant figure whose "spirit" infuses the lives of those who follow his example. But what does all of this actually mean? Who is Jesus really by Spong's lights? He is just another de-deified Jesus whose significance lies in his sagacious and vivacious presence and whose example infuses others with the passion and persistence to live a similar life. He is "Jesus the alive one, the loving one, the one who had the courage to be himself under every set of circumstances, was and is the life where God has been seen and can still be seen under the limitations of our finitude."[24] If it weren't so tragically sad, it would be comical. Spong's Jesus looks like the fruit of modern pop-psychology, one who has "the courage to be himself." He is an ancient self-help guru, a latte-sipping, Chopra-like Northeasterner who can't decide whether he fits better in nineteenth-century German liberalism or present-day postmodernism. It would seem that, when Spong's Jesus looks in the mirror, he sees none other than . . . John Shelby Spong!

---

22. Spong, *Why Christianity Must Change or Die*, 107.
23. Ibid., 116.
24. Ibid., 132.

## The Appetite of Naturalism

People often eat what they are hungry for. Simply put, our desires shape our choices. Many of us, through the prosperity afforded by much of the western world, have the luxury of choosing what we want to eat. This choice is typically driven by our appetites and our taste buds. What do we have a hankering for?! What are we in the mood for?! When it comes to the decision in the ideological kitchen to make a cream puff Christ to nibble on, the mood and the hankering are informed by the appetite of naturalism.

Naturalism basically says that the only things that are real are contained in our space and time continuum and consist of matter and energy. What this means is that non-physical things don't and can't exist. This is clearly seen in the definition of naturalism provided in The Cambridge Dictionary of Philosophy. The definition reads that naturalism is:

> The twofold view that 1) everything is composed of natural entities—those studied in the sciences (on some versions the natural sciences)—whose properties determine all the properties of things, persons included . . . and 2) acceptable methods of justification and explanation are continuous, in some sense, with those in science.[25]

This definition tells us that, on a naturalistic worldview, everything is composed of physical substances and explained only in terms of an appeal to those substances. This philosophy has had a deep and dangerous impact on our present world.

For example, the outflow of a naturalistic philosophy is seen clearly in the fields of biology and psychology through the works of Charles Darwin and B.F. Skinner, respectively. Darwin (1809–1882) saw the evolutionary story in terms of a sequence of events connected by natural laws. These natural laws, coupled with the existing physical conditions, formed causative agents for the next event to occur. The cycle of natural laws and consequent events creates the fabric of the naturalist story of biological development.

Skinner (1904–1990) understood human behavior to be the necessary outcome of a human's environment. An individual acts the way she acts because the factors acting on her are what they are. Skinner parallels Darwin here by claiming that even a human's actions or life events come

---

25. Post, "Naturalism," 596.

about by natural laws acting on them. Thus humans are not active free agents at all, but beings through which nature runs. So how then does a person change? The only way for someone to change is by changing their inputs. Doesn't this sound more like an automaton than a person?!

I mention these two examples because they are important on two counts. First, most of the historical development of the theologically liberal Christ recounted in this chapter has taken place over the lifetimes of these two figures. So they reflect the larger philosophical movement in western culture that has paralleled the study of Jesus analyzed in this chapter. Second, they show that naturalistic philosophy is no respecter of intellectual disciplines. If matter and energy are all that is, then you simply cannot have a supernatural Christ, and your philosophical presuppositions demand that you explain away anything that emerges as a data point to the contrary. So consequently healings, exorcisms, and miracles of any sort go out the window. It seems very clear to me that the engine of Jesus studies has often run on the fuel of naturalism, and those driving the vehicle have at times been cognizant of this fact and at times have not. But much like Darwin and Skinner, they have been led to their conclusions by a philosophy that does not allow for the entrance of miracle or supernatural activity.

In 1867 the English poet Matthew Arnold published "Dover Beach." It is a poem that reflects the naturalistic philosophical onslaught of the nineteenth century. The poem begins by describing, in rather naturalistic terms, the sea as it washes up on Dover Beach in its endless rhythms. His language makes one think of the ancient naturalism charted by Solomon in the first chapter of Ecclesiastes. Midway through the poem he uses the physical as an analogy to what is happening on the ideological landscape of his day. He pines:

> The Sea of Faith
> Was once, too, at the full, and round earth's shore
> Lay like the folds of a bright girdle furled.
> But now I only hear
> Its melancholy, long, withdrawing roar,
> Retreating, to the breath
> Of the night-wind, down the vast edges drear
> And naked shingles of the world.

And so faith, which once burned bright around the world, is running away from the force of naturalism that is in the process of rewriting the world's story. Arnold concludes:

> Ah, love, let us be true
> To one another! for the world, which seems
> To lie before us like a land of dreams,
> So various, so beautiful, so new,
> Hath really neither joy, nor love, nor light,
> Nor certitude, nor peace, nor help for pain;
> And we are here as on a darkling plain
> Swept with confused alarms of struggle and flight,
> Where ignorant armies clash by night.[26]

We are left to the randomness of naturalism where the world can have no real virtue. We are on a "darkling plain," as it were, where the natural forces clash in a survival of the fittest. Arnold has poetically caught the spirit of the age, and it is the wind of this spirit that crystallized the formation of a naturalist Christology which in turn led to the de-deifying of Jesus.

## The Cream Puff Comes to the Church Potluck

There may be no better observation to conclude this assessment of the liberal Christ than the one Schweitzer provided over one hundred years ago concerning Schleiermacher:

> The fact is that their "picture of Christ" does not agree with that which he wishes to insert into the history. When it serves his purpose, he does not shrink from the most arbitrary violence."[27]

While I do not believe that Schweitzer outran his own criticism, his characterization of such scholarship as "arbitrary violence" summarizes well the tragic formation of Cream Puff Jesus. The image of God the Son sits bloodied and beaten before the onslaughts of the naturalistically forged weapons of liberal scholarship. What will the church do to prevent such vandals from marring the portrait of Jesus Christ?

This chapter has traced the development of Cream Puff Jesus. We have seen the chefs who have had a hand in his preparation. We have seen those who yet remain in the kitchen preparing him for present-day consumption by many who already long for a Jesus who demands little from them. My fear is that on the whole we are indiscriminating eaters of spiritual ideas. As a boy I looked forward to church potluck

26. Arnold, "Dover Beach."
27. Schweitzer, *The Quest for the Historical Jesus*, 67.

luncheons in the small rural church I grew up in. Boys know nothing of counting calories and eating with their health in mind; only one thing matters: How does it taste? Similarly, precious old ladies are not counting calories as they bring their tasty delights to share with their brothers and sisters at the church social. But all is well and good in terms of great food, godly friends, and glorious fellowship. I wish we could say the same for the banquet of ideas shared in the halls of American churches, but, in truth, we cannot. Our next chapter serves as a response to this cream puff and as a call and consideration in how best to deal with this issue for the building up of Christ's body and for the preservation of truth. We must get this cream puff off our spiritual diet and equip others to do the same as best we can.

2

# Deconstructing a Cream Puff

*If it is true, as the scripture [sic] says, that "Jesus Christ is the same yesterday, today and forever," then we have no right to modify or alter those early portraits. We simply must not read back into those stories what we think ought to have been there.*

J. B. PHILLIPS

I GREW UP IN small town in a beautiful part of upstate New York. In many ways the community, like hundreds of others like it in the Northeast, has been weathered by much of the history of theological ideas and their development in the United States. Upstate New York felt the impact of the westward expansion of the First Great Awakening, but really came alive under the ideological entrepreneurialism fostered by the Second Great Awakening. Revivalism embedded itself deep into church culture and is still to be found in both fundamentalist and evangelical expressions of Christianity there. As the twentieth century rolled in, along came the Social Gospel wave. Rauschenbusch, mentioned in the previous chapter, was himself rooted in the upstate area. As a result the liberalism/fundamentalism split of the early twentieth century established clear lines of demarcation that are unmistakably vivid. These fissures still remain, religiously, and in many cases socially, dividing otherwise close-knit communities. Even the small hamlet I called home for my early years fell prey to embracing more than one Jesus.

The rural village of 1,200 souls has five churches in its "don't blink or you'll miss it" downtown. One is a United Methodist Church (UMC) that has felt the ebb and flow that is part and parcel with being a UMC congregation in North America these days. Given the church governing board's ability to move local ministers around, any particular congregation might be headed to the edge of the cliffs of liberalism or drawing back to a Methodism that would make both the church pioneer John Wesley and the indomitable circuit rider Francis Asbury smile. Another is an Episcopal church and, with the statements made regarding the Episcopal bishop John Shelby Spong in the last chapter, comment is relatively unnecessary. Additionally, there is a Roman Catholic church whose facility was at one time a Nazarene church. And finally two Baptist churches, one that has been clearly fundamentalist in its orientation and the other which seems to have journeyed over the years to a more modest brand of fundamentalism. This ecclesiastic town square shows a history and lives a present reality furnished by the rise of liberalism and the consequent reaction of fundamentalism.

The community's mainline churches are succumbing to the unrelenting march of time and its henchman "attrition." This is indicative of the demise of mainline churches dotting the United States which has caused no small amount of alarm at the hubs of these denominational superstructures. A report from the National Council of Churches in their 2010 yearbook of churches shows that of the twenty-five largest church bodies in the United States, all of the liberal Protestant mainline denominations experienced decline over 2009.[1] The US is not alone here and is merely decades behind its European counterparts. Does anyone think of anglicanism as wildly missional? Probably not, and this is a tragedy of the first order when considering its theological roots in reformation history. The Church of England is stagnant according to its own reporting. And its Canadian counterpart has declined by 53 percent over a forty-year period from 1961–2001 according to Christianity Today.[2]

Mainline liberalism is dying. But this is not overly encouraging news because its death is not resulting from a turnaround within theological liberalism. Certainly efforts are being made by evangelicals within mainline denominations and they are to be highly commended for this.[3] But

---

1. Goldberg, "Decline in U. S. Mainline Denominations Continues."
2. Blake, "Statistics Suggest Anglican Church of Canada in Huge Decline." para. 2.
3. The Association for Church Renewal is an attempt to network renewal groups across denominational lines. Additionally regional groups, for example in the United

for the most part the death is due to churches, leaders, and lay persons drifting so far afield that they actually become entirely irreligious or social religious entities rooted in humanism and humanitarianism. If you are reading this and are in a mainline denomination and feel called to stay and bring reform I hope this chapter will be helpful to you. It may even help you decide if and when it is time to leave. If you are in an evangelical church my hope is that this chapter helps equip you to steer clear of a slide toward liberalism and gives you and your church some thoughts on confidently responding to the gravitas of Cream Puff Jesus.

## The Unlivable World of Naturalism

An aged preacher once reflected on life as though God were absent, and he wrote:

> What does man gain by all the toil at which he toils under the sun? A generation goes, and a generation comes, but the earth remains forever. The sun rises, and the sun goes down, and hastens to the place where it rises. The wind blows to the south and goes around to the north; around and around goes the wind, and on its circuits the wind returns. All streams run to the sea, but the sea is not full; to the place where the streams flow, there they flow again. All things are full of weariness; a man cannot utter it; the eye is not satisfied with seeing, nor the ear filled with hearing. What has been is what will be, and what has been done is what will be done, and there is nothing new under the sun. Is there a thing of which it is said, "See, this is new"? It has been already in the ages before us. There is no remembrance of former things, nor will there be any remembrance of later things yet to be among those who come after. (Eccl. 1:3–11)

This is an ancient poetic description of naturalism. People come and people go but the natural world remains. Of course the preacher (known in Hebrew as Qoheleth) intuitively recognizes that if the world operates in this manner then the only game in town is meaninglessness. The ethical philosophy that teaches that everything is meaningless is called *nihilism*.

Friedrich Nietzsche (1844–1900) saw that nihilism was precisely where the naturalistic enterprise led and tried to rescue it from

---

Methodist Church, attempting to be pockets of evangelical reform abound. States like Virginia, Ohio, Mississippi, and others have state or even more localized efforts through publications and conferences in quest for a return to the denomination's roots.

meaninglessness, but he couldn't, and the world in which Nietzsche lived was shortly ravaged by two World Wars as one of his countrymen tried to walk out the humanist dream of the *übermensch*—superman—through ethnic cleansing and world domination. This is not surprising.

Nietzsche's last work was titled *Ecce Homo: How One Becomes What One Is*. His infamous last line sets the tone for naturalism's hostility toward the Christian worldview and its only real ethical option aside from nihilism. Nietzsche's triumphal declaration was "Dionysus against the Crucified."[4] But what did this mean?

Dionysus was a Greek god in the mythology that took on different shades depending on the particular mythological story being read. In Euripedes' *the Bacchae* Dionysus is vengeful and exacting. René Girard notes that in the mythologies "every time Dionysus appears, a victim is dismembered and often devoured by his or her many murderers."[5] Whether Dionysus is the victim or victimizer, carnage ensues. For Nietzsche then to say "Dionysus against the Crucified" was to say that there are only two options. One is indicative of the crucified Christ who was victimized by the sufferings of the world. The other is one that exercises the will to power and may need to dominate others in order to move life forward. At its most brutal form this plays out as an ethical Darwinism. At its mildest it is a philosophy of *humanism* which sees humanity as a uniquely evolved epicenter of cultural creativity and meaning. John Carroll insightfully called Nietzsche's last published words "the dying cry of humanist philosophy."[6]

Naturalism leaves us with two possible options to account for human life: nihilism and humanism. Humanism is clearly the more appetizing option, but it suffers from insufferable intellectual problems. Nihilism is the only logical conclusion left for the naturalistic world, but it cannot account for the observable in society and culture nor is it pragmatically livable. Let's critique both briefly.

Nihilism is logically untenable. First, *it is self-refuting*. The moment you define it the discussion is over: "Nihilism means that life is meaningless." But if the world is nihilistic then that statement can't mean anything. Second, *it has no explanatory power for how the world actually works*. We assume meaning as a basis for language, relationships, commerce,

---

4. Nietzsche, *Ecce Homo*, 1297.
5. Girard, "Dionysus Versus the Crucified," 822.
6. Carroll, *The Wreck of Western Culture*, 5.

and culture. Third, *it fails pragmatically.* It is unlivable. If society were nihilistic we would not have existed this long as a species. There would be no basis for morality, thus no basis for law, and no basis for order. Additionally there would be no way to evaluate whether something caused the species to flourish since the idea of "flourishing" has a goal or ideal of health that it is moving toward.

Nihilism is artfully and tragically depicted in the book and movie *No Country for Old Men.* In the film, ethically pregnant acts are seen as entirely random occurrences. This theme emerges in the worldview of the film. Twice, when Chigurh, the movie's serial killer, talks with his would-be victims, he has them call a coin flip to see whether or not he will kill them. In one encounter he informs the gas station owner and clerk that the coin and he (Chigurh) got where they are now the same way, by chance. Each time the would-be victim is operating from a different understanding, and a disconnect hangs in the scene between Chigurh's random worldview and their more traditional sense of the world's operation. Chigurh serves as an exemplar of how the world functions if naturalistic nihilism is true.

Humanism lacks the intellectual capital to write its own ideological checks. Evolutionary naturalism forms the basis for humanism. So this means that the evolved human creature has come about from random biochemicals, but somehow has the ability to make choices, appreciate art, create beauty, and understand moral consensus. But we must ask how this can be—it is simply impossible. Let's be clear here. The "will" on a naturalist account of things can only be described in material terms. It has no immaterial component to it. So the will itself is just a biochemical reaction of the brain that by its very nature must be random. So how do we get aesthetic order from naturalistic biochemistry? We can't unless we smuggle in concepts from another worldview. This is what makes humanism inconsistent. It can't account for the very life it espouses.

An illustration of this humanist attempt to assert meaning is found in the evangelical-pastor-turned-atheist Dan Barker. Barker has pointed himself toward trying to assert that life without God can still have purpose. He readily says that "there is indeed no purpose of life. There is purpose *in* life. If there were a purpose *of* life, then that would cheapen life." Presumably he thinks it would cheapen life because it takes out of autonomous human hands the authority to dictate the ultimate purpose for their own existence. The problem is that Barker has nothing to ground any notion of personal autonomy because his "mind" and "will" are just random biochemical constructs. But he tries to assert purpose by saying:

> Life is its own reward. But as long as there are problems to solve, there will be purpose *in* life. When there is hunger to lessen, illness to cure, pain to minimize, inequality to eradicate, oppression to resist, knowledge to gain and beauty to create, there is meaning to life.[7]

It is difficult to know where to begin with the problems plaguing Barker. Just a few of the questions that come to the surface are: What in Barker's naturalism makes the small quests—which supposedly give meaning "in" life—have any meaning themselves? In a random world where does he derive the authority to assert that any of the things (hunger, illness, pain, inequality, oppression) that he mentions as bad *are* bad? What is his standard of measurement? How does he account for anything that others would agree with him on as constituting "knowledge" or "beauty"? According to what standard is anything beautiful? Barker attempts to throw out any ultimate purpose while trying to hold on to intermediate purposes, but there ends up being no purpose for his purposes except that which he wants to randomly assert.

The failure of naturalism yields the failure of theological liberalism because it ends up providing the cream in the puff of liberalism's Jesus. His DNA has no divinity to speak of because the world isn't the kind of realm where supernaturalism is welcome. As long as the theology is carried in naturalistic railcars on the rails of academia and church life, it will never be able to hold the truths of history or any promise of real transformation. As church leaders and lay people representing Jesus to the world, it is important that we equip ourselves to slow the locomotive and maybe stop it altogether.

## The Incoherence of Naturalism with Theological Liberalism

There is a great deal of literature that deals with the errors of naturalism. Most of it directly interfaces with atheistic naturalism. Many of the same arguments are helpful to the discussion of theological liberalism simply because anything that destroys its philosophical underpinnings will inevitably cause upheaval in the system.

---

7. Barker, *godless*, 344.

*deconstructing a cream puff* 43

However, I want to share a few problems with naturalism that specifically cause a lack of coherency between it and the theology of liberalism. My encouragement to the reader is to get good material on atheistic naturalism and study it. But for the purposes of deconstructing Cream Puff Jesus it will be enough for us to show that the cream shouldn't be there at all.

Incoherence #1—Text

The theological liberal wants to see the Bible as important but not supernatural. It is "inspired" in the sense that my writing this book is "inspired." It comes from a place of personal encounter with God and devoted human passions. So Paul is an inspired writer, and so are C. S. Lewis and Anne Lamott. The text of Scripture is not "God-breathed" as orthodoxy teaches but instead is a human text of reflection on the experience of God. Marcus Borg puts it this way in describing the Gospels:

> Two statements about the nature of the gospels are crucial for grasping the historical task: 1) They are a developing tradition. 2) They are a mixture of history remembered and history metaphorized. Both statements are foundational to the historical study of Jesus and Christian origins, and both need explaining.[8]

Borg then goes on to explain what he means. The Gospels as developing traditions, were written sometime between AD 70 and AD 100. They were written down by different communities of Jesus' followers and reflect the tradition and setting of those communities. So in a very postmodern sense Borg sees them as conditioned by the culture and history of the community, not by the actual history of Jesus. In that sense the Gospels themselves are not concerned with the historical Jesus, but the Christ of the faith of seminal late-first-century communities.

The Gospels as history "remembered" and "metaphorized" are not actually concerned with accurate history as much as telling a story. Yes, some events, for Borg, really happened, but the way they are told and the details that are included are often metaphors intended to communicate the theology of that early community.

As a liberal, Borg's approach is very different than the orthodox understanding of the text. Borg and his cohorts at the Jesus Seminar and those de-mythologizers and de-constructors of liberal postmodern

8. Borg, *The Meaning of Jesus*, 4.

academia all think that any real history of Jesus is hidden somewhere behind the Gospels themselves, since the Gospels reflect the theological constructs of related but nuanced and even disparate bands of Jesus' followers. Hence the liberal quest for the historical Jesus.

Richard Bauckham has written an impressive tome called *Jesus and the Eyewitnesses*. His comments on this quest, and its attempt to get behind the Gospels themselves, are worth noting:

> From the perspective of Christian faith and theology we must ask whether the enterprise of reconstructing a historical Jesus behind the Gospels, as it has been pursued through all phases of the quest, can ever substitute for the Gospels themselves as a way of access to the reality of Jesus the man who lived in first-century Palestine . . . What is in question is whether the reconstruction of a Jesus other than the Jesus of the Gospels, the attempt, in other words, to do all over again what the evangelists did, though with different methods, critical historical methods, can ever provide the kind of access to the reality of Jesus that Christian faith and theology have always trusted we have in the Gospels. By comparison with the Gospels, any Jesus reconstructed by the quest cannot fail to be reductionist from the perspective of Christian faith and theology.[9]

Bauckham shows in his book that we can trust the Gospels as eyewitness material. This means that the Gospel writers either witnessed or were privy to direct witnesses and recorded the oral history communicated by those witnesses. There is no question that the Gospels are theologically driven narrative histories. But they are histories, not memories of communal traditions or metaphors glazed over the top of a hidden history.

The textual incoherence of liberalism is that it presumes to speak authoritatively about their textual deconstructions of alleged textual reconstructions while trying to reconstruct a Jesus they think needs to be deconstructed. Go figure.

### Incoherence #2—God

The predominant view of the liberal is that God is an evolving being. God does not possess a particular set of attributes to an infinite degree. Instead God is mutable. The theology is known as *process theology*. The term is self-explanatory: God is in process. He develops along with the

---

9. Bauckham, *Jesus and the Eyewitnesses*, 4.

world. In one of the more ignorant statements from a learned man that I have read, Christopher Evans states, "If there is an idea that helps one to understand the worldview of process theology, it is a belief that God cannot be put in box. Divine reality is in a constant pattern of change, which in its own way is a reflection of how creation is always changing."[10] But Evans actually shows that process theology does the very thing he tries to negate. God's immutability is precisely what distinguishes God from his creation. Cosmologically speaking it would be foolish to think that a God who suffers from the same mutable limitations of his creation could ever give birth to it to begin with. The cause would cease to be greater than the effect.

It is unclear to me why believing God is immutable is putting him in a box. Is perfect immutability more boxed in than imperfect mutability? If that which is immutable is also eternal and infinite what box can it logically fit in? The theologically liberal view of God seems incoherent. It extols God as great while trying to maintain essential continuity between him and his creation. This is a problem.

## Incoherence #3—Resurrection

The presupposition of naturalism is that if an event defies natural laws then it cannot happen. This pill has been completely swallowed by liberalism. As a result the resurrection is metaphorized—after all it is *theological* liberalism. There has to be a place for spirituality, but that metaphysic does not stand over or in relation to the physical; it maintains a completely separate identity. So for liberalism, Jesus resurrection was a spiritual raising of the dead but not a bodily raising of the dead. Interestingly the liberal churchmen cannot figure out why a bodily resurrection is such a big deal. Liberal Congregational pastor and philosophy professor Robin Meyers expresses the perspective through a couple of rhetorical questions:

> If the empty tomb is a metaphor and not a description of the resuscitation of a corpse, then shouldn't all the crosses in the world be turned in and melted down for scrap? Shouldn't all the churches be razed and an amnesty program implemented to allow everyone to turn in their Bibles without sanction?[11]

---

10. Evans, *Liberalism Without Illusions*, 85.
11. Meyers, *Saving Jesus from the Church*, 75–76.

He writes begging a negative answer. The irony of course is that Paul seems to answer his precise, slightly sardonic, questions in 1 Corinthians 15:12–19:

> Now if Christ is proclaimed as raised from the dead, how can some of you say that there is no resurrection of the dead? But if there is no resurrection of the dead, then not even Christ has been raised. And if Christ has not been raised, then our preaching is in vain and your faith is in vain. We are even found to be misrepresenting God, because we testified about God that he raised Christ, whom he did not raise if it is true that the dead are not raised. For if the dead are not raised, not even Christ has been raised. And if Christ has not been raised, your faith is futile and you are still in your sins. Then those also who have fallen asleep in Christ have perished. If in Christ we have hope in this life only, we are of all people most to be pitied.

So yes, it is all futile—raze the churches, turn in the Bibles and melt the crosses if Jesus did not rise *from the dead*. This phrase "from the dead" is important. The theology of liberalism attempts to spiritualize the language of resurrection. To be raised to life is seen as the language of spiritual exaltation and need not have a body attached to it at all. For most liberal theologians the bodily resurrection of Christ is denied or is seen as inconsequential to their theology (which I think ends up just being a passive/aggressive naturalism). New Testament scholar Marcus Borg confesses:

> For me, it is irrelevant whether or not the tomb was empty. Whether Easter involved something remarkable happening to the physical body of Jesus is irrelevant. My argument is not that we know the tomb was not empty or that nothing happened to his body, but simply that it doesn't matter. The truth of Easter, as I see it is not at stake in this issue.[12]

The problem for Borg and other liberals is that Paul's use of the Greek term for body, *sōma*, and his language of a resurrection from the dead (Greek: *ek nekrōn*) make it seem very implausible to conclude that the resurrection that Paul saw as vital to our future hope was a not bodily resurrection subsequent to a physical death.

---

12. Borg, *The Meaning of Jesus*, 131.

There is continuity in Paul's understanding between the body in this life and the next. In 1 Corinthians 6:13b–15 Paul is talking about the improper use of the body and he writes:

> The body is not meant for sexual immorality, but for the Lord, and the Lord for the body. And God raised the Lord and will also raise us up by his power. Do you not know that your bodies are members of Christ? Shall I then take the members of Christ and make them members of a prostitute? Never!

The idea that the Lord will "raise us up by his power" is tied before and after it in the context to the concept of body. The "us" he refers to is "us" in a bodily existence. The text is very clear about that. If we fast-forward to 1 Corinthians 15:35–38 we see Paul retaining the use of body (*sōma*) but explaining its post-resurrection future in more detail:

> But someone will ask, "How are the dead raised? With what kind of body do they come?" You foolish person! What you sow does not come to life unless it dies. And what you sow is not the body that is to be, but a bare kernel, perhaps of wheat or of some other grain. But God gives it a body as he has chosen, and to each kind of seed its own body.

A body (*sōma*) is sown and a body (*sōma*) is raised. The body that is raised has some different nuances to it, but it is characterized by Paul as a body nonetheless. So there is a continuity in essence but a discontinuity in detail between our pre-resurrection body and our post-resurrection body. This is important because this language of body adds to the fact that Paul says Jesus rose "from the dead"—which in Jewish thought absolutely would have included the notion of a body—and leads to the conclusion that when Paul talks about resurrection he is talking about bodily resurrection, whether it be ours or Christ's as our progenitor.

So to go back to where we started with Robin Meyers's seemingly rhetorical questions, we can conclude that the notion of bodily resurrection matters deeply and Paul's theology in 1 Corinthians serves to show us just that. The most magisterial work in my lifetime on the resurrection is *The Resurrection of the Son of God* by N.T. Wright. Commenting on 1 Corinthians 15 Wright states:

> Once more, there can be no question, granted the normal meaning of the words Paul uses, that what he has in mind is bodily resurrection. If we were to take the paragraph out of its context, it would be logically possible to understand it in terms of

'resurrection' meaning 'non-bodily survival of death'; but this is simply not possible historically or lexicographically.[13]

We cannot cherry-pick terms and define them according to our presuppositions. The theological liberal cannot get outside of his naturalism to consider that maybe the Bible is not restricted to his own plausibility structure. Our job is to upend that structure by showing the liberal who believes in a naturalized Christ that the text is a receptacle fit only for a supernatural Jesus.

## Incoherence #4—Miracles

Along the same line as the Resurrection, the naturalist in the church cannot account for the miracles of Jesus. They must either be explained away, as they used to be in the early twentieth century, or be seen as literary conventions of mythical stories told by early gospel communities and traditions as is now in vogue throughout academia.

It has often been asserted that a miracle is "a violation of nature's laws." The problem with this definition is that it stops the naturalist in their tracks because it smacks of being illogical. If every event is a result or function of a law of nature and the only category for a miracle is something that contradicts those laws, then a miracle is dismissed immediately because it doesn't fit within the plausibility structure of the naturalist. In the end their plausibility structure must change but defining a miracle properly might lend some assistance to the conversation. Perhaps the best definition of miracles is: "They are naturally (or physically) impossible events, events which at certain times and places cannot be produced by the relevant natural causes."[14] The importance of the definition is that it doesn't place a miracle in contradiction to nature; instead it includes but goes beyond nature. Analogously, the spiritual life is not irrational but is both rational and trans-rational—including but extending beyond rationality.

The denial of miracles shows again the theological liberals' naïve acceptance of naturalism. While adhering to a belief in God they place God in naturalist box. He assumes the limitation of the naturalist plausibility structure rather than defining humanity's plausibility structure. The liberal does not possess the epistemic teeth to consume the Jesus of

13. Wright, *The Resurrection of the Son of God*, 330.
14. Moreland and Craig, *Philosophical Foundations for a Christian Worldview*, 568.

history and so rewrites the narrative of the Gospels to exclude miracles. Remember Jefferson's "Bible." It seems incumbent on us to ask whether or not Jesus should be enslaved to post-enlightenment epistemology and modernist plausibility structures. J. P. Moreland and William Lane Craig hit the nail on the head, stating:

> Given a God who created the universe, who conserves the world in being and who is capable of acting freely, miracles are evidently possible. Indeed, if it is even (epistemically) possible that such a transcendent, personal God exists, then it is equally possible that he has acted miraculously in the universe. Only to the extent that one has good grounds for believing atheism to be true could one be rationally justified in denying the possibility of miracles.[15]

But very few theological liberals would go as far as atheism. So they accept the existence of God but simply redefine him as a finite being. It seems much more consistent once someone has opened themselves up to the idea of God to not artificially constrain him within the limits of naturalistic explanations.

## Incoherence #5—Purpose

Theological liberalism is not a purposeless enterprise. Much civic good has come from these liberal churches. Bellies have been fed. Roofs have been provided. Social evils have been battled. Race relations have been enhanced. The cries of the marginalized have been brought to the attention of politicians and government. Ecumenical partnerships have raised millions for humanitarian causes. Liberalism is anything but purposeless. But ironically its guiding philosophy, its intellectual currency, is entirely random and purposeless.

The one thing a naturalist cannot have is purpose. To use the Greek there is no *telos*, no ultimate end for which anything exists. Aristotle called it a final cause. It was the reason for the existence of something. The final cause of a table is "to have a place to eat" or "to have a place to sit and write a book." So what is the cause for the universe? The naturalist can only talk in terms of preceding dominoes, known as efficient causes. Think in terms of the scientific law of cause and effect. There must be an efficient cause to yield a particular result. So the naturalist cannot tell a story that

15. Ibid.

moves toward a conclusion. They can only tell a story that contains a series of efficient causes going nowhere because the moment a landing place is defined or described then we have a reason for the causes, which means we must have someone who designed the process to match the end. Since the naturalist has no room for God, they can have no room for purpose.

This is a major incoherence for the theological liberal. It assumes something its underlying worldview will not permit: *purpose*. The liberal church acts as though it has purpose but has no way of accounting for it. Its finite God is growing only at the pace of his natural creation. He could not have a planned-out map but liberalism assumes an ultimate good of some kind. It assumes that there is some merit to selflessness. It assumes that certain social habits move toward a better end than others. This is good. I commend them for it. But they only arrive at purpose because they borrow from another system. This is a great intellectual hypocrisy and shows that its pragmatic does not cohere with its presuppositions.

## Incoherence #6—Choice

The exercise of the will is an explicit assumption of the liberal church's appeal to social reform. The idea that appeals can be made to other human persons to make particular choices to act in the best interests of others is basic to liberalism. In fact this idea of human choice is so treasured that it causes liberals to abandon original sin altogether. Robin Meyers rejects original sin, calling it "a theology of entrapment, not liberation."[16] For Meyers, as for other liberals, this rejection is rooted in the idea that we are sinners by choice and not by nature.

The irony of course is that the same naturalism used to explain away miracles does not allow for the self-autonomy needed for human choice to exist. If all of life is a series of random, mechanistic, natural laws that enact events followed by natural laws that enact events followed by natural laws and so on ad infinitum how could there be anything denoting a will to choose? Nietzsche recognized the incompatibility of free will with his naturalism. He declared, "The concept 'sin' together with its associated instrument of torture which is the concept 'free will' were invented in order to confuse our instincts and make mistrust of them second nature!"[17] Animal instincts, not morally

---

16. Meyers, *Saving Jesus from the Church*, 110.
17. Nietzsche, Ecce Homo, 1288–1289.

responsible choices, govern the humanity espoused by naturalism. But this is at odds with the ethical demands of theological liberalism. The implicit naturalism guiding their hermeneutic belies their ethical impulse and sense of responsible human choice.

## Incoherence #7—Dignity

If naturalism is true, human dignity is not. But to their credit the theological liberal does see humanity with an intrinsic worth (their typical bifurcation of the value of life inside the womb from the value of it outside the womb notwithstanding). Their social impulse is born from a commitment to human dignity. This is commendable. However, if the world is a naturally running structure, then human worth is a completely arbitrary assertion. There can be nothing intrinsic to a human that makes him any more integral to the cosmos than a spider or a rose. He is just a more complex collocation of biochemical molecules. This is a boldfaced inconsistency that cuts at the missional heart of liberal theology.

## In Defense of Jesus' Deity

The fundamental theological problem plaguing liberalism is that it rejects the deity of Christ. This rejection clearly places it outside of orthodoxy and hence outside of what can justifiably be called "Christian." So when we are dealing with theological liberals who speak of themselves in terms of "Christian," we cannot accept it. To do so is to ignore both the text of Scripture and the historical consensus of the church in the name of modern pluralism and secularism. As Christians we say with literally millions throughout the last two millennia that Jesus is God in all of his fullness and to postulate otherwise out of ignorance is sub-Christian; to reject the claim blatantly is un-Christian.

Theological liberalism has two primary interpretations of Jesus. For some he was an apocalyptic prophet. This was especially popular with those in the late nineteenth and early twentieth centuries. It also has found a recent resurgence among some scholars. For others, like those in the Jesus Seminar, Jesus was a wise sage or a gentle cynic. By any liberal accounting, Jesus is not God. Robert Funk of the Jesus Seminar summarizes their perspective of Jesus, stating, "It is the vision that Jesus had of God's domain, not the myth of God incarnate, that is the bedrock of our discovery."[18]

What I marvel at most about liberalism's Christology is that they perceive his identity as incidental to following him. The content of Jesus' person seems relatively unimportant to and disconnected from the task of living like him. Meyers illustrates my point, saying:

> Christianity is now so fundamentally associated with the formula of fall and redemption, so focused on beliefs about Jesus instead of invitations to follow Jesus, that a new Reformation is needed. It will deal not with matters of doctrine and church order but with a recovery of the concept of transformation through the imitative wisdom of discipleship . . . Christianity was once and must be again, about following Jesus, not about worshiping Christ.[19]

Like most liberals, his false bifurcation between the Jesus of history and the Christ of faith frees him to separate doctrine and praxis.

Similarly, church historian Christopher Evans reflecting on Jesus' question to his disciples, "Who do you say that I am?" (Matthew 16:15) states:

> Part of the opportunity that liberal congregations may have in the future will not come through their ability to provide the "right" answers to this question. Rather, it will come through an ability of churches to take this question seriously: of what it means to follow Christ, and how the response to that question can not only enable congregations to honor traditions, but where age-old questions of faith and meaning can be engaged and received in innovative ways.

There are three brief things to note about Evans's quote. First, "right" is put in quotes. This is because the liberal cannot conceive the value of being right or wrong about historical fact. Also the conservative evangelical desire to be right about theology is devalued by the liberal. Second, liberals repeatedly imply that by not taking things literally they are taking them "seriously." This is a frequent jab at traditionalists as though conservative exegetes do not take the text or its admonitions seriously. Third, when "age-old questions of faith and meaning" are "received in innovative ways" some form of heresy almost always results. Theology is not a

---

18. Funk, *The Once and Future Jesus*, 10.
19. Meyers, *Saving Jesus from the Church*, 116.

discipline of innovation. For the liberal it is because God is in process, therefore just as technology changes with advancement, so must theology change as God advances and grows. But this is flawed to the core because of its conception of the mutable nature of God that I discussed earlier in the chapter.

Historic orthodoxy rejects this false separation of orthodoxy and orthopraxy. To have the latter we must possess the former. It is as basic as having the right coordinates before leaving on a trip. If we don't get Jesus right we will be following a Jesus of our own invention and he could be rather tasty.

## Claims

Did Jesus claim to be God in the text? The answer is clear: *absolutely*. The table below illustrates some central claims of Jesus that reflect his own self-perception. As one traveling in rabbinical fashion teaching people acquainted with the Old Testament, it is unthinkable that his statements of personal identification would not have been understood as clear claims to deity.

| Characteristic/Role | OT Attribution to God | Jesus's Claim |
| --- | --- | --- |
| Self-existence (aseity) | Exod. 3:14 | John 8:58 |
| Glory | Isa. 42:8 | John 17:5 |
| Eternality | Isa. 48:12 | Rev. 1:17 |
| Shepherd | Ps. 23:1 | John 10:11 |
| Bridegroom | Isa. 62:5 | Matt. 25:1 |
| Light | Ps. 27:1 | John 8:12 |
| Judge | Joel 3:12 | John 5:27 |
| Enduring Word | Isa. 40:8 | Matt. 24:35 |

In John 8:58 Jesus claimed, "Truly, truly, I say to you, before Abraham was, I am." The reaction by the religious leaders who heard him should put to death any doubt as to what he was claiming and what his hearers understood. Verse 59 reads, "So they picked up stones to throw at him, but Jesus hid himself and went out of the temple." Jewish religious leaders didn't stone gentle sages. They understood him to be committing blasphemy by claiming deity and they responded appropriate to their religious law and tradition.

## Conduct

Aside from his claims, Jesus' conduct befitted someone who was deity. He performed many miracles and rose from the dead. Of course the reality of these are disputed by liberals. Their perception of the Gospels and their naturalistic worldview cause them to explain away the plain readings of the text. But pre-modern writers and readers would all have understood Jesus' miraculous acts and their representations in the literature of the four evangelists to be claims to actual events. It is a post-enlightenment hermeneutical phenomenon that we now think the text is actually saying something different from its normative reading. For example, when Jesus walked on water (Matt. 14:22–33; Mark 6:45–52) the original readers' worldview would not have led them to conclude that he was actually walking in a shallow part of the lake or that it was a grand literary metaphor to say something else. They would have just assumed that the claim was "he miraculously walked on top of the water." Whether they believed it or not is irrelevant. They would have understood the description of the action to be claiming the miraculous.

## Character

Jesus' claims and conduct are buttressed by his character. Ironically this is where liberals and traditionalists agree. Jesus' moral character was pristine. In narrative portions of the Gospels accepted even by liberal critics Jesus is seen as guiltless. Pilate found no guilt in him despite the accusations of the Jews (Luke 23:4). Those crucified with him proclaimed his purity (Luke 23:41). The centurion exclaimed the innocence of Jesus upon observing his death (Luke 23:47). Apostolic writings understood him to be flawless and without sin (2 Cor. 5:21; 1 Pet. 1:19; 2:22; Heb. 4:15). His character should lead liberals to reexamine his claims but their presuppositions about the text and their plausibility structure that rules out the miraculous will not permit them to entertain any such concepts.

## Consequences

People don't die for mild cynics. People don't sacrifice their entire lives for remembered metaphorizations. They give themselves for radical beliefs about radical claims. Church history is its own testament to Jesus' identity, or at the very least, to how his identity was understood by generations from Peter and Paul to modern-day martyrs. Early followers of Jesus came from the ranks of monotheistic orthodox Judaism and polytheistic Gentile paganism. They were ideologically predisposed to not follow him. It seems difficult to explain how eyewitnesses ended up following him without having something evidentiary that entirely shook their world.

Those who followed on the heels of the Apostolic witness endured two centuries of sporadic persecution for the sake of Christ based upon the lineage stemming from eyewitness testimony. The medieval church pressed into barbarian, Mongol, and Moorish strongholds through mission efforts, often giving up their lives for the sake of the gospel of Christ. During the Reformation and on through the modern missions movement spurred by William Carey at the beginning of the nineteenth century, proclaiming true doctrine has mattered. The blood of the martyrs is more than the seed of the church as Tertullian famously quipped. It is a further vindication of the seriousness and centrality of Jesus' claim to be God. The absurdity of liberalism is not as much found in its disavowal of the deity of Christ as its attitude that such a notion is superfluous.

Apostolic Christology

The theological detail in which the epistles of the New Testament couch the identity of Jesus is testimony to the importance of the doctrine for the early church. Paul writes the Colossians and in chapter 1 utilizes hymnic material that itself may predate the letter. He says (emphasis mine):

> He is the image of the invisible God, the firstborn of all creation. For by him all things were created, in heaven and on earth, visible and invisible, whether thrones or dominions or rulers or authorities—all things were created through him and for him. And he is before all things, and in him all things hold together. And he is the head of the body, the church. He is the beginning, the firstborn from the dead, that in everything he might be preeminent. *For in him all the fullness of God was pleased to dwell*, and through him to reconcile to himself all things, whether on earth or in heaven, making peace by the blood of his cross (Colossians 1:15–20).

He later speaks of Jesus in the same letter, adding, "For in him the whole fullness of deity dwells bodily" (Col. 2:9). Paul is concerned that the christological precepts of early Christianity include a robust theology of Jesus as God in the fullest sense.

Additionally the author of Hebrews begins his portrait of Jesus with a theological prolegomena that leaves the understanding of deity undeniable. In Hebrews 1:1-4 a remarkable Christology is formed. Smack in the middle of it is a phrase in verse 3 that describes Christ as "the exact imprint of his nature." Two Greek words in this phrase are important. The author says that Jesus is the *character* of God's *hypostasis*. This means that the essential nature of God, his essence, being, or ontology is imbedded in the character of Jesus. The deity of Christ cannot be put more clearly.

The language New Testament writers use for Jesus gives us clear indication as to their understanding of his identity. Matthew says he is Immanuel, meaning "God with us" (Matt. 1:23). Peter and Paul both refer to him as "God and Savior"[20] (Titus 2:13; 1 Pet. 1:1). Importantly, Jesus is repeatedly called "Lord"[21] throughout the New Testament. For any first-century Jew this would have been understood as an attribution of deity to Jesus. He also is called "King of kings and Lord of lords" in Revelation 17:14 and 19:16. This phraseology hearkens back to Deuteronomy 10:17 where God is referred to as "God of gods and Lord of lords."[22] Finally, the title Savior is used repeatedly of Jesus in the New Testament[23] and of God, some eighteen times in the Old Testament.[24] It seems clear that the apostles understood and celebrated Jesus as fully God.

The affirmation of the deity of Jesus intensely impacts our representation of him and our service to him. If he is not God then he is impotent to rescue us from the destructive power of sin. Therefore all the social action in the world done in emulation of his character will be limited in its impact because it will not contain the power to change the human heart.

---

20. A helpful discussion completely accessible to any reader about the role of Granville Sharp's Rule in determining that two nouns are referring to the same person is found in Bowman and Komoszewski, *Putting Jesus in His Place*, 151-52.

21. Acts 4:33; 7:59; 8:16; 9:5; 10:36; 11:16-17, 20-21; 15:11; 16:31; 19:5; 20:35; 21:13:26:15; Rom. 1:7; 4:24; 5:1, 11, 21; 6:23; 7:25; 8:39; 10:9, 13; 13:4; 14:14; 15:6, 30; 1 Cor. 1:2-3, 7-10; 2:8; 4:5; 5:4; 6:11; 8:6; 9:1-2; 11:23, 27, 29, 32; 12:3; 15:31, 57-58; 2 Cor. 1:2-3, 14; 4:5; 8:9; 11:31; 13:14; Gal. 1:3; 6:14, 18; Eph. 1:2-3, 15, 17; 5:20; 6:23-24; Phil. 1:2; 2:11, 19; 3:8; 4:23; Col. 1:3; 2:6; 3:17, 24; 1 Thess. 1:1, 3; 2:15, 19; 3:11, 13; 4:1-2, 16-17; 5:2, 9, 23, 28; 2 Thess. 1:2,7-8, 12; 2:8, 14, 16; 3;6, 12, 18; 1 Tim. 1:2, 12; 6:3, 14; 2 Tim. 1:2, 8; Phlm. 1:3, 5, 25; Heb. 2:3; 7:14; 13:20; Jas. 1:1; 2:1; 1 Pet. 1:3; 3:15; 2 Pet. 1:8, 11, 14, 16; 2:20; 3:2, 10, 18; Jude 1:4, 17, 21, 25.

22. Also note Ps 136:2-3.

23. Luke 2:11; John 4:42; Acts 5:31; 13:23; Eph. 5:23; Phil. 3:20; 2 Tim. 1:10; Tit. 1:4; 2:13; 3:6; 2 Pet. 1:1, 11; 2:20; 3:2, 18; 1 John 4:14.

24. Bowman and Komoszewski, *Putting Jesus in His Place*, 175.

So yes, it does matter whether or not Jesus is God. Orthodoxy is the prerequisite for sound orthopraxy. Robert Bowman and Ed Komoszewski in their really helpful theological presentation of the deity of Christ make clear that knowing about Jesus' identity as divine must reach way beyond propositional knowledge. They write:

> If we are to experience a healthy relationship with God, we need to be intimately acquainted with the biblical teaching about the divine identity of Jesus. This involves more than merely knowing about, and agreeing with the doctrine of the deity of Christ, though that is certainly essential. It must become more to us than a line we say in a creed. We need to know what it means to say that Jesus is God and why it matters. We need to see Jesus as God. We need to think about Jesus and relate to him in the full light of the truth of his identity. We need to appreciate the significance of his divine identity for our relationships with God and others.[25]

Our need to value Jesus' deity is crucial in today's theologically chaotic context. We must be clear about the fact that Jesus was fully and entirely God in the flesh.

## Keeping the Cream Puff Out of the Church

Theological liberalism is based on naturalism and is internally inconsistent. Those incoherent tenets cause intellectual problems for the worldview in general and its view of Jesus in particular. As those who hold to Christian orthodoxy, we subscribe to the idea that Jesus is God. We see it clearly in the text as demonstrated above. Now there is a question that finally comes to the church and its leadership that must be addressed. What is to be done to equip the church to hold fast against the tide of liberal Christology? The answer is found in at least seven imperatives that must be undertaken.

## Teach the Central Tenets of the Faith

People in the local church desperately want to have their felt needs met. With all of the difficulties and challenges that we face in a fallen world this is entirely understandable. The Bible speaks to these felt

25. Ibid, 20.

needs throughout the text; however, it does so predicated upon a layer of doctrinal truth. This is the case whether we are dealing with personal brokenness, relational division, social evil, disappointments, emotional issues, addictions, and on and on. Broken people need the theology of the gospel. Disappointed people need the sovereignty of God. Addicts need to learn and believe in the power of the Holy Spirit. People plagued by the tensions of social evil need to know the meta-narrative of Scripture. In short, we need doctrinal preaching and teaching.

There is no question that we want to be relevant. And certainly speaking to the felt needs of people is relevant. But is doctrine irrelevant? I hope we don't think so. My dear friend Charles Ryrie has seen an awful lot through his many years. In his last, short book, he commented:

> *Relevant* means to have significant and demonstrable bearing on the matter at hand. *Practical* means "to relate to practice." Accusing doctrine of irrelevance or impracticality misuses both terms and assumes the Bible itself (from which our doctrine comes) is irrelevant and impractical. Of course, no one would want to make such a charge against the Word of God—at least not out loud.[26]

Unfortunately many pastors and teachers do make this charge indirectly and by their silence. I am deeply concerned about this. Preaching should never be stale or a form of dead orthodoxy, but it had better include a healthy dose of orthodox theology. People need spiritual meat to survive in times where the devil is looking to eat their lunch. If Sundays continue to be solely about milk we will find our people malnourished and ready for the world, the flesh, and the devil to pick them off. People need to be behaviorally changed. However, such change cannot occur unless a change first takes place in their thought patterns. No change can come to a person's thought patterns without their presuppositions being challenged and at times reframed. In this sense there must be an apologetic aspect to our preaching. We need to show people their need, show them how a deep and rich God can fill it, give them the necessary content and tools to appropriate the truth of God, and convince them that applying it is worth it. All of these are part of good preaching.

---

26. Ryrie, *Ryrie's Practical Guide to Communicating Bible Doctrine*, 3.

## Engage Naturalism at a Popular Level

I have discussed naturalism throughout much of this chapter in one form or another. As church leaders we must understand that by the very fact that we serve in the western world, the default human mind is largely naturalistic. We cannot change this overnight. It is embedded in almost every area of our culture. But we must expose it or it will be a silent killer to the world of the Spirit in our midst. My attempt to show the incoherent worldview of theological liberalism was an attempt to put on display what happens if we pull back the curtain on naturalism. We will find that it doesn't fit with what we say we believe, but ironically, it does dictate quite a bit of our practice.

I assume, like most people, when you get a headache your first thought is to take a pill to kill the pain. Isn't it interesting that for most of us our first impulse is not prayer? I certainly am not saying we shouldn't take the pill, but doesn't our first impulse usually portray our default understanding? In life we tend toward looking for and expecting natural causes. Even in the church we tend to operate as though God is present but we are seemingly unsure what it would look like if he really showed up in power, and we are often not overly convinced that he will. This needs to change.

Here are some practical ways to engage naturalism on a popular level in the local church. First, raise the bar of expectant prayer. People need to look to God in a manner that actually believes he engages the natural world. Second, as a church leader you need to read and study so your faith can be intellectually robust. Third, take on the naturalists in preaching and teaching. There is little worse than a church that seems afraid of the intellectual corridors of naturalism and atheism. Show the church that there is nothing to fear. Fourth, refer to pop-cultural media that attempts to smuggle in naturalistic themes. Engage it in teaching, small groups, and discipleship and train people to uncover it and see it for what it is.

## Embrace Intensive Discipleship

At the church I pastor we have thrown a lot of our eggs in the basket of intensive, gender-based, adult discipleship. Discipleship does not happen by accident. We need intentional ministry modalities focused on holistically helping people as they journey the long, twisty, narrow road of kingdom living. It is my belief that a formal approach to discipleship is crucial for the local church.

Here is how we do it at Lifeline Community. I will share how our men's discipleship works just to illustrate the general concept. We have two levels of discipleship. One encompasses the disciplers (or disciplers-in-training) and the other consists of those being discipled. Once a week early in the morning I meet with our disciplers. This is a time for me to pour into them. I take them through material that is rigorous and intended to stretch them both intellectually and personally. We have spent extensive time doing work in theology, apologetics, ethics, spiritual formation, rudimentary logic, and philosophy as well as other disciplines. Each morning the men come prepared to discuss the material for that day. Additionally one of them prepares a devotional reflection from a particular passage of Scripture that is planned out on a schedule ahead of time. They start the morning sharing what God has taught them from the text. We then go into our discussion of the material at hand. We also spend time in prayer and sharing with each other.

The men who attend that meeting are involved in discipling other men within the church. They do so anywhere from one-on-one to one-on-five. They have a set curriculum that they utilize with these men that starts with practical issues in the life of a man and moves toward deeper issues of spiritual theology. In this forum we stress transparency, accountability, and community. The net effect is that these discipleship groups become essential to the spiritual journey of these men. Ultimately our hope is that men in these small cohorts will desire to move forward and be disciplers and eventually transition to our disciplers training module. We have seen it work very effectively with both our men and our women. We have tweaked it a bit for our women to attempt to zero in on the best structured modality for their lives. But all in all it retains a similar pattern.

There are a few presuppositions that I have that root me in this modality. First, if you do not call people to something that demands enough that they could fail, it is impossible for anyone to actually succeed. If no one fails then it is highly likely that the mechanism is not excising anything from anyone. This only feeds our natural bent to be minimalists in terms of our spiritual growth. Second, ambiguity is the death of ministry. If we think discipleship just happens because people come Sunday morning or go to a small group or go through a class, we are fooling ourselves. The flesh is relentless and subtle. Discipleship provides an intensity of focus and relationship that serves as a great weapon against the evil one. Third, people long for community, and a structured approach to discipleship creates a context that is very difficult for someone to simply bail on. In that sense it is a great safeguard if someone throws themselves into it. Fourth, it is a great place for the gospel to be regularly on display as brokenness is made visible and covered by selfless love through mutual relationships pointed toward the glory of God.

Recapture the Value of Social Action

Liberalism was birthed in an effort to lay hold of social action. The problem was they left behind the gospel—the most vital component to make social action effective and enduring. As we will see, fundamentalism made the mistake of swinging the pendulum too far in the other direction and left social action to those touting a social gospel. One of the attempts of the emergent church has been to return to a focus on social action. The problem is that they are not sufficiently breaking from the tenets of the liberal social gospel. In recent years a growing focus of churches committed to the true gospel is figuring out how to share that gospel while valuing social action.

At the level of the local church we need leaders who will value the dignity of humanity. We need leaders who recalibrate their ethic to a biblical one that recognizes the high premium the Bible places on caring for the poor and needy. We need churches that will refuse to leave behind the verbal proclamation of the gospel of the forgiveness of sins and entrance into kingdom life while filling empty stomachs, caring for hurting people, meeting the needs of social niches, and planning to care for orphans and widows.

## Encourage Integrated Thinking

People tend toward compartmentalization. They create categories like academic and practical or like orthodoxy and orthopraxy. While sometimes these are helpful for conceptualization and presentation of facts, they are rarely helpful for application. For example, if I say I believe in the sovereignty of God over all things, then I am said to be "orthodox" in my perspective of his control of the universe. But if I fret and worry over the safety of my children when they are away from me I am said to be failing in orthopraxy. Yet belief and knowledge surely constitute more than mere assent to a set of facts. They also contain experiential and habituated practices. So what tends to happen is we draw a solid line between thinking and doing when at best a dotted one exists and at times no line exists at all. Romans 8:6 tells us, "For those who live according to the flesh set their minds on things of the flesh, but those who live according to the Spirit set their minds on the things of the Spirit. For to set the mind on the flesh is death, but to set the mind on the Spirit is life and peace." There is a deep connection between the focus and content of our mind and fidelity and content of our actions.

At the level of the local church, leaders need to bridge the chasm between the isolated realms of orthodoxy and orthopraxy. Teachers need to be integrationists. They must make the connections between deep theology and deliberate living. People make choices that are always connected to worldviews of one shape or another. The choice is never in a vacuum. Consequently teachers, preachers, disciplers, and leaders must help people connect their choices to theology; otherwise, those choices will not only be disconnected from God but they will be connected to something else.

In preaching and teaching we take from the historical move through the theological and land in the homiletical or applicational. There will be more about this process later in the book but for now we need to recognize that our people need to see the middle step. They need to know from whence the application comes, not merely what it is.

In addition to preaching and teaching we need to be sure that in our repertoire of small-group ministry, discipleship cohorts, counseling ministry, youth and children's ministry, and various other modalities, we ask the "why" question. Unless we ferret out reasons for specific behaviors we will never be able to show the gospel's answer for those attitudes and modes of thought that brought about the behavior.

## Reclaim Our Cultural Posture

In one sense pastors have lost respect, and it is both very sad and very bad. It is sad because the pastoral office is a type of priestly role. Please do not misunderstand. All believers are priests in the sense that they have direct access to God and do not need a human mediator. But in another sense pastors represent God to his people. They are under-shepherds. They open the Word of God and have the responsibility to accurately represent to God's people in the present situation what God said in space and time to his people long ago. They are bearers of truth in the fullest sense of the word. That is to say, they bring embodied souls to connect with reality in such a way that those persons leave transformed. They carry out "holy orders" as it were.

But today the office has been sold out by many of its practitioners. Pastors are CEO types. They are upper-management folk interfacing with middle-management directors who interface with real people. We have all of these catchphrases like, "The church rises and falls on leadership," or "You don't have a money problem in your church; you have a vision problem." These are just catchy ways of telling men in ministry, "If you don't attend mechanistic conferences on sociological growth principles and innovative marketing techniques you are failing your church and being an irresponsible leader." This pastor-as-CEO is destructive because it makes the office revealed in the text of Scripture into something that is not revealed in the text of Scripture. In this way pastors have capitulated to cultural corporate and economic norms instead of getting a scriptural job description.

This is not the only way the office has been despised. In an effort to be among the people and meet them where they are at, many have minimized the life of the mind in the pastoral role. To say that this is killing us would be an understatement. There was a day when the local church pastor in a community was seen as a primary intellect in community affairs. His thoughts on ethics were valued. His voice on civics was heard. His philosophical perspective had gravitas. Now we live in an age where young people desire ministry (not very acquainted with its demands, I might add) and assume that their desire should cash out in opportunity. Now people care more what Tom Cruise thinks about kids on medication than their local clergy. They care more about Oprah's metaphysic than their local pastor. Dr. Phil is seen as an expert on marriage but not their local church elders. And why is this? There are at least five reasons.

First, *men and women have rejected the church's call to holiness so they reject the prophetic witness to holiness*. This first issue will almost always be with us to some degree or other. Second, *men and women in vocational ministry disconnected the value of rigorous orthodoxy from orthopraxy and we are now paying the price*. My previous remarks on integrated thinking should be revisited here. Third, *the life of the mind in general has been shunned*. It seems foolish to some for a pastor to read philosophy, to stay culturally informed, to be abreast of comparative religions, to study ethical frameworks, to be an apologetic expert, and to be informed on the history of ideas. As a result ministers forfeit their own cultural position. Fourth, *some have bought into the cultural isolationism of fundamentalist thinking.* There will be much more about this to come in chapters 3 and 4. Fifth, learning has been divorced from theology rather than captured by it. If our goal is transformation then we must seek to bring philosophical thought, scientific thought, historical thought, ethical thought, religious thought, sociological thought, and psychological thought in conversation with and ultimately under the umbrella of theology as "the queen of the sciences." The Puritan Richard Baxter wrote to pastors long ago, saying:

> If tutors would make it their principal business to acquaint their pupils with the doctrine of salvation, and labour to set it home upon their hearts, that all might be received according to its weight, and read to their hearts as well as to their heads, and so carry on the rest of their instructions, that it may appear they make them subservient unto this, and that their pupils may feel what they aim at in them all; and so that they would teach all their philosophy in *habitu theologico,* — this might be a happy means to make a happy church and a happy country. But when languages and philosophy have almost all their time and diligence, and, instead of reading philosophy like divines, they read divinity like philosophers, as if it were a thing of no more moment than a lesson of music, or arithmetic, and not the doctrine of everlasting life, — this it is that blasteth so many in the bud, and pestereth the church with unsanctified teachers.[27]

Baxter is not rejecting other bodies of knowledge and the importance of them. He is simply saying that they must be brought into the sanctified imagination afforded a theologically astute mind.

## Mitigate the Relationship Between Science and Faith

Many lay persons in the church have the idea that science and the Bible are somehow opposed. I think this is in large part due to young-earth fundamentalism that cynically treats the scientific community as a subversive entity. This is unfortunate and unfair. It also has severely impacted the church's ability to represent the Christ and his kingdom to the scientific intelligentsia with any modicum of success. That some feel this is acceptable and a result of "standing up for truth" is alarming and paints the church as led by ideological rednecks. This needs to change. And,

27. Baxter, *The Reformed Pastor,* 59–60.

actually, I would contend that unless we do so, we will find ourselves simply ignored by adherents to Cream Puff Jesus.

This does not mean that we have to hold the same convictions about origins of the universe, modes of biogenesis, and the nature of human persons as many in the scientific community do. But it does mean that we had better be able to engage the scientific community with some level of intelligence, a lack of ideological myopia, and a heart bereft of hostility. If you doubt whether Christians or creationists are guilty of misrepresenting science, just analyze not the content but the presentation of the film *Expelled* featuring Ben Stein, or read some of the acrimonious rhetoric from the pens of many young-earth creationists. I think we can and need to do better. It starts with the church.

One way of engagement is for church leaders to acquaint themselves with the issues in the philosophy of science. Most of us lack the technical training to be scientists, and yet we certainly have the opportunity to think about how we think about science. Contrary to many atheistic scientists and naturalistic apologists, science is not a purely objective, data-driven discipline. Scientific observations must lead to normative conclusions that must in turn be interpreted by people both inside and outside the scientific community. As Nancy Pearcey and Charles Thaxton observe:

> Moreover, contemporary historians argue that it is impossible to neatly separate out something called "pure" science from the "external" religious and metaphysical influences that supposedly "contaminate" it. Fundamental decisions within science are necessarily affected by extra-scientific commitments. The facts that a researcher considers scientifically interesting in the first place, the kind of research he undertakes, the hypotheses he is willing to entertain, the way he interprets his results, the extrapolations he draws to other fields—all depend upon prior conceptions of what the world is like.[28]

Faith and science are not inimical to one another. When pastors act as though they are, they belie the statement "all truth is God's truth." To say that science and faith need to be "reconciled" is the equivalent of saying that special revelation and general revelation need to be reconciled. But this would be absurd because both are spheres of God's dominion.

---

28. Pearcey and Thaxton, *The Soul of Science*, 74.

Church leaders need to treat them both as such and keep rigorous engagement open with the scientific community.

## Conclusion

Cream Puff Jesus vacates Christ of his deity and renders him impotent. As much as the theological liberal cries out that Jesus is, in some way, a figure of the present, in reality he cannot be one from their vantage point. Instead he *was* an apocalyptic prophet of history or a wise and gentle sage. We can learn from his example and even follow in his reformist footsteps. But make no mistake, he functions as fodder for inspiration or a model of how to live but he elicits no actual personal transformation of the heart. As a result social justice movements can only go so far.

The cream in the puff is naturalism and it must be expunged by critical thinking and by exposing its necessary conclusions. This is not merely the job of Christian academics but of church leaders. Theological liberalism's naturalistic subtext creates key incongruities with some of its ideological claims. These incongruities show that naturalism fails miserably to account for the plight and promise of the human species. Consequently, the most expedient option for theological liberals is to recognize their naturalistic assumptions and reject them in exchange for a robust supernaturalism that looks with expectation on an organic Jesus who died for sinners and rose from the dead and lives forever exalted reigning over his kingdom.

# 3

# No Carb Jesus

## The Christ of Fundamentalism

*So you want to know where a man stands with God? You have only to ask him one question: What do you think of this university?*

BOB JONES SR.

*You can't handle the truth!*

JACK NICHOLSON AS COLONEL NATHAN JESSUP

I WENT ON A no carb diet once . . . once . . . did I mention I only did it once? I can still remember the night I exploded at dinner after having three straight days of Canadian bacon covered in melted cheese (that was six years ago, and I don't think I have eaten any since). I sat at the table with my fork in one hand and my knife in the other, looked at my wife, two children, and a dear friend we had visiting us in town from Texas, slammed my utensils on the table and chanted in rhythm "*I want bread! I want bread! I want bread!*" It was not a pleasant experience for anyone in the house.

The premise behind a "no carb" diet is that by limiting access to foods high in carbohydrates you allow your energy to come from fat being burned off rather than the sugar from the carbohydrates in your system. So by reducing your carbohydrate intake you lose weight, because you are giving your cells an alternate source of fuel for energy via the fat in your body. Makes sense, right? Well, sort of. The problem is that it has created a public perception in some that carbohydrates are somehow the enemy, when in truth they are an essential fuel for life. We need carbohydrates, they are essential, but we just don't need them exclusively.

Believe it or not the no-carb craze found its origination not in South Beach, but up in the Arctic with Eskimos in the early portion of the twentieth century. An explorer named Vilhjalmur Stefansson lived among the Eskimos off and on for a time from 1906 to 1918, subsisting on a diet of only meat and water. His tastes adapted and his health remained strong. At the outset of his experience he did not care for fish, but over time he began to gain a taste for it and even began to prefer boiled fish—and the Eskimo delicacy of rotten fish—over baked fish. Subsequent to his time with the Eskimos he participated in dietary studies at Bellevue Hospital in New York to further his theses about issues of human nutrition that had developed in the Arctic. Reflecting on his journey in a series of articles in Harpers Weekly running from November 1935 to January 1936, he began with the following:

> In 1906 I went to the Arctic with the food tastes and beliefs of the average American. By 1918, after eleven years as an Eskimo among Eskimos, I had learned things which caused me to shed most of those beliefs. Ten years later I began to realize that what I had learned was going to influence materially the sciences of medicine and dietetics.[1]

Steffanson's experience, testimony, and subsequent involvement in dietary experiments began the forays into a no-carb world which popular programs like the Atkins diet and the South Beach diet built into commercial weight-loss juggernauts. Such diets can whip you into shape quick but usually serve as a poor long-term alternative to a traditional balanced diet.

I have observed a parallel idea emerge in terms of spiritual health among many Christians. Often those who ate the worst spiritual food and who came to Christ out of the most radical ethical junk food imaginable respond by enacting the strictest spiritual diet possible. It is usually laced with a no-carb overreaction to the excesses of their past. While this is often a helpful corrective at the outset, it makes for a poor approach to enduring as a disciple of Jesus. The danger is not found in the zealous

---

1. Stefansson, "Adventures in Diet: Part 1."

departure from former things but the rabidness and myopia that often contributes to the filter for what is acceptable in their new-found Christian life. And frankly this overreaction could easily be viewed as a relatively harmless and fairly natural step in the process of being made new in Christ and maturing in the new life of his kingdom. However, the real issue emerges with grave seriousness from sectors that ought to know better. And this is my concern here when considering the emergence of a No Carb Jesus. The Jesus who dwells in rigidity seems to be the primary cameo of the Christ of Christian fundamentalism.

There is a sense that has evolved in fundamentalist circles that only certain portions of the spiritual diet matter, a sense that the "meat of the matter" is truth and that the ethos of life is a carbohydrate of sorts that is non-essential or maybe even inconsequential to spiritual health. This may seem like an overstatement, but in practicality I think it is not. Both my study of history and my own personal experience bear this out. In fact, I think this lack of a traditionally balanced spiritual diet is absolutely toxic and is to be blamed for much of the failure of the church in its gospel mission and for feeding some reactionary movements that now threaten historic Christianity. This false dichotomy is a separation of the *how* from the *what*, a separation of the *disposition* of Jesus from the *doctrine* of Jesus. Such a bifurcation is a blight on true Christianity and serves only to push people away from the Christ of history.

## A Necessary Nutritional Change

So how did such a dichotomized Christianity evolve? How did the *how* get separated from the *what*? The answer is found in a pendulum swing that has been regrettably all too common a story on display throughout Christian history. Throughout the history of the church actions produce reactions that often find their identity mainly as foils to the individuals or ideas they are reacting to. In some ways this is the kernel of truth embedded in Hegel's dialectic. Often as a thesis is put forward and gains a following an antithesis emerges that also gains a reactionary following. Eventually they end up producing a modification of the original idea and its counterpart. Again, this is called a synthesis.

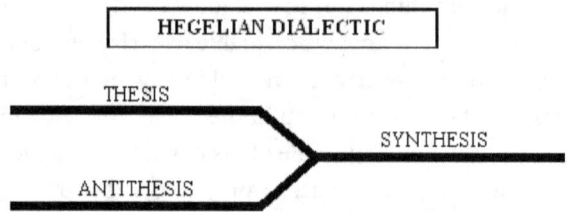

Liberalism provided a thesis, and fundamentalism became the antithesis. This was not an unhealthy development at the outset because liberalism, as we have already seen, needed some major corrections. However, the movement came to be too defined by what it had reacted to rather than what it positively purported. Consequently, the Jesus that emerged was one whose doctrine was on the whole rather healthy but whose disposition was severely lacking. So the fundamentalist answer to that infamous question "What would Jesus do?" was defined by Jesus' rebuke of others and his more spirited statements like those found in Luke 12:49–53:

> I came to cast fire on the earth, and would that it were already kindled! I have a baptism to be baptized with, and how great is my distress until it is accomplished! Do you think that I have come to give peace on earth? No, I tell you, but rather division. For from now on in one house there will be five divided, three against two and two against three. They will be divided, father against son and son against father, mother against daughter and daughter against mother, mother-in-law against her daughter-in-law and daughter-in-law against mother-in-law.

Of course this text is true enough, but the mantle of Christ-likeness is woven with more than one thread. And the misapprehension and misappropriation of Jesus' disposition has left a serious and perilous pit in the midst of what is often a fertile doctrinal field.

With this in mind the task now emerges to sketch the development of this Jesus in an effort to better understand how to reclaim what has been lost. We will do so by briefly highlighting the factors that contributed to the rise of fundamentalism, recounting the history of its growth and observing the present tenets that characterize it.

## Factors

There are many factors that play into the rise of fundamentalism. However, the shortest and probably most accurate summary to a complicated history is simply to say that it was a reaction to the rise of liberalism. It was a nutritional alarm that went off when the body began being fed a string of cream puffs from the hand of liberal spiritual chefs. The spiritual health of the body of Christ began to be compromised by liberalism and many, attuned to lack of health, responded by taking radically appropriate measures.

At least three important issues at the heart of the liberal agenda came together and fueled what became known in the early twentieth century as "Fundamentalism." The first of these was the role of *higher criticism* and its assault on the biblical text. This was mentioned in the first chapter as I dealt with the various quests for the historical Jesus that have taken place subsequent to the writings of David Strauss and the theology of Schleiermacher and Ritschl. The second issue was the strong influence of the *social gospel*. Furthering Ritschl's ideology that Christianity was primarily to be concerned with present morality, men like Walter Rauschenbusch and Shailer Mathews brought home to the church the implications of a Christ devoid of deity but deeply concerned about human morality. This was particularly true in terms of mutual concern for one another and outreach to the marginalized. The third issue was the growing influence of *Darwinism* in the intellectual life of western culture. Its role as a theory of origins challenged traditional interpretations of the Genesis account and acted as a handmaid to the tenets of higher criticism in the deconstruction of the text of the Bible. Its place in the launching of fundamentalism was cemented by the Scopes Trial in 1925, in which a public school teacher was put in trial for teaching Darwinism. These three factors created a concern among a large constituency of American Christianity that the church was losing its moorings and that fidelity to long-held essential doctrines was being threatened.

## Historical Beginnings

Out of the concern generated by these factors emerged the movement that came to be known as fundamentalism. The term "fundamentalist" was coined by Curtis Lee Laws in 1920. Laws was an editor for a publication called *The Watchman Examiner*, and he used the phrase to describe those ready to do battle for the fundamentals of the faith. If this description adequately defined present-day fundamentalism then I would have no objection with it, particularly as these early adherents came to define the fundamentals. In fact their understanding of the fundamentals of the faith had already been codified in rather lengthy expression through a series of volumes aptly titled *The Fundamentals* published from 1910 to 1915. *The Fundamentals* served as a collection of thoughts on a large number of doctrines and topics ranging from the liberal misuse of higher criticism to theological and apologetic matters to addressing other movements that had nothing to do with liberalism. Nonetheless it did act as a sort of theological banner that could be waved proclaiming where the objectors to this upsurge of liberalism stood.

Those carrying this banner were not monolithic in their theology, but they did rally together as scholars and pastors opposed to the influence of liberalism and its post-enlightenment approach to life in the modern world. Perhaps historian George Marsden's description says it best: "Fundamentalism was a loose, diverse and changing federation of co-belligerents united by their fierce opposition to modernist attempts to bring Christianity into line with modern thought." [2] So first and foremost it was a reactionary and, in my estimation, absolutely necessary movement whose focus was to retain a commitment to the core of historic Christian dogma.

It should be noted that fundamentalism emerged as an American movement responding to ideas of European origin. This may be one of the reasons why fundamentalism as conceived of by British thinkers like James Barr and Harriet Harris is often treated as one with evangelicalism. Harris, in her book *Fundamentalism and Evangelicals,* interacts extensively with Barr's critique of both, which he sees as one and the same. Both authors home in on the fundamentalist doctrinal commitment that evangelicals have for inerrancy, and therefore conclude that they are linked because of this mutual commitment. However, it seems to me that they have missed that the real point that separates evangelicals from fundamentalists is not primarily doctrinal but dispositional. It is historically ignorant to conclude that a mutual affinity for inerrancy unites the two movements when in fact they divided over dispositional discontinuity and a departure regarding doctrinal taxonomies.[3]

2. Marsden, *Fundamentalism and American Culture*, 4.

3. Harris is admittedly much softer and more rounded in her critique than is Barr's work *Fundamentalism*. Harris herself states the following: "Evangelicalism predated

The establishment of fundamentalism as a movement in the western world was at the beginning of an enormous cultural shift. World War I wrapped up in 1918 and left deep scars of fear and insecurity on the human psyche. In fact, the first half of the twentieth century was so dominated by war and poverty that it set a trajectory of insecurity and cynicism which flowered into the postmodernism that is such a crucial part of the landscape of society today. In this corporate mentality came modernist ideas like the three factors mentioned earlier, along with the additional nihilistic baggage of Nietzsche's thought that extended Darwinian naturalism to its logical conclusion that life is devoid of meaning. Standing for historic Christian thought amidst this raging confluence of ideologies called for leadership of both able mind and disposition. Such a man was found in Princeton scholar J. Gresham Machen.

Machen served as a professor of New Testament at Princeton from 1906 to 1929. He later left with a number of other faculty from Princeton and founded Westminster Theological Seminary. Machen gave intellectual teeth to the fundamentalist movement that was often viewed as being largely anti-intellectual. Machen was a scholar and was not as overreactive to the winds of liberalism as some were. In fact, in many ways he was not a typical fundamentalist. This may be what gave him a wider and more receptive hearing as the best spokesperson for the cause. While strongly objecting to the march of liberalism, he held views out of step with others who would be considered by many as part of his constituency. For example, he believed in a form of theistic evolution, differing with many others considered as fundamentalists by the broader culture. He was a political libertarian, opposing many in the conservative church by standing against prohibition. Additionally, he was not a fan of revivalist preaching and methods that captivated many churchgoers of his day.[4]

fundamentalism and is likely to survive beyond it. Various evangelical movements co-operated in the fundamentalist coalition of the 1920's, and various evangelical movements emerged out of that fundamentalist episode. Clearly evangelicalism is too wide a phenomenon to be equated with fundamentalism. Moreover British evangelicals have not exhibited militant or separatist attitudes to the same degree as American fundamentalists. Yet these considerations do not make it inappropriate to suggest that contemporary evangelicals are 'fundamentalist' in Barr's sense. Barr's principal argument is that many evangelicals reflect a fundamentalist mentality regarding scripture." Harris does distance herself a bit from Barr by stating, "To propose, however, that evangelicals share fundamentalist ways of thinking is not to equate evangelicalism with fundamentalism." Harris, *Fundamentalism and Evangelicals*, 56.

4. Hart, "When is a Fundamentalist a Modernist? J. Gresham Machen, Cultural Modernism, and Conservative Protestantism," 614–17.

Machen's definitive diatribe against liberalism was published in 1923 under the title *Christianity and Liberalism*.

In this work, Machen gave an incisive assessment of the blunders of liberalism. He deftly analyzed liberalism's faulty concepts of the major matters of Christian doctrine. He accurately saw the root of liberalism subsisting in the soil of naturalism. In his introduction he noted:

> The movement designated as "liberalism" is regarded as "liberal" only by its friends; to its opponents it seems to involve a narrow ignoring of many relevant facts. And indeed the movement is so various in its manifestations that one may almost despair of finding any common name which will apply to all its forms. But manifold as are the forms in which the movement appears, the root of the movement is one; the many varieties of modern liberal religion are rooted in naturalism—that is, in the denial of any entrance of the creative power of God (as distinguished from the ordinary course of nature) in connection with the origin of Christianity.[5]

Having identified naturalism as the foundation, Machen saw the construction of liberalism's edifice for what it was. He spent the rest of the book assessing and dismantling the walls of higher criticism and its assault on the biblical text, the walls of a deconstructed Christology, and the walls of a social and moral soteriology and ecclesiology.

Machen's influence sparkled in part because he could not be dismissed as lacking intellectual clout. He was a Princeton scholar of the first order and was not given to hyperbolic reaction or oversimplification. He employed clear-cut reason with an adroit hand. In 1937 even the mordant satirist H. L. Mencken, who was himself no friend of Christianity, lauded Machen's offensive against the theologically liberal intelligentsia in an obituary in the Baltimore Sun, stating:

> Dr. Machen argued them quite out of court, and sent them scurrying back to their literary and sociological *Kaffeeklatsche*. His operations, to be sure, did not prove that Holy Writ was infallible either as history or as theology, but they at least disposed of those who proposed to read it as they might read a newspaper, believing what they chose and rejecting what they chose.[6]

---

5. Machen, *Christianity and Liberalism*, 2.
6. Mencken, "Dr. Fundamentalis," In North, *Crossed Fingers*, Appendix A.

Machen lent credibility to the response to liberalism, something that was much needed in light of what many saw as a debacle for fundamentalism in the 1925 Scopes Trial.

In the secular media, fundamentalists took it on the chin. They were largely perceived as anti-intellectual, back-woodsy Bible-thumpers. This perception probably emanated from a couple of realities. First, liberalism seemed to make its primary appeal to the cultured highbrow. With their penchant for higher criticism, social awareness, and scientific inquiry, the liberals set the stage to appeal to a particular constituency. This made fundamentalism a foil movement perceived to reject progress and wave the banner of old-time dogma. Second, fundamentalism had two primary loci of effectiveness. One was in the north with Machen and other Princetonians. The other, however, was in the south, now commonly known as the Bible Belt. Here the movement was more grassroots, more the product of the popular culture. In the north, fundamentalism was a reactionary reformist movement; in the south it was simply the old standard. The south was more rural and easier to push aside as lacking the requisite sophistication for new ideas and progress.

In 1925, John Scopes, a high school biology teacher in Dayton, Tennessee, was put on trial for teaching Darwinism. The trial, in the minds of many, served to cement this cultural chasm and its import into the emerging perspective of fundamentalism. More significant than the trial itself was what the trial came to mean for a culture trying to find itself amidst the ecclesiological and philosophical tensions of the early portion of the twentieth century. The trial was surrounded by a circus-like atmosphere and was the first trial carried live on national radio. It became immortalized in the play "Inherit the Wind," written in 1950 and first put on display in 1955. Five years later it was adapted to the big screen. While the play and movie did not directly cite the Scopes Trial, the trial served as the historical basis for the theatrical presentation. Historically, the play intended to combat the intellectual paranoia of post-World War II America. However, part of its legacy was found in the caricatures it created of the defense attorney Clarence Darrow and the statesman William Jennings Bryan, a fundamentalist who joined the prosecution. Neither Darrow nor Bryan worked alone, but history canonized them as the leaders of the warring factions. The trial ended prematurely when Darrow requested that the jury return with a guilty verdict so the case could then be heard before the Tennessee Supreme Court. However, just prior to its end, a famous confrontation took place between Darrow and Bryan that only fed into popular stereotypes as Bryan floundered under Darrow's interrogation. This was only exacerbated by the fact that Bryan was then unable to cross-examine Darrow or deliver his closing remarks.[7]

The fissure between fundamentalism and liberalism was becoming clear and pronounced. In the north a doctrinal and intellectual response to liberalism was provided by Machen. However, the intellectual climate provoked a creation of new institutions rather than the reformation of old ones. This trajectory of engagement by extraction, rather than engagement by endurance within the failing institution, afforded a culture that later fundamentalism would take to extremes—ones that Machen and others of his ilk likely never intended. In the south, the gap only widened at the popular level as a result of the role of Bryan at the trial in Dayton. Fundamentalism as a movement was now distinct from its liberal counterpart, though a bit unorganized as it approached the years of the Great Depression and World War II.

## The Nature of the New Diet

One of the defining features that helped carry fundamentalism was the founding of institutions of higher learning. This proved crucial in rearing up a new generation of people to carry the agenda forward, yet it only further darkened the lines between fundamentalism and broader culture. A number of schools had been started a decade or two earlier, but some significant institutions sprung up in the mid- to late 1920s that gave real momentum to the counter-liberal movement. Machen's break from Princeton created the founding of Westminster Theological Seminary in 1929. The dispensational tradition found a hub for its development in the founding of Dallas Theological Seminary by evangelist Lewis Sperry Chafer in 1924. In 1927, a Southern Evangelist named Bob Jones started a university that would bear his name and eventually become a flagship institution for a unique and defining brand of fundamentalism. These schools, and several already existing institutions like Wheaton College and Moody Bible Institute coupled with the robust Bible Conferences that met in various portions of the country, provided real steam to the movement through the nation's economically lean years.

7. For an intriguing look at what Bryan would have said in his closing statement and in his expected cross-examination of Darrow based upon Bryan's speeches leading up to the trial and the transcript of his undelivered closing argument, consult the article "Revisiting the Monkey Trial" by Todd C. Riniolo and Lorenzo I. Torrez,

As fundamentalism glided through the 1930s, there arose the clear need to establish a more united front. Unity is always a difficult task, but it was doubly difficult to bring together individuals and institutions that had both staked their claim as a reactionary movement to liberalism and created a self-perception as the guardians of doctrinal truth. However, many individuals began to recognize that more could be accomplished together than apart. As a result, in 1942 the first meeting of the National Association of Evangelicals (NAE) was held with 147 delegates. The impetus for bringing people together across denominational lines was largely the work of J. Elwin Wright, who had been instrumental in bringing evangelicals together in the New England area. He, along with Harold Ockenga, pastor of Park Street Church; Will Houghton, president of Moody Bible Institute; and several others, led the formation of this united front.

They were not, however, enthusiastically joined by all fundamentalists. Some felt that this new organization was too lax in its associations and not strident enough in its opposition to liberal coalitions like the Federal Council of Churches.[8] The most noteworthy dissenter was Carl McIntire who spent most of his life in Collingswood, New Jersey, across the Delaware River from Philadelphia, and founded the Bible Presbyterian Church. McIntire was a staunch fundamentalist whose identity was closely tied to what he stood against. In many ways he was at the forefront of a divide that would come swiftly to the fundamentalist cause primarily over the issue of ecclesiastical separation. The NAE was not particularly interested in courting McIntire either. In fact, one of the key factors in the formation of the NAE was a desire to be less bombastic. They sought to form an identity based on a positive yet conservative position rather than one rooted in a posture of militancy and isolationism. Martin Marty and Scott Appleby note as much in speaking about the formation of the NAE:

> To a person, however, they had trouble with the face fundamentalism wore. They were convinced that fundamentalists were misplacing the scandal of Christianity. Non-converts and others who might be attracted to conservative evangelical witness

---

8. The Federal Council of Churches was formed in 1908 and was later merged with other similar organizations to form what is now the National Council of Churches. The present organization retains its liberal form including such heterodox organizations as the Reorganized Church of Jesus Christ of Latter Day Saints (now called Community of Christ) and The Swedenborgian Church.

were being alienated by the brusque manners, the militancy, the shocking intentions of the McIntire types. [9]

While Marty and Appleby are mostly correct, it should be noted that one of the 147 delegates at the initial gathering in St. Louis would shortly leave the ranks of his fellow evangelical associates and become one of the most influential propagators of militant fundamentalism. His name was Bob Jones.

Jones was from southeastern Alabama and became an evangelist at a young age. In 1927, Jones, a Methodist, founded Bob Jones College. The school's first campus was located in Panama City, Florida. It later relocated to Cleveland, Tennessee and eventually found its home in Greenville, South Carolina. Jones was initially on the same page with the NAE's philosophy of retaining conservative convictions while allowing some the freedom to remain in denominations battling liberalism as possible lights of change. Jones himself retained his membership in the Southern Methodist Episcopal Church as several battled liberalism's influence. But Jones and his son Bob Jones Jr. did not maintain this marriage with the NAE for very long. The Joneses and the NAE were heading two different directions and the influence of three men shook the ground enough that people began to align on various sides of the fissures.

In 1947, Carl F. H. Henry wrote a defining book entitled *The Uneasy Conscience of Modern Fundamentalism*. An introduction was scripted by his like-minded friend and Fuller Seminary colleague Harold J. Ockenga, the first president of the NAE. These two placed a fork in the road of early fundamentalism because of the course they felt the movement was on. They became the scholarly point of the sword that began to press on the fundamentalism of the late 1940s, seeking a realignment of its objectives. The perfect complement to their academic pursuits came in the inimitable figure of the young evangelist Billy Graham. Graham's populist appeal, combined with Henry's journalistic abilities and Ockenga's statesmanship, created a triad that pressed fundamentalism into self-evaluation and caused some to jump ship and walk a different path.

In 1948, Harold Ockenga, made clear that he was proposing a "new evangelicalism" in his leadership of the organization. This "new evangelicalism" emanated from a repudiation of what fundamentalism had become in its development from the mid-1920s to the mid-1940s. He cited three areas that this new branding differed with much of what fundamentalism had become:

---

9. Marty and Appleby, *The Glory and the Power*, 67.

A repudiation of the doctrine of separation
A summons to greater social involvement
A determination to engage in theological dialogue with liberalism[10]

Briefly looking at each of these three in turn will help create a deeper understanding of the issues at the heart of the fissure that created modern evangelicalism and modern fundamentalism.

## It's All in the Seasoning

Emeril Lagasse is known for his culinary prowess. He is an acclaimed chef and has starred in literally thousands of television episodes on a number of networks teaching people how to cook and disseminating his recipes to households all over America. He is most known for a signature move he has when cooking. At a critical juncture, when he adds some spice or seasoning to his recipe, he startles the audience by exclaiming *"Bam!!"* as he tosses a dash of this or that on a piece of food. He knows that those crucial additions make all the difference to the palate and he celebrates their additions with a *"Bam!!"* here and a *"Bam!!"* there.

The three areas mentioned above define the flavor of modern evangelicalism and modern fundamentalism. Each segment of Christianity has created a distinct flavor to their theologies of Jesus and the church that make for a unique taste as these three seasonings create very distinct experiences of engagement.

## Bam!! #1: Separation

First and undoubtedly central was the issue of separation. This was the fundamentalists' focal point as seen in their own historical assessment of their rejection of the new evangelicalism. In 1973, fundamentalist historian and Bob Jones University church history department chair George Dollar wrote *A History of Fundamentalism in America*. In it he attempts—in classic fundamentalist style—to kick theological posteriors and take names. Particularly insightful into the psyche of the separatist is his chapter entitled "The Face of Fundamentalism, 1973." Here we find a fundamentalist giving his take on the state of the church in his day—1973—and what fundamentalists should be concerned about. He

10. Beale, *In Pursuit of Purity*, 262.

states positively the doctrines which fundamentalists must assent to, in part saying:

> The historic fundamentalist accepts literally the teachings of the Bible concerning the conduct of the church, the two ordinances of baptism and the Lord's Supper, *the relationship of believers to the systems of the world, separation from worldly things* and the demands of the Bible for service and obedience on the part of every truly re-born believer ... The historic fundamentalist not only holds to the exposition of the Bible in its every affirmation and attitude *but also sets himself to expose every affirmation and attitude not found in the Bible*. His negatives, like his affirmations, are as many as those of the Bible. *To expose is as vital to his faith as to expound the truths of the Scriptures*. Truly he has no creed but the Bible.[11] emphasis added)

Additionally, he went on to list twelve dangers facing fundamentalism, the last of which is their stance on separation. Subsequent to this, Dollar followed through with his own admonition to others by listing people and organizations contemporary to him that warranted caution and others that ought to be accepted. He broke the organizations into three categories: militant fundamentalists, moderate fundamentalists, and modified fundamentalists. The militant class holds to separation as an essential doctrine for ecclesiastical purity and therefore warrants his endorsement. His closing paragraph in the chapter, like the book itself, is telling of the self-perception militant fundamentalists have of what comprises real fundamentalism (emphasis mine):

> Nevertheless, despite their inevitable shortcomings, lists of organizations within *professing* fundamentalism must be made and continue to be made so that *genuine* fundamentalists will know where to direct their support. There is a general drowsiness among the saints at present, who have been so lulled into sleepy self-satisfaction that few are inclined to believe there is any danger at all. Most offer their support and blessing indiscriminately to the militant, the moderate and the modified. How much compromise can be allowed before non-cooperation is a Biblical demand? *To obey the Lord in the responsibility of separation will demand keenest discernment and a willingness to follow Biblical convictions wherever not only apostasy but also compromise has taken hold.*[12]

11. Dollar, *A History of Fundamentalism in America*, 265.
12. Ibid., 288–89.

The emphasis and role played by the doctrine of separation is at the heart of what comprises fundamentalism and makes it distinct from evangelicalism. This was the claim staked by the Bob Joneses. They wrestled with the direction of the fundamentalist movement as the 40s wore on and began to grow weary of its direction; as Henry and Ockenga transitioned it from the late 40s into the early 50s. But the philosophical cauldron boiled over when Graham, a former Bob Jones University student, put on his definitive evangelistic crusade in New York lasting from May 15 to September 1, 1957. Graham's event was sponsored by the ecumenical Protestant Council of New York, a group which contained liberal churches. Graham famously permitted participation from Roman Catholics in his crusade effort. He allowed for some politicization of the crusade with an appearance of then-Vice President Richard Nixon at an event in Yankee Stadium on July 20.[13] Such engagement with non-fundamentalists left a bad taste in the mouths of the Joneses and only made clear their fears of where these "new evangelicals" were headed. In his insightful book on the Joneses' legacy in fundamentalism and the separatist movement, *An Island in the Lake of Fire*, Mark Taylor Dalhouse notes:

> . . . without question, Graham's 1957 crusade was a watershed event in the deepening division between fundamentalists and new evangelicals. Graham's inclusion of liberal Protestants in his evangelistic efforts was a microcosm of the new evangelical strategy of reestablishing dialogue with those once dismissed as "modernists."[14]

This dialogue was of no interest to those rejecting the agenda proffered by the new evangelicalism. Soon two paths would be clearly established: one taking the moniker "evangelicalism," and the other retaining the old descriptor "fundamentalism." Although each path could hardly be characterized as unified, these two labels do suffice to create two definable rubrics identifying these divergent perspectives within Christian orthodoxy.

---

13. Billy Graham Center, "Crusade Timeline."
14. Dalhouse, *An Island in the Lake of Fire*, 83.

## Bam!! #2: Social Involvement

A second point identified by Ockenga was the church's role in the sphere of social issues. For Ockenga and Henry, the neglect of social action in the early years of fundamentalism felt like a failure. They keenly sensed the need for the church to hold to doctrinal purity while persisting in meeting the earthly needs of people. These needs were raw in the American psyche, having just come through the Great Depression and having just witnessed the intense devastation foisted on the globe by the colossal conflict of World War II. The American political engine was now directed toward rebuilding what had been torn down, and the question loomed as to what role the church was to have in the economic and social plight facing the culture. The bane of the fundamentalist movement up to this point was, according to this new evangelicalism, its lack of active social concern. Perhaps Ockenga put it most succinctly in his introduction to Carl Henry's definitive piece in 1947 when he wrote, "The church needs a progressive fundamentalism with a social message."[15] But to the ears of many fellow fundamentalists, such language spelled compromise.

The ties between theology and morality were so tight for many fundamentalists that engagement in a cause that either required or suggested work with an individual or organization holding to an aberrant theological paradigm was unacceptable. Often the theological citadel of the rabid fundamentalist was defined more by his juxtaposition to lesser matters of Christian dogma or social ethics than to the core components of Christian orthodoxy. This, in part, was what Henry was expressing concern about in his book. In fact, aspects of Henry's book read eerily prophetic some sixty-five years later. Consider the statement from early in the book as an artifact of his historical concern (one I still share with him six decades removed):

> It is not fair to say that the ethical platform of all conservative churches has clustered about such platitudes as "abstain from intoxicating beverages, movies, dancing, card-playing and smoking," but there are multitudes of fundamentalist congregations in which these are the main points of reference for ethical speculation. In one of the large Christian colleges, a chapel speaker recently expressed amazement that the campus newspaper could devote so much space to the all-important problem of

---

15. Henry, *The Uneasy Conscience of Modern Fundamentalism*, xx.

whether it is right to play "rook," while the nations of the world are playing with fire.[16]

Setting aside the fact that I was a regular Rook player in my Christian college dormitory, it occurs to me that the chapel speaker and I share a mutual amazement. This obsession with individual nuances of personal holiness in clearly non-essential matters to the minimization of involvement in serious issues of global well-being has been all too typical of fundamentalism throughout the years subsequent to the schism of the 1950s. In an effort to recast the idea that fundamentalism through the 1970s and mid-1980s was not concerned about social issues, one fundamentalist journal chronicles the articles of social import emerging from fourteen years of Bob Jones University's publication *FAITH For the Family*. However, the author's attempts fall painfully short and only expose the reality that fundamentalism's leading lights had little concern for the social issues that weighed heavy on the collective conscience of the masses and that likewise adhered to a biblical concern for social ethics. The author's main explanation for this is that the fundamentalists were so driven by theological integrity that they under-engaged sociopolitical issues. He dismisses this neglect as merely a matter of priorities, stating near the end of the article, "Fundamentalists chose in favor of the theological, and it may appear that they were rejecting any presence in the political arena. In reality, however, they were simply going about it in accordance with their own predetermined guidelines."[17] But this is entirely unhelpful. This amounts to saying they chose this path because this is the way they thought. But this is not much of an explanation and certainly provides no vindication for the false dichotomy between theological and sociopolitical concerns. Can one really expect to focus on theological realities, ignore sociopolitical ones, and pretend he has a robust theology at all? Ironically, the fundamentalist concern for morality only fed one direction: from morality to theology. They were concerned that their theology would be stained by a lack of morality rather than allowing their worldview to flow the other, more biblical direction. Morality is the outflow of theology and so the new evangelicals rightly asserted that a theology that was unconcerned with moral and social renewal was not a full theology at all. The danger is not that morality will rob theology but that

---

16. He devotes an entire chapter to the subject entitled "The Apprehension over Kingdom Preaching." (41–54).

17. Mayes, "Fundamentalism and Social Involvement."

a weak theology will have no sway over social morality. This defensive posture led to a false bifurcation and drove Henry and Ockenga in their quest to ensure that this new evangelicalism retained a holistic devotion to the doctrine of Jesus.

Henry's picture of Jesus diverges from the fundamentalist portrait in a couple of ways. First, we can note an eschatological difference. Henry noted in his work that Jesus was deeply concerned with kingdom preaching. For Henry this meant a present reality of the kingdom, not just a future reality of the kingdom indicative of the fundamentalist dispensational perspective of the mid-twentieth century. While it seems to me that many writers tend to overplay the role of dispensationalism in the lack of present social concern, it no doubt was likely a factor in the theological underbelly of many. If the kingdom is solely thought of in terms of future restoration, and if Jesus' rapture of the church comes in the context of cosmic upheaval, then why concern ourselves much with the here and now? Henry stepped away from what he saw as an under-realized eschatology to one that embraced both present and future redemptive activities as part of the kingdom of God.

Second, Henry has a practical theology of Jesus that understood him to be a socially involved and concerned Messiah. At one point in his book he highlights Matthew 11:4–5 and Luke 7:22, which both read:

> And he answered them, "Go and tell John what you have seen and heard: the blind receive their sight, the lame walk, lepers are cleansed, and the deaf hear, the dead are raised up, the poor have good news preached to them."

He then comments, "In view of so central a passage, it is difficult to find room for a gospel cut loose entirely from non-spiritual needs . . . There is no room here for a gospel that is indifferent to the needs of the total man nor of the global man."[18]

Third, he crucially refuses to see social action outside of the redemptive work of Jesus. In this he is thoroughly in concert with his fundamentalist forbears.[19] Again and again he draws the reader back to the idea that

---

18. Henry, *The Uneasy Conscience of Modern Fundamentalism*, 34–35.

19. Note Machen, *Christianity and Liberalism*, 152–56. Here in his definitive work, Machen lends no credence to the idea that social concerns ought not be the concern of the church. He states: "The 'otherworldliness' of Christianity involves no withdrawal from the battle of this world; our Lord Himself, with his stupendous mission, lived in the midst of life's throng and press. Plainly, then, the Christian man may not simplify his problem by withdrawing from the business of the world, but must learn to apply

the gospel is work of redemption. In this he asserts that non-Christian solutions are inadequate because they have no means for the redemption of fallen creatures and only this ultimately reforms society.[20]

## Bam!! #3: Intellectual Inquiry

Finally, the third element in the division between the new evangelicalism and fundamentalism was their respective reactions to liberal academia. On the one hand, the new evangelicalism deemed such intellectual engagement in the public square as crucial for the broader goals of cultural transformation. In contrast, those who carried the fundamentalist label after the 1950s took a very different approach to culture and intellectual inquiry.

At this time of transition in the mid-twentieth century, Fuller Seminary, with Henry and Ockenga, certainly led the way in engaging critical liberal scholarship. Perhaps no one held the intellectual bar with such capability as Edward J. Carnell. Carnell died at the relatively young age of forty-seven, but in his brief years he accomplished quite a lot. He wrote on mainly two fronts. On the one hand he defended conservative protestant orthodoxy against its liberal counterparts in academia. He was well tested in his ability to engage the intellectual elites of modern liberalism, having studied theology and philosophy at the doctoral level at Harvard University and Boston University respectively. This educational background, coupled with his familial background as the son of fundamentalist Baptist minister, equipped him to deal on both fronts. He was known for his vigorous, and at times harsh, criticism of fundamentalism while at the same time laboring to defend the faith in the face of the liberal elites. This made him somewhat a casualty of history. He stood in a middling position as a sort of pioneer of evangelical engagement to come.[21]

---

the principles of Jesus even to the complex problems of modern industrial life. At this point Christian teaching is in full accord with the modern liberal Church; the evangelical Christian is not true to his profession if he leaves his Christianity behind him on Monday morning. On the contrary the whole of life, including business and all of social relations, must be made obedient to the law of love. The Christian man certainly should display no lack of interest in 'applied Christianity.'" Machen, *Christianity and Liberalism*, 155.

20. Some relevant passages in *The Uneasy Conscience of Modern Fundamentalism* include: 36, 72–73, 78, 87.

21. Concerning Carnell, George Marsden notes: "Carnell's intellectual contributions should be viewed in this context of the new evangelicals' larger hopes to transform the culture. Like Graham, Carnell hoped to help turn the nation around by

While Carnell represented the new evangelicalism's penchant for intellectual engagement, the Joneses typified fundamentalism's alien mentality. Their concern for purity of doctrine led to a hedgehog mentality that valued ideological protection over critical engagement. As Dalhouse observes, "The Joneses . . . feared that the new emphasis upon research, critical thinking, and dialogue with liberals was diverting evangelicals from their primary mission of evangelizing. Liberals were to be converted, not debated."[22] This last statement betrays a characteristic of fundamentalism that evidences itself in more than one arena. There is a deliberate prioritization of the individual over the community. This manifests in its general lack of concern for social ills, as well as its focus on individual conversion with little thought to defeating the greater cloud of liberal theology responsible for much of the confusion oppressing the minds of the masses. Individual evangelism should not be divorced from the need to engage and refute the broader forces that keep individuals in the dark. The latter lays the strategic groundwork for the former.

The assessment above is not intended as an exhaustive history but as essential historic bullet points for apprehending the formation of the Christ of fundamentalism. Certainly there are groups that I know well who fit somewhere between the two poles,[23] but by describing things as I have my hope has been to make clear the soil from whence this Jesus has grown. In the years since the definitive schism of the 1950s, we have seen the rise—and some might say fall—of the Moral Majority, which

---

effectively presenting essential gospel teachings, while jettisoning what he considered the counterproductive peculiarities of fundamentalism." Marsden, "Edward J. Carnell," In *Makers of Christian Theology in America*, 485.

22. Dalhouse, *An Island in the Lake of Fire*, 69–70.

23. While being admittedly generalist in this brief accounting of the schism which created evangelicalism and fundamentalism, I don't want to be too simplistic. Not everyone fits into tidy categories. In fact, one of the more uncomfortable postures was held by my own alma mater, Dallas Theological Seminary. Dallas found itself somewhere between the two camps of fundamentalism and evangelicalism. In principle its concerns then resemble my concerns now even though we the specific issues at play today are different than they were then. Writing about Dallas, historian John Hannah reflects that "in the 1950's, the school was neither in the fundamentalist camp nor the emergent evangelical camp, yet it was criticized for being too fundamentalist by the evangelicals and too evangelical by the fundamentalists." John Hannah, *An Uncommon Union: Dallas Theological Seminary and American Evangelicalism* (Grand Rapids: Zondervan, 2009), 157. In a sense it could please no one. The main concern of Dallas and other institutions like it was their desire to hold fast to the doctrines of the faith but also to carefully represent the ethos of Jesus as well.

was its own interesting attempt to engage culture in political reformation. It crafted its own political Jesus. It merged a brand of fundamentalism's iconoclastic, hard-edged Christ with a Jesus concerned about specific social issues like abortion and the retention of traditional marriage. For some reason the needs of the poor seemed to still lack emphasis, even though for the New Testament Jesus they seemed to be important.

Additionally and in response to the Jesus of fundamentalist modernism and impotent Jesus of present-day evangelical pop culture, a postmodern Jesus has come on the scene and two chapters in this book will be devoted to this reactionary Christ. But for now it will suffice us to say that the Jesus of fundamentalism still remains rigid and cold. And the roots of Machen in the early twentieth century seemed to have been reconfigured in the late 1950s to create a Christ that selectively resembles the Jesus of the Bible.

## The Food Critic

A good food critic has more than one category of analysis. He looks at the good and the bad, rendering as even and unbiased an assessment as possible. I have no illusions that I make a particularly unbiased critic. I do, however, think that I am at the very least experienced and informed enough to critique the Jesus of fundamentalism.

I was raised on the sunny side of the mountain of fundamentalism in upstate New York. I am very grateful for what it gave to me. I learned the Bible early on. I heard its stories, felt the flannel graph, sang the children's songs, attended the revival meetings, recited the memory verses. I felt the love of the community and listened to the word of God proclaimed every week without fail. I attended Bible college and look back on those who formed me then as key contributors to God's work in my life. I had the privilege of investing in ministry with some of the most passionate people I have ever met, some of whom were exceptions to the rule. It was, on the whole, the mountain's sunny side.

But I was also witness to another side, a darker side, whose error has marginalized many from ever embracing the love of Christ. A side whose victims bloviate in online chat rooms and often tack on to their fundamentalist upbringing new worldviews of agnosticism and atheism. A side whose self-righteous, self-aggrandizing disposition has fostered alienation in the name of standing strong for truth and left many a potential believer more distanced from the gospel than before they met these "truth speakers." A side whose No Carb Christ was held up as a model of health but who in reality could only be ingested for a season without causing the life to convulse with a lack of needed spiritual sugars. For a healthy life entails more than doctrinal protein; it must also consist of the sweetness of a Christ-reflecting disposition. Perhaps an anecdote from family will illustrate my point.

My grandfather was a man's man. He fought in World War II in the Pacific theater driving supplies up the Burma Road from Rangoon to Kunming in an effort to help supply the Chinese as they battled Japanese forces. In his younger years he was a pretty rough-and-tumble customer whose stories alone might make for an interesting read. He made his civilian living as a long-haul truck driver until arterial sclerosis took away his ability to maintain that career. He perseveringly endured over twenty surgeries and was finally left with just a stump for a right leg. In the midst of these life-altering trials—the premature retirement, the loss of a leg, the pain of operation after operation—he was visited by a local pastor from one of the Baptist churches in town. Now, to be sure, my grandfather had never been a very religious man. He was not particularly interested or disinterested in God. Like many he was a man living his life aloof from certain weightier matters, the kind of man Qoheleth warns in Ecclesiastes to refrain from chasing the wind. So there he sat, just the kind of man in just the kind of physical situation with just the kind of spiritual need to benefit greatly from a strategic visit with a shepherd who represents the Good Shepherd. But there was one serious fly in what should have been the ointment of grace: a minister devoted to No Carb Jesus.

Pastors are to be "ambassadors," people who represent the One sending them in a manner indicative of his character. This pastor failed and the consequence of that encounter has long lingered in my family. Upon entering my grandparents' home he informed my grandfather that the reason he was having his leg amputated was that he was a wicked sinner. True enough. The same could be said of me and every person I have ever met. That idea is as orthodox and central to Christian theology as anything I have ever considered. This minister could rest assured that he had carried the doctrine of Jesus accurately out on his pastoral visitation. But something happened in the encounter. My grandmother was also present and clearly heard his pronouncement of doctrinal veracity. But in an ironic twist her heart was not pierced by the arrow of truth; instead, she became enraged and proceeded to usher him out of the house (likely with some choice words of her own that would restrict me from Christian publication).

This encounter forms a lingering question: Was the pastor right or wrong in his pontification that my grandfather's loss of his leg was the result of sin? Well, in a general sense yes, the same way that every physical malady that befalls any human is the result of the sin of Adam. But that is not what the minister meant. He intended to draw a direct connection, like the disciples in John 9, between specific sins and physical judgment. So I ask again: Was he right? Maybe. Maybe not. I don't know if he was right about his sin causing his leg to be amputated any more than Pat Robertson knows about the cause of Hurricane Katrina or the Haitian earthquake. But one thing is true of No Carb adherents: They apparently have been ceded special status as armchair prophets, postulating the motives of the divine mind. What I do know is that while that minister may have left feeling like he proclaimed the truth, what he actually did was presume to know the mind of God and relate in an unbiblical manner to people he was called to, all the while probably feeling like he had just been persecuted for bearing witness to the truth. Somewhere between the front door and the living room the disposition of Jesus took a backseat to the doctrine of Jesus and believe me, it was no help in winning the hearts of my grandparents to the gospel.

## Conclusion

I once knew of a well-educated minister in the Northeast (who is now with the Lord) that used to refer to fellow Christians that disagreed with him on substantial theological issues as "our cousins in the Lord." If this were't so tragically sad it might have been funny. Does God see people as his "nephews or nieces" rather than his children? Should the Lord's Prayer begin "Our Uncle in heaven, hallowed be your name"? Should I be so myopic as to want brothers and sisters who don't think like I do removed one familial step from me? Such condescension makes light of the doctrine of adoption, deals haphazardly with the unity of the church universal, and contains an unfortunate hubris that allows one to sit in the ecclesiological catbird's seat picking off those who dare to disagree. While I am deeply troubled with the Tasty Jesuses represented in this book, I am careful to acknowledge that there are only two categories regarding our relationships with others: either we have a sibling relationship in Christ or we don't. In his wisdom God affords us no second-tier relationships in his family. If he did, we surely would retreat from one another rather than stand in the unchanging (and at times uncomfortable) kinship demanded between mutual heirs of a common kingdom.

My hope in this chapter and the next is both to call and warn. I want to call my fundamentalist friends to reassess whether or not they have really laid hold of a complete picture of Jesus. Additionally, I want to warn the unsuspecting within the folds of fundamentalism and those yet to be impacted by its Jesus. Be careful that the economy of Jesus' evaluation of true disciples is yours as well. After all, it was he who declared "By this all people will know that you are my disciples, if you have love for one another" (John 13:35). Ironically, this same Jesus saved his harshest rebuke for those who thought that they had dotted every doctrinal "i" and crossed every doctrinal "t." There is no place for mealy-mouthed theologians but neither can we accept doctrinally precise but dispositionally discordant representatives of the Christ who modeled for us perfect orthodoxy and perfect orthopraxy.

4

# Enjoying the Fruitfulness
# of a Carbohydrated Christ

*You can safely assume that you've created God in your own image when it turns out that God hates all the same people you do.*

ANNE LAMOTT

MY GRANDMOTHER TOLD ME a story from her youth that is at the same time comedy and tragedy. She grew up in the same small town that I spent my early years in. In fact, basically her whole life has been spent in this community. When she was in her pre-teen years in the 1930s the town had a theater where people could go and watch films. In the mid-1930s, of course, film was itself a controversial new entertainment technology that the church had to grapple with. It is no secret that fundamentalism has struggled a bit (the understatement of the decade) to relate to the entertainment industry and the stamp it continues to make on culture. As people filed into the local theater, they were watched by the local pastor of the Nazarene church across the street. His name was Pastor Butt (which makes the story all the more comical).

Pastor Butt would watch from the balcony of his home in the upstairs apartment over the church and eye all the "sinners" going to the evening movie, likely hoping that none of them were members of his congregation. One particular weekend the Nazarene church was having a revival meeting and members were praying down front, calling for revival. One of the members named Roxy was deeply "moved" to begin calling down judgment and fire upon the town because of all the sinners in the community. Roxy, pounding her fist, railed against the unrighteousness in true fundamentalist fashion, asking God to send down fire on the brazen and seditious townspeople. As she bellowed her plea the town fire siren rang out. Indeed fire had come! But, to whom? In an ironic twist that can only be characterized as divine, Roxy's own kitchen was on fire!

At first I wondered if the story was more small-town apocrypha than real history. But, as I have probed, my grandmother's knowledge of event details leads me to believe that it really happened. Regardless, it communicates a deep hypocrisy that has been the perceived modus operandi of significant portions of fundamentalism. Many stand askance of it because it seems to propagate one thing (often doctrine) while ignoring other meaty matters (often disposition). And frankly the concern is more than anecdotal. Certainly hypocrisy is no respecter of persons. Believe me, I know all too well the hypocrisy of my own heart. However, it is one thing to be a hypocrite but quite another to be hypocritical about your hypocrisy. This "second-order" hypocrisy, as I call it, creates a double standard. It actually highlights a pertinent and pressing failure of fundamentalism to hold up under its own standard of being a biblically healthy representation of Christ.

My hope in this response chapter is to articulate some ideas that need to be noted and acted upon to reshape this faulty vision of what Jesus wants his church to be. I also hope to provide some practical suggestions for not only how individuals ought to respond but how the local church itself can steel up its faithful to properly add the disposition of Jesus to the crucial doctrines of the faith.

## Emphasizing Adverbs

I am in search of an adverbial Christianity, a religion of ethos. I recall reading Philip Yancey once and I took note of him citing an old Puritan saying that went, "God loveth adverbs." For those of you grammatically challenged just remember that adverbs "add" to the verbs. They tell us what the action is like. They create the aroma of the moment. They define the nature of what is done. They create our take-aways from interpersonal engagement. The difference between "she rebuked me graciously" and "she rebuked me harshly" tells more than just how she rebuked me.

Adverbs play a role beyond syntax. They exist beyond grammar. It would be good to mention a few things about the powerful import of adverbs.

*Adverbs tell a story about the heart.* They force who we are out of hiding and make public the state of our souls. They are more than footnotes to living. They form the vehicles for everything from holiness, freedom, and trust to discrimination, marginalization, and manipulation. Since Christianity is fundamentally a transformation from the inside out, the real story of who and whose we are is a narrative writ large in adverbs. Therefore, if we are not attuned to the fact that they act as a thermometer of the inner man or inner woman, we may find ourselves swept up in a grand delusion about the real condition of our own spiritual lives.

*Adverbs take on a prophetic character.* They prepare for a particular response. Adverbs till the soil of the heart and lay the groundwork for the development of such essential relational properties as trust, vulnerability, mutual appreciation, joy, and sorrow. They set the relational and communicative table with knife and salad fork or sword and pitchfork. Their power to invoke a response is as real and regular as the earth's rotation, and anyone who doubts this either has his head willfully in the sand or suffers from a social awkwardness that requires more help than this book can afford. Because this is true we often have to take some responsibility for the response of others. No, we do not "make" them do anything, but let's be realistic, we do deeply influence others, and no action happens in a vacuum. Obtuse approaches to human relationships only end in disaster. Ask any husband who has not yet figured out his adverbs!

*Adverbs reflect our identity.* The Bible is rife with rich meaningful descriptors begging us to place the control center of our soul in a posture reflective of God and his kingdom. In fact, it is only when our adverbs reflect the rule of God in Christ that we can even begin talking about the benefits and blessings of the kingdom life. In Colossians 3 Paul speaks of this kind of life zeroing in on the orientation of the soul. He references both heart and mind and the need for both to be caught up in the life of God. And then in verse 3 he poignantly states, "For you died, and your life is now hidden with Christ in God." In what sense have I died? My death is a death to self, to my flesh, to the baser proclivities of my nature. It is what John Owen called the mortification of the flesh. And it is in this mortification, this battle to the death with death, that life springs anew in blossoms of adverbial proportions. Why does this happen? It happens because my life is now hidden with the Son in Trinity. My life is being taken over by the attributive properties of trinitarian wholeness. No, I am not becoming God, but I am beginning to resemble my Father's character and my relationships are beginning to look like that model divine community. This is simply the way life is in his kingdom because the kingdom takes on the character of the King. In fact, after a number of exhortations to personal holiness and admonitions to act rightly toward each other, Paul shows his deep concern for this aroma of ethos (Col. 3:12–17):

> Therefore, as God's chosen people, holy and dearly loved, clothe yourselves with compassion, kindness, humility, gentleness and patience. Bear with each other and forgive whatever grievances you may have against one another. Forgive as the Lord forgave you. And over all these virtues put on love, which binds them all together in perfect unity. Let the peace of Christ rule in your hearts, since as members of one body you were called to peace. And be thankful. Let the word of Christ dwell in you richly as you teach and admonish one another with all wisdom, and as you sing psalms, hymns and spiritual songs with gratitude in your hearts to God. And whatever you do, whether in word or deed, do it all in the name of the Lord Jesus, giving thanks to God the Father through him.

His concern is with *how* they clothe themselves, not *that* they clothe themselves. His concern is with *how* they admonish one another (with the word of Christ richly inhabiting life), not *that* they admonish one another. His concern is with *how* they sing (with a heart full of gratitude), not *that* they sing. His concern is with *how* they do deeds (giving thanks[1]), not *that* they do deeds. Simply put, mature Christians learn, know, and grow in their capacity to direct their adverbs properly.

The use of adverbs reminds me of when I used to coach high school basketball in Texas. I was the first varsity assistant in a successful program for four years. The head coach was a good friend and very knowledgeable both in terms of the game itself but also in terms of how to teach young men how to play it successfully. More times than I could possibly count a player would ask about a specific situation and where he should be on the court in that particular situation. My friend was always careful to teach the principles of any defense or offense thoroughly and go over it multiple times, but as these individual situations would arise, and players would be out of position and asking repeatedly where they should be

---

1. The Greek term here is a present participle which constitutes a continual idea. The disposition of thankfulness is to be perpetual.

positioned on the court, he would usually answer the same. He would look at them and say "Figure it out!" . . . in a way only a coach can.

What I found interesting is that this wasn't because he didn't know where they were to be, it wasn't because he was too lazy to tell them where to go, and it wasn't because they didn't legitimately need to get in a different posture or position. It was because he knew that in the game they could not be told where to be all of the time; practice was their lab to figure it out, but *they* needed to figure it out. That was something that he couldn't do for them. The mark of their basketball maturity in the system he had designed was adaptability to the given situations that may or may not arise. I think this is a poignant illustration for the use of adverbs in relational life. Mature people have learned *how* to respond, not just what to respond with. There is no paint by numbers approach to Christian living even though book upon book, sermon upon sermon, and children's curriculum upon children's curriculum seems to imply otherwise.

*Adverbs tell the story of discipleship.* This scent of intangibles, these relational pheromones, are the indispensible qualities that make for a truly Christian life. But this crucial component of spiritual health seems to have been seriously under-emphasized in our concepts of outreach and disciple-making. This de-emphasis has contributed to the hostilities that many have toward fundamentalism. Ironically, some fundamentalists throw the masses' rejection of their gospel and doctrinal message aside as simply a rejection of the truth, and wear this rejection with pride as a sort of battle scar. They seem almost oblivious to the fact that they were not rejected because of the propositions themselves but because of the caustic adverbs that surrounded it. The package is important because we are not relaying information to automatons. We are sharing truth and hope with complex souls called "persons." The cause of the gospel and the drive for discipleship is not aided by trying to cram information down anyone's throat. However, it is enhanced by information amalgamated with interactive relationship and properly distributed with the recipient's nature in mind.

Peter clearly had this issue as a concern in his first letter. He wrote to people who were isolated and suffering. They knew what it felt like to live as strangers or temporary residents in a place they did not really belong.[2] Their identity as minority truth-holders in a world that did not receive

---

2. In 1 Peter 1:1 his addressees are identified as "exiles," later in 1:17 he exhorts them to live in reverent fear during their "exile," and finally the two Greek terms already used come together in 2:11 where he identifies them as "sojourners" and "exiles."

them and did not understand them is evident. They easily could have had the same proclivities of a marginalized self-identity that often pervades certain forms of fundamentalism. Knowing this, Peter engages them with a particular sensitivity to their suffering, but he is always mindful that, amidst their societal pressure, they must respond with a proper temperament. So in 1 Peter 3:14–16 we read:

> But even if you should suffer for righteousness' sake, you will be blessed. Have no fear of them, nor be troubled, but in your hearts honor Christ the Lord as holy, always being prepared to make a defense to anyone who asks you for a reason for the hope that is in you; yet do it with gentleness and respect, having a good conscience, so that, when you are slandered, those who revile your good behavior in Christ may be put to shame.

Part of what it means to "in your hearts honor Christ the Lord as holy" consists of how we respond to people who may be inquiring about or even be opposed to our faith. The "how" is typified by two attitudes: gentleness and respect. The first term "gentleness" is also used in 2 Timothy 2:24–25 to speak of a very similar situation.

> And the Lord's servant must not be quarrelsome but kind to everyone, able to teach, patiently enduring evil, correcting his opponents with gentleness. God may perhaps grant them repentance leading to a knowledge of the truth;

In 2 Corinthians 10:1 Paul employs the same term to describe an attitude of his that resembles the demeanor of Christ: "I, Paul, myself entreat you, by the meekness and gentleness of Christ—I who am humble when face to face with you, but bold toward you when I am away!" So for Peter to call his readers to respond to others with gentleness was the same as appealing to them to put on the character of Christ in this particular situation. So this is the other side of Peter's "honor Christ the Lord as holy." Make no mistake, this needs to be taken seriously by fundamentalists who long to share the gospel with the world and trumpet the call for personal holiness. This same apostle calls his readers to "be holy" (1 Peter 1:16). But he will not let his readers turn the call for holiness into a theological hammer to drive wedges of distance between them and the culture at large around them. While they carry their alien identity (1 Peter 1:17; 2:11) they are also called to maintain an ambassadorial status. Our alien identity is never held to the exclusion of our ambassadorial role. We cannot have our interactions characterized by severity or austerity and declare that we do so because we are passionate for the holiness of God. Such an approach only defames the name of the One we claim to revere.

## Carbing Up on Adverbs

Practically speaking, those of us teaching and preaching must begin to emphasize the "how" from the pulpit as much as we emphasize the "what." So much of the health of the body of Christ is incumbent upon the health of interpersonal communication. As if relationships weren't complex enough, the challenge of getting our adverbs right is only exacerbated by the social-media revolution of the present day. We live in a world where there are seven hundred Facebook status updates per second and six hundred Twitter posts per second.[3] In 2010 there were 294 billion e-mail messages sent every day.[4] It was estimated in 2010 that by that year's end 6.1 trillion text messages would be sent.[5] Never before has there been more potential for errors in how we relate to one another. So if there is one area we need to spend time teaching and preaching on at the local church level, it is how we relate to one another. This is vital advice to all of our churches because certainly fundamentalists do not have the corner on the market when it comes to poor communicative patterns. Nonetheless the issue is deeply relevant to a spiritual psychology that sees imitating Christ as too often best expressed by harsh rebuke and tends to define itself by what it is against rather than what it is for.

## Engaging Hubris

By its very nature hubris destroys it subject. It becomes intoxicating and spellbinding for those enveloped in its grasp. It nibbles at each of us, and one of the great tasks that each of us has is, like Cain in Genesis 4, to master it before it masters us. But it is a sly monster. My brother-in-law once had a fellow student inform him that he "prided himself in his humility." Apparently the oxymoronic nature of such a comment skipped by the young man, but his careless remark is indicative of the subtleties of pride as it contends for control of the soul.

---

3. McGee, "By the Numbers Twitter Vs. Facebook Vs. Google Buzz."
4. Pingdom, "Internet 2010 in Numbers."
5. Reisinger, "6.1 trillion, "text messages to be sent in 2010."

Fundamentalism has been guilty of falling prey to hubris, which accounts for at least some of the backlash that it has received. Again it becomes too easy to simply charge everyone who disagrees with us as guilty of "rejecting the truth." The visceral responses that certain brands of fundamentalism receive have very little to do with truth or untruth but are absolutely rooted in feelings of being marginalized by arrogant people. In a chapel message at Bob Jones University, Bob Jones Sr., the school's founder, once declared, "So you want to know where a man stands with God? You have only to ask him one question: What do you think of this university?"[6] This is hubris, pure and simple. As good as Bob Jones felt about the state of his university, he wrongly saw it as an adequate mirror of the God of the universe. The absurdity of the statement is almost comical, but the laughter ceases when we contemplate the depth and danger of the problem. Many of the "rebellious" people that have abandoned their fundamentalist heritage were running more from the Christian soldiers than from Christ himself. Tragically, the good doctrine that much of fundamentalism espouses gets thrown out the window as these rebels run from the acerbic attitude of the fundamentalist.

Ironically this "fundamentalist danger" was alive and well in Jesus' day, and we know exactly how he responded to spiritual arrogance. Matthew 23 shows us Jesus' concern for his followers' well-being as they were under the influence of the Jewish religious leaders of the day. This text is one of the most direct and brusque extended statements in all of the Gospels. He turns his open rebuke of the leaders into a classic "woe oracle" reminiscent of the prophets. This would not have been lost on religious leaders with a clear grasp of the Scriptures. Of particular interest is the manner in which he begins the oration in verse 2: "The scribes and the Pharisees sit on Moses' seat, so practice and observe whatever they tell you—but not what they do. For they preach but do not practice."

In the wisdom of Jesus we find the first problem with hubris: *it produces hypocrisy by calling others to a standard that it is both unwilling and impotent to uphold.* It writes punctilious checks that its preachers are not prepared to cash.

Later in the same proclamation Jesus pulls out yet another problem with hubris that has been utterly cancerous to the testimony of the gospel today. In verses 23–24 he says:

---

6. Dalhouse, *An Island in the Lake of Fire*, 7.

> Woe to you, scribes and Pharisees, hypocrites! For you tithe mint and dill and cumin, and have neglected the weightier matters of the law: justice and mercy and faithfulness. These you ought to have done, without neglecting the others. You blind guides, straining out a gnat and swallowing a camel!

The second problem with hubris is that *it redirects us from what really matters.* "The weightier matters" Jesus refers to are the matters that are of greater importance. This idea becomes critical to a later criticism of fundamentalism. For now, we need just note that Jesus is correcting the fact that these religious bean counters (actually spice counters) are missing the forest for the trees. They have emphasized the measurables while ignoring the meaty intangibles like "justice and mercy and faithfulness." The same thing happens in our day when the real spiritual substance gets neglected because religious leaders are more concerned with whether or not someone is going to the movies rather than whether or not they are pursuing purity; whether they have taken a drink of alcohol rather than whether or not they have a self-control problem; whether they smoked a cigarette rather than whether they have a problem looking out for the well-being of others; whether they dressed appropriately for worship rather than whether their heart was attuned to God's voice in the service; or whether the drums were too loud rather than whether their praise was too quiet. I am sure you get the point. Jesus wants us to push past our obsession with form and find our musings on more substantive matters of spiritual vitality.

Paul reinforces this idea in Romans 14. Here he discusses how Christians ought to relate to one another when they are at odds over matters of strong opinion, where they find themselves convicted of a particular course of action regarding an item of debatable spiritual value. For Paul, in his day, the issues revolved around what people ate and what days they observed as special or holy. Today we have different issues of disagreement but Paul's admonitions remain relevant. Consider one of his statements in verse 17: "For the kingdom of God is not a matter of eating and drinking but of righteousness and peace and joy in the Holy Spirit."

These words cut both ways. The individual who feels great liberty within matters of preference needs to be reminded that their character in acting (righteousness, peace, and joy) is the primary concern of God's kingdom, not that they get to do what they want to do. The person who feels that participation in those activities would be sinful likewise needs to take into account the same character or ethos of the kingdom rather than mistaking the physical matter (eating and drinking) for the kingdom matter (righteousness, peace, and joy).

A third problem with hubris is that *it produces an attitude of condescension toward others*. In Luke 18:9–14, Jesus told a parable about a Pharisee and a tax collector who went up to the temple to pray. The Pharisee sees himself as greater than the tax collector who, in his mind, is indicative of sinful men who live to satisfy their baser urges. In contrast, the tax collector is gifted at the art of accurate self-assessment. He possesses that most underrated of virtues known as healthy introspection. What else can we say about one who kneels before his Maker and meekly cries out "God, be merciful to me, a sinner!" How drastically different are the two characters in this short parable?!

The tip of the spear of this story was directed by Jesus toward "some who trusted in themselves that they were righteous, and treated others with contempt" (Luke 18:9). We should note that this term for "contempt" is also used biblically to describe the attitude of Herod and his soldiers toward Christ (Luke 23:11) and insightfully by Paul to speak of an attitude that ought not be present from one believer to another as both deal with matters of Christian liberty (Rom. 14:10). The latter use cuts right to the core of the problem that is often faced as No Carb Jesus seeps his way into the life of the local church. As a pastor, this is an enormous concern for me. Self-righteousness is a deterrent to discipleship because it rips at the heart of what it means to have a teachable spirit and assaults the relational comfort vital to healthy corporate worship and mission. To take people somewhere missionally, as a leader, they must be teachable and to take them somewhere in unity they must have a healthy relational dynamic. But both mission and unity wither under the toxicity of self-righteousness.

## Carbing up on Humility

At the local church level hubris can be mitigated in a few ways. First, *the pastoral staff and elders need to model what it means to be teachable*. As a wise leader Solomon understood this when he wrote:

> Whoever heeds instruction is on the path to life, but he who rejects reproof leads others astray (Prov. 10:17).

Or again:

> By insolence comes nothing but strife, but with those who take advice is wisdom (Prov. 13:10).

Yet again:

> Listen to advice and accept instruction, that you may gain wisdom in the future (Prov. 19:20).

I cannot expect anyone in my church to be willing to receive instruction if I am not actively and visibly receiving it as well. A leadership that has all the answers and needs no guidance becomes suspect when they always want to dispense what they seem ill-equipped to receive.

Second, *only place teachable people in positions of influence.* One of the worst things that can happen at the level of leadership in a local body is when someone rises to prominence, often by the force of their personality and gifting, but does not own a teachable heart. This is the very first thing I look for when pouring into a future leader. It monopolizes some of my initial conversations with them. As we meet I have my vice sniffer out and now, after years in ministry, I know all too well the scent of obstinacy; with my first whiff of it I run the other way. That is all you can do. You cannot teach the unteachable. You cannot correct the uncorrectable. You cannot give answers to those who have them all. What they need is a brokenness that only God can provide in the crucible of life. It is not my job to give that to them, but only to be ready to use them should their Father decide to tear down so he can build up. As William Tyndale once said:

> If God promise riches, the way thereto is poverty; whom He loveth, him He chasteneth; whom He exalteth, He casteth down; whom He saveth, He damneth first. He bringeth no man to heaven, except He send him to hell first. If He promise life, He slayeth first: when He buildeth He casteth all down first. He is no patcher; He cannot build on another man's foundation.[7]

Third, *make guided self-assessment part of your inspection tools for ministry volunteers and staff members.* It has been rightly said that we should inspect what we expect. So if we expect someone to be teachable we need to create formal and informal mechanisms to be sure that this is happening. Some formal mechanisms might be things like:

- Fostering opportunities for ongoing education

---

7. Demaus, *William Tyndale: A Biography,* 184.

- Creating staff-based learning communities where issues are regularly discussed
- Providing modes of ongoing training for lay staff that stretch them in cognitive learning, not just in ministry skills
- Requiring an annual learning plan from staff and other volunteers that would promote and maintain accountability for life-long learning
- Holding a regular, scheduled review process where teachability can be discerned by questions about present learning and modes of personal introspection

Informally, we need to make the value of being teachable regularly present in our staff and church ministry discussions. We need to share what we are learning. We need to acknowledge the insight of others both within and outside of our body. We need to acknowledge when we have been wrong and share what we learned that brought us correction. As a pastor/theologian, I personally experienced a major shift in one area of my theological development while serving as a lead pastor. Aside from the actual theological shift and its consequences, it really demonstrated to the church that I am teachable. I was willing to say that I was wrong. I am not willy-nilly in my theological ideas and would encourage no one to be so, but being open to research an issue and admit you were wrong as a leader only contributes to your ability to exhort those you lead to reconsider their faulty presuppositions.

Establishing a Hierarchy of Theology

Now we have to return to an important phrase that Jesus used in Matthew 23, and, in doing so, we will strike at what seems to me to be the epicenter of fundamentalism's ideological error. The glitch in the system that often plagues fundamentalists is their lack of regard for a healthy doctrinal hierarchy or theological taxonomy. The mindset often taken by the fundamentalist reasons this way: Because all truth is God's truth, all truth is worth fighting for, and therefore worth guarding like a dog guards a bone—thus typifying the idea of being dog-matic! This issue must be reassessed by the fundamentalist and, more importantly for our purposes, it must be guarded against by evangelicals with a strong commitment to truth. Fundamentalism has not only been guilty of going further than the Bible in terms of practical restrictions on the ethical life, but also in terms of the vigor with which specific doctrines are held.

## Perspicuity

The reformers put forward the doctrine of the perspicuity of Scripture. To say something is perspicacious is simply to say that it is clear or lucid. The reformers combated a Roman Catholic church that left interpretation solely in the hands of the priests and prelates. Therefore the idea that Scripture could be clearly understood by the common man was crucial to the contention that the Bible should be in the hands of the common man. William Tyndale's famous statement in an argument with one loyal to the Pope, as they haggled over the validity of getting the Scripture beyond just Latin and into the vernacular tongue of the English people, is indicative of the reformers' collective thoughts on this matter. John Foxe records the incident:

> It was not long after but Master Tyndale happened to be in the company of a certain divine, recounted for a learned man, and, in communing and disputing with him, he drave him to that issue, that the said great doctor burst out into these blasphemous words, and said, "We were better to be without God's laws than the Pope's." Master Tyndale, hearing this, full of Godly zeal, and not bearing that blasphemous saying, replied again, and said, "I defy the Pope and all his laws;" and further added, that if God spared him life, ere many years he would cause a boy that driveth the plough, to know more of the Scripture than he did.[8]

Tyndale's passion for the Bible in English was the same as Luther's passion for the Bible in German. They wanted every person to be able to encounter the text for themselves because they believed it to be clear enough to be understood at a basic level by everyone. Of course this doctrine needs a necessary qualification, and they, no doubt, understood this. *The clarity of Scripture does not imply that everything is equally clear.* Our interpretive filters are fallen. The sin of man has produced predictable negative noetic effects on our abilities to grapple with truth. Our Edenic and our post-Edenic minds are not in the same boat. As a result, hubris raises its head again and leads us to reach beyond the Bible or to hold more firmly to ideas that are less clear or ideas that we have less information about. *The Reformation doctrine of perspicuity was not a way of saying everything is equally clear but a way of saying everyone can understand the central message of the text with a healthy awareness of the fallibility of our human filters.*

8. Foxe, *The Acts and Monuments*, 117.

## Crucial Questions

This discussion about the clarity of Scripture is important because if we are not thinking in degrees then we will reach beyond the text itself. Our job is to hold doctrines with a force that is governed by the answers to three questions.

*What baggage might I be bringing to the interpretive task?* Without a healthy humility in our hermeneutics we become people who canonize our own interpretation. This is a danger for everyone who comes to the text because all of us, not just the fundamentalist, are sinful creatures. Sometimes I hear people say things like, "I just believe what is in the Word!" or, "It is right there in the Word!" or, "I just believe in the authority of the Bible." But these statements are actually unhelpful in in-house discussions about doctrine because all people claiming an evangelical or a fundamentalist adherence are going to proclaim their reliance on the Word of God and their subjection to its authority. The issue often is not that we have a low regard for the Bible so much as we possess a high regard for ourselves.

*How clearly is it revealed?* Not all doctrines are equally apparent. This is true for at least three reasons. First, some doctrines have more information in the text of Scripture to build on than other doctrines. The specifics of Christology have much more material to work with than the specifics of angelology even though both Christ and angels are revealed in the text. Second, the distance in culture and setting means that some things will not be as apparent to me as other things depending on my context as a reader. The goal of any interpreter ought to be the determination of the author's intended meaning. To achieve that end the interpreter must wade through his own culture, recognize places of disconnect from the biblical culture, and see what the text is saying in its culture and then bring that message to relevant application in his present context. Sometimes this process places us different distances away from the text's historical meaning. For example, the intent of teaching is the same throughout the centuries, namely, that others would learn. So the idea that the church should have capable teachers is pretty universally accepted. But in contrast the purpose of a head covering is not as clear. Is the text descriptive or prescriptive in the wearing of one? Consequently some women still wear them in worship and others do not. This difference in interpretation is borne from the fact that the role of head coverings and the role of teaching are not equally clear even though both are

*enjoying the fruitfulness of a carbohydrated christ* 105

found in the text. Third, some truths are embedded in genres of literature that are simply more difficult to understand. Would anyone really argue that the symbolism of Revelation is as clear as the injunctions of Paul or the Law of Moses?

*How crucial is it to the establishment and verification of other doctrines?* Doctrines vary in importance on two fronts. On the one hand some are more essential as building blocks for other concepts of Scripture. A good example of this is the Trinity. It forms a fountainhead from which a number of other, crucial ideas flow. Without it, other doctrines begin to go sideways. On the other hand, some are more crucial for us as we live in God's kingdom. It is genuinely more crucial that I understand the substitutionary atoning work of Jesus than whether I believe the earth was created in six literal days or not.

## An Appeal and an Apologetic

How we answer the three questions above will dictate what kind of hierarchy of theology we construct. However, I want to be clear because I believe this idea to be absolutely vital to the health of the church. The main issue at stake for the fundamentalists is not so much what kind of hierarchy they construct (although in another sense that is crucial) but simply that they construct one. A frequent fundamentalist rejoinder to creating any area of grey in theological or philosophical discussions comes in the form of a question that goes something like, "Yeah, but where do you draw the lines?" That is a good and necessary question, but it is asked dismissively, as if to say since we can't know definitively where to draw the lines, we will just create the safest path to the most error-free theological assessments and practical applications possible. It devolves into a better-safe-than-sorry approach to doctrine and life. But this is actually not responsible at all. It is like deciding to keep your child from ever driving a car (a temptation for us parents) rather than teaching them how to drive a vehicle responsibly. So my appeal is simple: *Formulate your theology on a hierarchy of commitments that reflects a humility concerning your ability to be certain and that takes into account the clarity and emphasis that the Bible places on the issue.*

But why should anyone concern themselves with this? I would like to give you several reasons in order to create a cumulative case for such an approach to theology. First, *a hierarchy of theology helps us choose discernment over defensiveness*. Paul exhorted Timothy to "keep a close watch on yourself and the teaching. Persist in this, for by so doing you will save both yourself and your hearers" (1 Tim. 4:16). This is an important word to pastors, like me, called to shepherd God's people. But it is not an impatient word; it is a calculated word. It is measured and vigorous. The term for "keep watch" is used in the Septuagint primarily to speak of "waiting" or "refraining."[9] Its contexts are situations where decisions need to be made. I highlight this because the two fatal flaws of the fundamentalist engagement with theology and Christian living are a defensive posture in terms of hermeneutics and an impatience with individuals to change. There will be more to come about the latter, but for now, we need to focus on the former.

Often, Christians do theology by defense. By this I mean that instead of a proactive engagement with the text they form their presuppositions and thoughts in a reaction to contemporary abuses of the text. I see this in my own setting of ministry in the "Mormon Belt." Often, apologetic works critiquing Mormonism choose whichever interpretation of a given text lands them furthest from Latter-day Saint theology, rather than one that actually best adheres to the historical and grammatical meaning of the text itself. Biblical accuracy gets sacrificed at the expense of ideological safety.

I have been guilty of the same error in my own theological development. For example, I used to take a view of the gifts of the Spirit that held to the idea that the supernatural gifts had largely ceased. This cessationist view was mainly driven by the fact that I had only witnessed abuses of the gifts in churches that seemed to have little regard for adhering to any biblical restraints or conditions placed upon their exercise. I had very little textual arguments for my position because, frankly, not many exist. I had some historical arguments, but the lens I viewed history through was preconditioned by my experience. It was a really poor way to do theology. I was doing it by defense. It was like concluding that if a man killed another man with a shovel then I would not use it to dig a hole. But wouldn't that be ridiculous!? One person's abuse of something should not define anyone's use of it. In fact, I am convinced that many fundamentalists have rejected the supernatural gifts for this very reason, and from one theological traveler to another I would beg them to reconsider.

---

9. Gen. 8:10, 12; 1 Kgs. 22:6, 15; 2 Kgs. 4:24; 2 Chr.18:5, 14; Job 30:26

A hierarchy of doctrinal commitments helps us be less defensive because we begin to see how much things matter. When we see this more accurately we don't overreact to views on less important matters that may not fit our views. Instead we are willing to wade through and have generous conversation knowing eternity is not at stake in the discussion.

Second, *a hierarchy of theology recognizes that the "slippery slope" argument fails*. I would be able to put my children through college if I had a dime for every time the "slippery slope" argument is appealed to. It goes like this. When a disagreement arises someone says, "Well brother, if you open that Pandora's Box you are going to be on a slippery slope and the next thing you know, you will be going liberal." Similar to my previous point, it takes a posture that rejects discernment in place of defense. The real problem is it doesn't actually acknowledge that all of life is a slippery slope and everyone is choosing to draw lines somewhere on the slope. The presupposition is flawed. You cannot pretend to get off the slope or avoid; it you can only be a biblical steward of your decisions on it.

Third, *a hierarchy of theology reflects Jesus' own view*. We need to cycle back to Matthew 23. In verse 23, as mentioned earlier, Jesus rebukes them because they "have neglected the weightier matters of the law" that he identifies as "justice and mercy and faithfulness." He goes on to say, "These you ought to have done, without neglecting the others." He is careful not to speak slightingly against the law, but he is also careful to recalibrate their thinking in terms of what is "weightier" or, simply put, that which is more important. If the issues of Old Testament theology (the Law) were not all equal in gravitas, then wouldn't the same be true of theology in general?

Let me make an important addition. It would be easy to conclude that I am suggesting that some things matter and others don't, and that is not my point. I am actually trying to steer away from the categorical approach to theological thinking that says everything is equally important (the fundamentalist error) or everything is equally unimportant (the liberal error). We should note Jesus' full statement in Matthew 23:23, "Woe to you, scribes and Pharisees, hypocrites! For you tithe mint and dill and cumin, and have neglected the weightier matters of the law: justice and mercy and faithfulness. These you ought to have done, without neglecting the others." The last part of the verse makes clear that Jesus' point is not that the tithing demands of the law do not matter at all, but they did not matter *as much*. Your view on election matters but not as much as your view on the deity of Jesus. Your view on the role of women in the church matters but not as much as your view of Bible's truthfulness.

Fourth, *a hierarchy of theology helps synergize and clarify the mission of the church*. If every thing is a major thing, then we will shoot at our target with buck shot rather than a streamlined bullet. I think this has cost the mission of the church of fundamentalism. If the Jesus of fundamentalism is as concerned about the age of the earth as he is the doctrine of the atonement then his followers will be as vigorous in fighting for the one as the other.[10] And this turns out to be an incredible waste of energy!

Carl Henry saw this coming in his pivotal book mentioned in the previous chapter. It is unfortunate that his words were not heeded by his fundamentalist counterparts. He wrote:

> The evangelical may often believe too much, but the sweep of his ideology at least includes the great essentials. The time has come now for fundamentalism to speak with an ecumenical outlook and voice; if it speaks in terms of the historic Biblical tradition, rather than in the name of secondary accretions or of eschatological biases on which evangelicals divide, it can refashion the modern mind. But a double-minded fundamentalism—which veers between essentials and inessentials—will receive little of the Lord, and not much of a hearing from the perishing multitudes.[11]

The failure to make a distinction between "essentials and inessentials" is both distracting and debilitating to the central mission of the church to make disciples of Jesus. Ironically, in an effort to stay away from the distraction of social involvement, the fundamentalist has found a different distraction in less important matters of Christian dogma. It might be fair to ask which is a more biblical distraction: feeding the homeless or arguing over the age of rocks?

Fifth, *a hierarchy of theology reflects humility rather than hubris*. Years ago I remember my father telling me that if he was going to make an error in ministry, he would choose to err on the side of love rather

---

10. An unfortunate example of a lack of hierarchy that pulls at the mission of the church is found in the emphasis of some at the Institute of Creation Research and their attempts to make young earth creationism a litmus test for orthodoxy. Note such articles as John D. Morris, "How Does Old Earth Thinking Affect One's View of Scripture's Reliability?" (found at http://www.icr.org/article/1183/302/ accessed 2012-17-24); or Henry Morris, "The Compromise Road" (found at http://www.icr.org/article/281/ accessed 2012-17-24).

11. Henry, *The Uneasy Conscience of Modern Fundamentalism*, 59–60.

than legalism. That's a gold nugget of ministerial wisdom that has stuck with me. We will all make mistakes in relating to people, but when we do, which way will we be leaning? When it comes to doctrinal dispute, humility is the personal posture that love takes. This doesn't mean that we lack conviction or that we don't formulate valid and sound arguments to buttress our points, but the disposition we do all of these with must be defined by humility.

Finally, *a hierarchy of theology recalibrates the biblical doctrine of separation*. Please notice that I referred to it as a *biblical* doctrine because it definitely is. Many evangelicals are silent about the call for separation but the Bible is not. Fundamentalism has something important to teach evangelicalism here, and evangelicals will do well to listen.[12] In concert with fundamentalism, Paul makes clear that the Jesus of the Bible is a separated Jesus. Consider 2 Corinthians 6:14–18:

> Do not be unequally yoked with unbelievers. For what partnership has righteousness with lawlessness? Or what fellowship has light with darkness? What accord has Christ with Belial? Or what portion does a believer share with an unbeliever? What agreement has the temple of God with idols? For we are the temple of the living God; as God said, "I will make my dwelling among them and walk among them, and I will be their God, and they shall be my people. Therefore go out from their midst, and be separate from them, says the Lord, and touch no unclean thing; then I will welcome you, and I will be a father to you, and you shall be sons and daughters to me, says the Lord Almighty.

Paul's questions in verses 14 through 16 are intended to show the disparity between Christ and entities associated with him (righteousness, light, believers, and their bodies) and Belial and entities associated with him (lawlessness, darkness, unbelievers, and idols). Belial is taken from the Hebrew term for "destruction"[13] and may be an ancient reference to the god of the underworld in ancient lore. In any event, the point of the text is to say that Christ's followers are to be distinct in lifestyle and in

---

12. For a fair fundamentalist treatment of the doctrine of separation, see Fred Moritz, *Be Ye Holy: The Call to Christian Separation*. While I certainly do not agree with Moritz on all his points and would take exception to inconsistencies in how his judgments land, I nevertheless commend him for his soft stance on second-degree separation (although I wish he would have gone further) and his clear concern for the attitude of the separatist. This was a refreshing word, and one I wish his constituency would take with greater weight.

13. Note 2 Sam. 22:5 and Ps. 18:4.

some measure of association from unbelievers. Paul conflates two Old Testament passages, Isaiah 52:11 and Ezekiel 20:34, to make his point in verse 17 when he says "go out from their midst and be separate from them." Both texts speak of the nation coming out of exile and separating from the culture in which they have been embedded for years. The call to follow Christ is indeed a call out of exile and out of a culture that has little room for Jesus.

So we are to be separate . . . but the story does not end there. And it is the rest of the story that causes the fundamentalist Jesus to stall out. Perhaps Dick Staub has offered the most practical template and doable solution to the conundrum of the church's relationship to the world. In his book *The Culturally Savvy Christian*, Staub proposes that our relationship as Christians to the world should be characterized by three different roles: aliens, ambassadors, and artists. Aliens stand apart from the world and their testimony is rooted in their apartness. In a word, they are separate. Ambassadors are sent to be relational engagers for the grand purpose of relating from one kingdom to another. At times relational lines of communication need to be strung so that serious spiritual messages can be passed with an amicable aroma. Artists are people who change the culture from within. They are the ones who produce forms that provoke thought and spur inquiry. They do not stand without but within the world and provide rhythms of creative internal reformation. All three are needed to provide effective holistic engagement with the world.

Peter sees us as aliens in 1 Peter. Paul sees us as ambassadors in 2 Corinthians 5. Jesus evinced an artist's approach engaging Judaism from within coming to bring the Law to its fruition, not its abolition. He said as much in his grandest sermon, "Do not think that I have come to abolish the Law or the Prophets; I have not come to abolish them but to fulfill them" (Matt. 5:17). The biblical approach is a holistic approach. It includes separation but looks beyond it as a sufficient narrative to talk about engagement with the world.

An excessive emphasis on the doctrine of separation has plagued fundamentalism since before the schism of the 1950s. It was an enormous factor in the schism itself, particularly in the visceral reaction to Billy Graham's New York crusade in 1957. In the previous chapter I highlighted the fundamentalism of Bob Jones because it typifies separatist fundamentalism and its efforts to create a No Carb Jesus. At the conclusion of a chapter entitled "Separatism Unleashed," chronicling the role of the Bob Joneses through much of the 1940s and 1950s, Mark Taylor

*enjoying the fruitfulness of a carbohydrated christ* 111

Dalhouse summarizes separatism's place in their post-schism world. He observes:

> Separation became, after the events of that sixteen year span, the Joneses' way of dealing with the rapidly changing American religious environment . . . Separatism became, for the Bob Joneses, much more than ecclesiastical separation. It afforded them the opportunity to deal with the increasing change characteristic of American society in the 1960s and 1970s.[14]

That same approach remains. At present, Bob Jones University has four thousand students and six different schools within the university. A perusal of their website highlights their emphasis on biblical separation. In fact, in a list of publications under the heading "Preacher's Corner," the concept of biblical separation is given its own category. I mention this only to demonstrate that in the stratification of issues for the fundamentalist, separation remains near the top.[15]

This emphasis is not without consequence. The Jesus of fundamentalism finds some of his most significant texture in this doctrine. It has bred a view of Jesus that can be seen in the rhetoric of fundamentalist literature. "Rebuke" gets the press clippings rather than "restoration." The process of confrontation is emphasized over the goal of reconciliation. As a result the pervading ethos feels rooted in law, and failings are met with criticism. The relational default is flavored by an abrupt and harsh approach that has too little room for gentleness and grace. Certainly there are exceptions and the mountain of fundamentalism does have a sunny side, but the temperature in the room often feels a little too cold and separatism tends to enforce its will on the thermostat.

## Carbing Up on a Healthy Hierarchy

My thesis is that in order to carry the doctrine of Jesus and the disposition of Jesus in lockstep we need to implement a hierarchy of theology and let that define the theological culture of our local churches. This can only happen by choosing a strategic and purposeful path to that end. My sense is that many reading this would say a hearty "Amen!" to the idea of establishing a taxonomy of theological commitments, but

14. Dalhouse, *An Island in the Lake of Fire*, 87.

15. The article is found at http://www.bju.edu/academics/college-and-schools/seminary/preachers-corner/publications/separation/ (accessed 2012-17-25).

the truth is we are often bent toward overstating our own preferences and opinions. So a reconstitution of how we talk about our theology is essential and needs to be placed in front of our people early on in their engagement with the local church. It needs to be recycled in sermons. It needs to find its reinforcement on church blogs and websites. It needs to be rehearsed in our small groups and discipleship efforts. It needs to be modeled by leadership and staff as they agree and disagree about secondary and tertiary matters.

Here are two practical suggestions. First, add to your statement of faith two categories, "Things that matter to us that may not matter to you," and "Things that may matter to you but don't matter all that much to us." We do this at our church and it provides an opportunity for two things when I go over our statement of faith with new people checking out our church. It affords our staff the opportunity to sniff out hijackers who have a pet issue or agenda that they want to push in the church, and creates a non-threatening but honest way for us to share that we are not interested in accommodating theological special-interest groups. It also lets us discuss our commitment to viewing theology as in a stratified hierarchy and communicates to our guests and new attendees the culture of how we do theology.

Second, create a visual representation communicating your hierarchy of commitments and make it a topic of discussion in small groups and discipleship contexts. As you do so, it will help if you communicate that the purpose of this is to assist the church in gaining healthy parameters for fellowship and a more definable criterion for missional partnership with other individuals, churches, and ministries. Below is a suggested rubric that you might find helpful for doing so, along with some examples of doctrines and issues that could be placed in each category.[16] The point of the chart is not in the specific items on the right but in the broader categories on the left. Each church will likely fill in the right column differently, but all must keep in mind that any theological taxonomy has to be determined by interacting with the three crucial questions highlighted earlier in the chapter.

16. A well-argued Internet paper by a former professor of mine, Dan Wallace, was very influential in this conceptual paradigm. Some of the basic verbiage is Dan's, and I share it. The suggested doctrines are mine. I think the importance of it for this book rests in its attention to how doctrines ought to practically be stratified if we are to take into account their implications for mission and fellowship. That is precisely my concern in addressing this issue of fundamentalism. Wallace's paper is entitled "My Take on Inerrancy" and can be found at http://bible.org/article/my-take-inerrancy.

| Level 4<br>Speculative Doctrines/Issues | i.e. Who are the sons of God and the daughters of men in Gen. 6?, authorship of Hebrews |
|---|---|
| Level 3<br>Debatable Doctrines/Issues of Some Import | i.e. the extent of the atonement, the age of the earth, timing of end-times events |
| Level 2b<br>Doctrines/Issues Essential for the Unified Practice of a Local Church | i.e. the role of women in the church, general commitments to Calvinism or Arminianism, continuationism or cessationism regarding the spiritual gifts |
| Level 2a<br>Doctrines/Issues Essential for the Health of a Local Church | i.e. biblically qualified leadership, inerrancy, the role of ordinances/sacraments |
| Level 1<br>Doctrines/Issues Essential for Eternal Life | i.e. Trinity, nature of Christ, substitutionary atonement, bodily resurrection, the reality of a second coming, the reliability of the Bible |

## Executing the One Anothers

One of the most under-utilized components of Scripture is the *one anothers* of the New Testament. There are thirty-five of them in Scripture. Twenty-four are positive in nature and serve as points of action we ought to implement in our relationships with others. Eleven are negative and are given to us in the text as points to avoid in our relationships with each other.

In John 13:34, Jesus gave what an acquaintance of mine calls the "Eleventh Commandment."[17] "A new commandment I give to you, that you love one another: just as I have loved you, you also are to love one another." Jesus' injunction here typifies the message of his preaching and the sense of his ministry. His commandment is a powerful synthesis of what ought to characterize the Christian's relational life. One clear and distinguishing property of the Jesus of the New Testament is that he is guided by the principle of love. Now I need to be clear about what

---

17. Don McMinn has done some great work on these *one anothers* and produced two really useful workbooks to help embed some of them in the lives of believers. I credit him with the term "the Eleventh Commandment" and his work has been integral to the formulation of my own thoughts on the subject.

I mean when I use the term love, since it means a number of different things to different people. The best definition I am aware of for love comes from philosopher Dallas Willard. I have fully adopted his definition since I think it best captures the pervading biblical sense of the various Hebrew and Greek terms found in the text. He says that love is "acting in another's best interests."[18] That is a great description and one worth each believer internalizing.

So if we are to love in the spirit of this definition, then we need to have some guiding principles to apply to specific situations we might encounter as we relate to our fellow humans. In his sovereign wisdom God has provided these in the form of the various *one anothers* of the New Testament. In short, they are the situational modes through which love is expressed to others. They become the tubes that transmit love to people in particular circumstances. Or yet another way of saying it might be to simply state that when love lands in a given context, it shows up as one or more of these *one anothers*. Consider the following examples. If you are discouraged the best way that I can love you (read: "act in your best interests") is by applying the principle "encourage one another" (1 Thess. 4:18; 5:11, 14). If you feel rejected by people the best way I can manifest love to you is to apply the injunction "accept one another" (Rom. 15:7). Conversely, if someone is mistreating me, an expression of my love for them is to not "grumble against one another" (Jas. 5:9). Love shows up contextually as one of these *one anothers*.

Below is a list for your reference of all the *one anothers* found in the New Testament:[19]

---

18. Dallas Willard, "Knowledge of Christ in Today's World". This is an eight-part audio lecture series whose worth cannot be overstated.

19. I have chosen to cite these in the verbiage of the New International Version.

## enjoying the fruitfulness of a carbohydrated christ 115

| Positive "One Another" Statements | Negative "One Another" Statements |
|---|---|
| "members of one another" (Rom. 12:5) "being devoted to one another" (Rom. 12:10a) "honoring one another" (Rom. 12:10b) "being of the same mind toward one another" (Rom. 12:16; 15:5) "loving one another" Rom. 13:8; 1 Thess. 3:12; 4:9; 2 Thess. 1:3; Heb. 10:24; 1 Pet.1:22; 1 John 3:11,23; 4:7,11,12; 2 John 5) "edifying one another" (Rom. 14:19) "accepting one another" (Rom. 15:7) "instructing one another" (Rom. 15:14) "greeting one another" (Rom. 16:16; 1 Cor. 16:20; 2 Cor. 13:12; 1 Thess. 5:26;1 Pet. 5:14) "waiting for one another" (1 Cor.11:33) "caring for one another" (1 Cor. 12:25) "serving one another" (Gal. 5:13) "carrying one another's burdens" (Gal. 6:2) "bearing with one another" (Eph. 4:2; Col. 3:13) "being kind to one another" (Eph. 4:32) "submitting to one another" (Eph. 5:21; 1 Pet. 5:5) "esteeming one another" (Phil 2:3) "encouraging one another" (1 Thess. 4:18; 5:11,14) "confessing sins to one another" (Jas. 5:16a) "praying for one another" (Jas 5:16b) "offering hospitality to one another" (1 Pet. 4:9) "fellowshipping with one another" (1 John 1:7) "admonish one another" (Col. 3:16) | "lusting for one another" (Rom. 1:27) "judging one another" (Rom. 14:13) "depriving one another" (1 Cor. 7:5) "biting one another" (Gal. 5:15a) "devouring one another" (Gal. 5:15b) "destroying one another" (Gal. 5:15c) "provoking one another" (Gal. 5:26a) "envying one another" (Gal. 5:26b) "lying to one another" (Col. 3:9) "hating one another" (Tit. 3:3) "slandering one another" (Jas. 4:11) "grumbling against one another" (Jas. 5:9) |

By executing on the *one anothers* of Scripture we keep ourselves from over-emphasizing things like separation and under-emphazing the proper use of our adverbs. These relational paths laid out for us in Scripture fit with the heart of the biblical Christ, and when applied with balance will keep us from frustrating ourselves and others with a rigid, No Carb Jesus.

## Carbing Up with the One Anothers

At the local church level, here are a few ways to really encourage the implementation of the *one anothers*. First, *employ them in marital counseling*. I once began meeting with a couple that was on the cusp of divorce. They had seen a secular counselor who told them upon assessment that if their marriage were rated on a scale of one to five, with a five indicating divorce, they were at a four and a half on the scale. One of the exercises I had them do in response to one of our meetings was to list two *one anothers* that they thought would be helpful if implemented by them in their marriage. I then asked them to list three tangible ways that they would put each *one another* into action the next week. They did as instructed and followed through with their plans. It is no exaggeration to say that this revolutionized the climate of their relationship. In particular, the wife's commitment to enact "greet one another" when her husband came into the house from work created an environment of warmth and openness that caused them to relate to each other in a much more healthy way. It was a palpable reminder to me of the power of the Word when applied without ambiguity to human life.

Second, *let the one anothers form the curriculum for family worship or family devotions*. In our home we gather at night for a time in the Bible and prayer as a family. I lead this and try to make it short, simple, and practical. One of the most effective tools I have found to engage my family during this time is the *one anothers*. Open your Bible as a dad or mom and read a *one another* with the family. And then just begin asking questions like "How can you live this out within our family?" "How will this help you in your relationships with your siblings or friends?" "How does it make you feel when someone treats you this way?" You can also create some fun action plans or challenges out of these *one anothers* to help keep them on the front burner of your family.

Third, *infuse them into your church culture* through highlighting one at staff meetings or bringing them into the matrix of your accountability in discipleship. You also might consider utilizing a small-group study that focuses on these *one anothers*.[20] It would be difficult to imagine a church that implemented these principles well resembling a No Carb Jesus.

## Conclusion

Hidden in the middle of Luke's Gospel is a lesser-known parable of Jesus. It is about a fig tree that doesn't bear any fruit. In the parable, the fig tree is likely Israel, and the subject matter is the timing of its judgment because of its fruitless reception of Jesus. The language of the parable and its context in Luke communicate something interesting about the ministry of Jesus, giving us a glimpse into a carbohydrated Christ.

Luke precedes this parable with Jesus making a strong call for repentance. In fact, if you only read Luke 13:1–5 you might get the idea that Jesus wasn't too hot on relational or spiritual carbs. He is direct and unequivocal in his assertion that his audience is sinful and unless they repent they will perish. When I read the text I hear Jesus with a lingering southern drawl and a deep resonant voice calling for brokenness. This text smells like Billy Sunday's sawdust trail and seeps with the sweat of Charles Finney's anxious bench.

But then there is an interesting addition to this picture in Jesus' parable. Luke 13:6–9 reads:

> And he told this parable: "A man had a fig tree planted in his vineyard, and he came seeking fruit on it and found none. And he said to the vinedresser, 'Look, for three years now I have come seeking fruit on this fig tree, and I find none. Cut it down. Why should it use up the ground?' And he answered him, 'Sir, let it alone this year also, until I dig around it and put on manure. Then if it should bear fruit next year, well and good; but if not, you can cut it down.'"

There are two characters: a "man" and a "vinedresser" likely employed by the man. The problem in the parable is the fruitlessness of the

---

20. Some resources include: Don McMinn, *The 11th Commandment: Experiencing the One Anothers of Scripture*. There are actually two workbooks available. Gene Getz, *Building Up One Another*. Getz also has two additional books in the same "One Another" series. Gerald L. Sittser, *Love One Another: Becoming the Church Jesus Longs For*.

fig tree and becomes the topic of discussion between the two characters. What will they do with it? The man wants to cut it down, but the vinedresser takes a different approach, a more patient approach. He proposes that they give it another year and that they care for the vine and nurture it and hope for the best. This parable of optimism and patience comes as surprise when bookended to Jesus' strong call for repentance. However, isn't this precisely what we should expect from a Christ who values holiness but does so measured by the virtue of patience and longsuffering? Jesus does more than drop stern truth-bombs. He calls a nation to repentance but knows that the disposition or posture of engagement must be permeated with optimism rather than cynicism. He chooses to give a story that hopes for restoration rather than one that simply resolves on rebuke.

Jesus once told a confused Philip that if he had seen him he had seen the Father. And here in Luke we see the heart of the Father shining through the teaching of the Son. The patience of God shows up in a Jesus who tolerates the foibles of the disciples, who hangs out with sinners and rebukes the prideful casuists, who is willing to let those following him learn and grow at a painstakingly slow pace, a Jesus who receives again friends who wounded him deeply. My prayer is that those who bear the label "Christian" would indeed be little Christs by holding fast his doctrine but with a disposition that can legitimately offer the whole Jesus to the whole world.

# 5

## Smorgasbord Jesus

### The Christ of Postmodernism

> Jesus is supracultural. He is present within all cultures, and yet present outside of all cultures. He is for all people, and yet he refuses to be co-opted or owned by any one culture. That includes any Christian culture. Any denomination. Any church. Any theological system. We can point to him, name him, follow him, discuss him, honor him, and believe in him—but we cannot claim him to be ours any more than he's anyone else's.
>
> ROB BELL

My grandfather made soup. As a kid I felt there was something special about his soup. In fact, in our family all you have to say, to this day, is that we ate some of "Grandpa's Soup." To say the label is to whisper words of magic and whimsy. It is to paint a portrait of a one-legged man feeding long, thick orange carrots and green celery stalks from his garden into a stainless-steel grinder with a crank handle. It is to envision his tattooed forearm, with his charcoal button-up shirt rolled up on it, turning the crank, effortlessly grinding the vegetables into a bit-sized purée. It is to entice the tongue with phantom tastes of soup with a splash of vinegar sopped up with buttered bread. To say the label is to reach beyond the amalgamation of garden delights and finely ground beef into the nostalgic and mythical corridors of childhood memory. It is to re-imagine and re-invigorate the memory of a man beloved for more than his soup. Maybe that's why a litmus test for people marrying into the family was whether or not they liked "Grandpa's Soup." In hindsight it doesn't seem all that fair. Should someone be excluded from the tribe because they have a different palate? Probably not . . . but since the chef has been gone some twenty-plus years now, at least it gave him a sort of posthumous say in who was joining the crew. Of course no one takes this too seriously, but I would be lying if I said it wasn't secretly important to me that my wife compliment the stew.

By now you might be wondering how an old man's soup could have such gastronomical clout. What hidden ingredient made it dance in our mouths? What spice intoxicated our aromatic senses, causing such devoted madness? Well, the short answer is . . . nothing. In fact I remember when the truth came home to me. One day, while mentioning the soup, my wife said something to the effect of, "You know it's really just vegetable beef soup." *What!!?? Insanity!!!* Who was this invader? Was this the woman I married? Was this the lady who dipped the bread in the preternatural pot when we dated? Her seemingly innocuous statement instantiated itself in my brain as a threat to the beautiful nostalgia of my youth. How dare she!!?? But alas . . . my precious wife was right . . . it was just vegetable beef soup. The consistency was different but the elements were the same. The texture was a little unique and the man who made it remains a giant, but in truth the mishmash known as "Grandpa's Soup" is vegetable beef.

Dallas Willard used to say "reality is what you run into when you're wrong."[1] Whether it is the crassness of soup or the sophistication of theology, reality has a way of bending us back and getting us thinking strait about the way things are. I thought of titling this chapter "Cream Puff Jesus 2.0." The truth is that the veggies of liberalism went through the postmodern grinder, and the shaft has been cranked by a number of people, but the elements have basically remained the same. But this Jesus demands a different kind of attention because he comes to us in this puréed form and because our cultural taste buds have changed.

We are not in the same cultural morass as we were in the late nineteenth and early twentieth centuries. In and of itself, this is a significant reason for us to look with fresh eyes at what can be called a postmodern Jesus. He is post-modern in that his evolution comes out of, goes beyond,

---

1. Willard, "Knowledge of Christ in Today's World."

and is a reaction to modernism. Classical liberalism is deeply rooted in modernist assumptions. In fact we saw in chapter 1 that the basic philosophical premise for theological liberalism was naturalism. Naturalism is a thoroughly modern notion that roots factual knowledge in the material sciences alone. By contrast, postmodernism rejects crucial aspects of the modernist story and attempts to distance itself from the factual assumptions that are rife within modernism. There will be more about this to come, but for now it is important simply to note that for something to be postmodern it must be reacting to something that is a tenet of modernism. For something to be a tenet of modernism we can simply say that it is an intellectual data point that is part of an era stemming from the period of the Enlightenment which occurred in western history in the seventeenth and eighteenth centuries.

## The Evolution of the Smorgasbord

In chapter 1 I discussed the rise of the Enlightenment. We need to go back to that briefly to begin to understand how postmodernism has become what it is today. Probably the most famous statement regarding postmodernism was made by Jean-Francois Lyotard in a book called *The Postmodern Condition*, which he wrote in 1979. What he said reduced postmodernism in its simplest form as "incredulity towards meta-narratives."[2] That statement synthesizes postmodernism on a couple of levels. For one it shows that postmodernity, as mentioned above, is a reaction. It is grounded in incredulity, which is an unwillingness to embrace something. Second, the unwillingness to believe is directed at grand stories that govern or direct human life, namely, "meta-narratives." I want to briefly summarize how western culture came to the place where Lyotard's concise summary of postmodernity could ring so true.

The Cream Puff Jesus of liberalism came from Kant through the German theologies of Schleiermacher and Ritschl and into the social action of the early twentieth century, finally culminating in the textual deconstruction of mainline liberalism as evidenced by the Jesus Seminar and others. As I demonstrated earlier, the philosophy of naturalism carried theological liberalism all the way to the bank and completely withdrew from the textual accounts the deity of Jesus. But naturalism wasn't alone in carrying culture forward. In fact, another movement took Kant's

2. Lyotard, *The Postmodern Condition*, xxiv.

ideas a bit of a different direction. In classic Hegelian fashion, the thesis of "mechanistic naturalism" in one brand of the Enlightenment found an antithesis in the Romanticism of yet another brand. Both aspects of the Enlightenment rightly trace their roots to Kant.

As a movement taking on a different trajectory than the naturalism fed by Darwin, Romanticism was concerned with the individual's subjective experience of reality. It centered on emotions rather than mind as the primary interface with the real. Kant had his twelve categories of mind that individuals utilized to construct the phenomenal world in which they lived. These twelve categories were shared by all humans. It was from this that Kant suggested we could have common experiences and talk with one another about a common sensual reality that we experience. This commonality made science at least rphenomenally objective. The scientific method itself starts with observation. For Kant, what makes this a viable starting point to talk concretely about the world is the shared categories of mind we all have. But the romantics cultivated a different nuance to Kant's thinking by focusing on the knowing subject. They emphasized the individual's experience of the world. Their focus was on the emotional properties of humanity. This philosophy of life trickled down to issues of personal satisfaction and ethics. Gene Edward Veith summarizes this well, "The romantics exalted the individual over impersonal, abstract systems. Self-fulfillment, not practicality, was the basis for morality."[3]

The location of the self at the center and the obfuscation of impersonal systems are deeply important to the manufacturing of the present postmodern mindset. For the romantics, the issues were about feelings, not facts. When one thinks of romantics, one cannot help but consider the works of key literary figures and artists. The currency of Romanticism was poetry and prose, not chemistry and calculations. In contrast, the other branch of Enlightenment philosophy rooted itself in the hard sciences of Newton and later that of Darwin. In fact, by the end of the nineteenth century, Romanticism was fading away as the bulldozer of naturalism made its way across the ideological plain attempting to destroy every metaphysical foray in its sight, be it the arts, morality, or religion.

But alas, the twentieth century put a colossal wrench in the machine of naturalism. It came in the form of two World Wars that exposed the ethical dangers of the science of technology and the evils of autocratic

---

3. Veith, *Postmodern Times*, 36.

power. The quest to optimize humanity in Hitler's own militaristic natural selection and his abuse of other cultures by means of tyranny left an optimistic world decimated. The scorched earth that remained in the hearts of humanity was riddled with personal pessimism and skepticism about others. The naturalism that had captivated the minds of the intelligentsia was no longer satisfying to a world that had watched atomic bombs go off in Japan, smelled the scents of Auschwitz, and listened to taps in front of too many white crosses.

There were two main philosophical reactions to the ethical plight of the two World Wars: logical positivism and existentialism. Logical positivism began after World War I and taught that for anything to be accepted as true and meaningful, it needed to be verified by experience and evidence. This carried forward the heritage of naturalism. It did so by leaving ethics alone in one sense. It privatized ethics as a subjective matter that could not be spoken of with any sense of rationality. The ensuing ethical philosophy of the logical positivists was known as "emotivism." Emotivism taught that the only thing we can say about whether or not something is right or wrong is how we feel about it. We can say that we *feel* it is wrong to torture three-year-old children for fun, but we can make no principled statement in *fact* about its being wrong. So what becomes clear is that logical positivism carried forward the naturalist distinction between facts and values that had been carried forward all the way from Kant.

Existentialism really emerged after World War II. Its great proponents were men like Jean-Paul Sartre and Albert Camus. There is no uniform strand of existential philosophy. Søren Kierkegaard lived years before in the nineteenth century, but many think he "should be considered the first modern existentialist."[4] He was a theist, whereas Sartre and Camus were atheists. Kierkegaard saw man's connection with God as supra-rational. He was a fideist who understood man to reach God not via rationality but via faith. In contrast, the atheistic existentialist sees the distance between man and God as unbridgeable because certitude is impossible. So instead of postulating faith as a bridge his conclusion is to eliminate God altogether.

There are three existentialist themes that dominate Sartre in particular that play important roles in present-day postmodernism. These are "his extreme individualism, his emphasis on freedom and responsibility,

---

4. McBride, "Existentialism," 296–97.

his insistence that we and not the world give meaning to our lives."⁵ Veith gives a good summary of how these three ideas of individualism, free choice, and meaning come together in the existentialist milieu:

> Meaning is not to be discovered in the objective world; rather, meaning is a purely human phenomenon. While there is no ready-made meaning in life, individuals can create meaning for themselves. By their own free choices and deliberate actions, human beings can create their own order, a meaning for their life that they and they alone determine. This meaning, however, has no validity for anyone else. No one can provide a meaning for someone else. Everyone must determine his or her own meaning, which must remain private, personal, and unconnected to any sort of objective truth.⁶

By endowing individuals with the power to establish meaning, existentialism formed the basis for postmodern thought.

To arrive at the postmodernist expression which is so influential today in the emergent church movement, only one more thing needed to be added to existentialist ideas. Sartre so strongly emphasized the autonomous freedom and responsibility of the individual. This individualism has found strong emphasis in today's postmodern culture; however, it also needed a communal connection. The connection came through a perspective of truth as a social construct. If individuals were to survive they needed to form community. If they were to have community, then they needed to arrive at conclusions about reality to govern life as a community. The 1960s ushered in this communal wave. People distraught with the authoritarianism of their parents' generation wanted to express themselves as individuals. But even individuals need other individuals and so the unbridled expressionism of the 1960s produced communal living situations to suit and celebrate the unorthodox views, practices, and styles of an entire generation. In the shadow of the Vietnam War, the United States government was seen by this generation as a regime of manipulative power. Slogans like, "Hey hey LBJ, how many kids did you kill today?" "Power to the people," and "Do your own thing" spoke in turn of the suspicion of the government, the primacy of individual choice, and the supremacy of personal autonomy and morality.

---

5. Solomon and Higgins, *A Short History of Philosophy*, 277.
6. Veith, *Postmodern Times*, 37–38.

There was a philosophical underbelly to the 1960s. The two World Wars showed that Nietzsche's nihilism and concepts of social power were prophetic in many regards. In the same line of thought as Nietzsche, twentieth-century philosopher Michel Foucault reacted to the power plays of totalitarian regimes in the first half of the century. He understood knowledge—whether it was in the subject of morality, the use of language, or the study of history—as a socially engineered idea. Power then came in the form of the socially constructed manipulation of knowledge. An objective claim on morality, a particular use of language to explain an idea or a law, and the telling of history were just the stories of people both capable and guilty of dominating others. Foucault was in midlife as the 1960s emerged, and his philosophy serves as an intellectual foray into the ideas that guided the quest of that generation all the way up to our present. When Lyotard made his famous statement in 1979, with which we began this historical summary, he was analyzing the ideological atmosphere of his day. Like him, Foucault's philosophy was born from the analysis of his life situation. In that sense it wasn't theory. It was an interpretation of observations he was making about society and its systems at large. Christian philosopher James K. A. Smith, who is sensitive to the postmodern context, writes:

> His claim about the relation between power and knowledge is not an a priori or abstract claim; rather, it is a claim that bubbles up from his analyses of concrete institutions and ideals such as hospitals and prisons, notions of madness versus reason, or the history of sexuality. Thus Foucault's claim is always made on the basis of case studies-where the axiom is not applied to a case but rather arises from it. If Foucault thinks that power is knowledge, it is because the history of modern institutions bears that out.[7]

Noting that this philosophy stems from the observation of society is important because it contributes to the cynical impulse of postmodernity toward structure and hierarchy. This impulse is carried on in the pragmatics, ministry philosophy, and theology of the emergent church.

This historical summary comes to a close with the realization that the individualism fostered by existentialism, the egalitarianism that has resulted from a rejection of hierarchy and structure, the cynicism toward systematic or objective notions of knowledge, and the communal

---

7. Smith, *Who's Afraid of Postmodernism?* 87.

longings of these autonomous agents have converged into an oxymoronic smorgasbord of ideas. Solomon and Higgins observe:

> Postmodernism has invited an obscurity and a pretentiousness almost unmatched in the long, often obscure, and pretentious history of philosophy. In its attack on dogmatism, it has too often become dogmatic. In its insistence on style, it has often become "stylized," conformist, and unimaginative to the point of tedium.[8]

Needless to say, consistency is not a postmodern virtue.

As postmodernism has flowered out in the emergent church movement several things have happened. Theology has become a collocation of preferences. Scriptural texts and church traditions have been cynically deconstructed. Community has been valued as a place where my individual expressions of spirituality garner appreciation and find validation. And ecclesiology has been reshaped to fit secular social values while thirsting for genuine relationships. Perhaps now we can look at the emergent church movement with greater understanding of its present concerns and its ideological heritage and with sensitivity to its popular appeal.

## The Emergent Church

Time has filtered the streams of the emergent church. What started as an initial frustration with traditional and commodified evangelicalism has branched out into different responses. A few years ago Mark Driscoll wrote a popular article for the Christian Research Journal that proposed that there were now four streams (he called them lanes) that the emergent church movement had branched out in. The four he proposed were: "Emerging Evangelicals," "House Church Evangelicals," "Emerging Reformers," and "Emergent Liberals."[9] Of the four, the first three tend to stay within the realm of historic Christian orthodoxy; the last . . . not so much. Each appeals to certain postmodern sensibilities with their own uniqueness. Emerging Evangelicals appeal with their sense of hipster culture. House Church Evangelicals appeal with their structure-light ecclesiology and their sense of organic community. Emerging Reformers appeal with their theological aesthetic of the glory of God and their

---

8. Solomon and Higgins, *A Short History of Philosophy*, 301.
9. Mark Driscoll, "Navigating the Emerging Church Highway."

commitment to meet the global needs of the poor. "Emergent Liberals" appeal to the most-raw postmodern sensibilities of egalitarian culture, individual spiritual expression, hermeneutical suspicion, and a dislocation from a pervasive socio-religious meta-narrative.

My concern is this last stream that Driscoll rightly labeled "Emergent Liberals." For simplicity's sake, from here on out I will simply refer to them as "emergent" since it seems to me that they are the stream most prominently associated with the term as the filtration process of time has worked its magic over the last decade. The emergent church's appeal to postmodern affections and its divergence from historic orthodoxy converge to create a dangerous movement that is reshaping both Christ and Christianity. I want to take the four points of appeal mentioned above and burrow a little deeper on each so we can see how they show up in present emergent voices.

## Four Flavorful Appeals

Flavorful Appeal #1: A Dislocation from Orthodoxy

In the last chapter, I proposed a hierarchy for theology. The basis of this proposal was that all doctrines are not equally important, and all doctrines are not equally clear in the text. It is true that some have been too haughty with their theological dogmatism. Hence the need for a clear hierarchy of doctrines that actually changes the rigor and vigor with which theological beliefs are held. However, the nature of the emergent church as a recycled form of liberalism comes out in their approach to theology as they swing the pendulum the other way. It is not that each doctrine matters to an equal degree of importance, but rather that each doctrine tends to matter to an equally insignificant degree. Some will accuse me of exaggeration, and maybe there is some truth to that. However, it is important that we make clear that, at the very least, everything is up for grabs doctrinally as far as the emergent church is concerned. In his book *Velvet Elvis*, leading emergent figure Rob Bell says as much:

> I embrace the need to keep painting, to keep reforming. By this I do not mean cosmetic, superficial changes like better lights and music, sharper graphics, and new methods with easy-to-follow steps. I mean theology: the beliefs about God, Jesus, the

Bible, salvation, the future. We must keep reforming the way the Christian faith is defined, lived, and explained.[10]

It doesn't get more to the core of Christian faith than the five areas of theological inquiry mentioned by Bell. And it is important to note the issues for Bell (and the emergent movement in general) do not merely revolve around how doctrine is applied, but how it is "defined." Yes, it really is all up for grabs.

I think this is further illustrated by the introduction to one of Brian McLaren's (the undisputed godfather of the emergent movement) books, *Everything Must Change*. In the introduction McLaren explains the title. As he does so, he introduces the goal of his book, which is to get his readers to reconsider a new "framing story" over the one typically proclaimed by Christianity. He describes what he means by the phrase:

> By *framing story*, I mean a story that gives people direction, values, vision, and inspiration by providing a framework for their lives. It tells them who they are, where they come from, where they are, what's going on, where things are going, and what they should do.[11]

In philosophy this is basically called a worldview. So he is suggesting that what needs to change for his readers is their present Christian worldview. That not only is a tall order, but a risky one. To change your beliefs on certain issues or doctrinal matters may have minimal importance to the core of your faith, but to say that the entire way you frame reality and your role in it needs to change is cataclysmic. This certainly doesn't mean he is wrong. I just want to be clear about what the stakes are. So then what about our "framing story" (a.k.a. worldview) needs to change? In the next paragraph he goes on to further explain:

> In searching for a better framing story than we currently proclaim, Christians like myself can discover a fresh vision of our religion's founder and his message, a potentially revolutionary vision that could change everything for us and for the world we inhabit. We can rediscover what it can mean to call Jesus Savior and Lord. When we raise the question of what exactly he intended to save us from. (His angry Father? The logical consequences of our actions? Our tendency to act in ways that produce undesirable logical consequences? Global self-destruction?) The

---

10. Bell, *Velvet Elvis*, 12.
11. McLaren, *Everything Must Change*, 5–6.

popular and domesticated Jesus, who has become little more than a chrome-plated hood ornament on the guzzling Hummer of Western civilization, can thus be replaced with a more radical saving, and, I believe, real Jesus.[12]

So what needs to change? According to McLaren it would seem that our view of Jesus and our view of the atonement need to. But now we are meddling with the foundation of Christian theology. We are wrestling with what Christ died for. When it comes to the emergent movement, things long assumed in tradition to be core matters of the Christian faith are up for grabs. The doctrine of the atonement is as much up for discussion as how many angels can stand on the head of a pin. To steal a title from another one of his books, should we incorporate a "generous orthodoxy" into our worldview? McLaren thinks so. In fact, in that book he begins describing the seven Jesuses he has encountered on his faith journey. His conclusion upon describing them is to exhort us to celebrate the diversity of the Christian representations of Jesus. He recommends "that we acknowledge that Christians of each tradition bring their distinctive and wonderful gifts to the table, so we can all enjoy the feast of generous orthodoxy—and spread that same feast for the whole world."[13] But what if liberalism's Jesus and my Jesus say the exact opposite? Apparently it is no matter. We should close our logical eyes and celebrate the naïve joy of a pluralistic Christology.

Christology is not alone among doctrines being minimized or altogether erased by the emergent movement. Samir Selmanovic writes a chapter in a book called *An Emergent Manifesto of Hope* that claims to be a book that brings its readers "the voices of those who are shaping the emergent conversation."[14] His chapter is titled "The Sweet Problem of Inclusiveness." In it he makes the following assertion:

> When we say that only Christ saves, Christ represents something larger than the person we Christians have come to know. He is all and in all. And Christ being "the only way" is not a statement of exclusion but inclusion, an expression of what is universal. If a relationship with a specific person, namely Christ, is the whole substance of a relationship with the God of the Bible, then the vast majority of the people in world history are excluded from the possibility of relationship with the God of the

---

12. Ibid., 6.
13. McLaren, *Generous Orthodoxy*, 66–67.
14. Pagitt and Jones, *An Emergent Manifesto of Hope*, 5.

Bible, along with the Hebrews of the Old Testament who were without a knowledge of Jesus Christ—the person. The question begs to be asked: would God who gives enough revelation for people to be judged but not enough revelation to be saved be a God worth worshiping? Never![15]

This is stunning. To move beyond the person of Christ and into the symbolism of what he represents is the substance of the matter? Is our trust in an idea? Is our savior a person or a moral ethos? Does John not tell us that Jesus "exegeted" the Father?[16] Didn't Jesus set his *person* up as the only way to the Father?[17] In a type of emotive argument, all too common among emergent writers, Selmanovic creates a context where the God painted by historic Christian orthodoxy so repulses his sensibilities he confesses he could not worship him.

Another nuance that the emergent church makes to the scope of soteriology comes in the form of a "Christian" universalism. Rob Bell's much talked-about book *Love Wins* had postmortem universalism as its premise. Bell's concept is that the love of God will outlast the vilest sinner so that free creatures in hell will one day respond to God's love and quit their rebellion against him. If C. S. Lewis was right and hell is locked on the inside then there is not only hope for the alienated, but also the expectation that God's enduring love for them will ultimately be more stubborn than their rebellion.

In addition to Bell, an even more theologically rigorous attempt at universalism is now being made in the name of so-called trinitarian theology. The focus here is not on God's love enduring postmortem, what I might call the *length* of God's love. Instead the focus is on God's love in Christ including all people now: what I might call the *breadth* of God's love. Its proponents range from the popular writer William Paul Young, author of the highly acclaimed work of fiction *The Shack*, to the less known theologian C. Baxter Kruger.

15. Ibid., 194–95.
16. John 1:18 says "No one has ever seen God; the only God, who is at the Father's side, he has made him known (exēgēsato)."
17. In John 14 the dialogue between Jesus and his disciples is a foundational text for the doctrine of exclusivism, and with good reason. Right after responding to Thomas's question by proclaiming "I am the way, and the truth, and the life. No one comes to the Father except through me" (6), he gets another question from Philip, who wants to see the Father. Jesus responds to this question, saying in part, "Whoever has seen me has seen the Father. How can you say, 'Show us the Father'? Do you not believe that I am in the Father and the Father is in me?" (9b–10a).

Kruger's understanding of the work of Jesus is that he reversed the curse for all. Jesus' death was the culminating work of his entire life, which was focused on reversing the curse, and in his life and death "the Fall of Adam and Eve has been undone, Adamic existence has been thoroughly converted to God, fundamentally reordered into right relationship with God."[18] We must be careful to not misunderstand and think Kruger is merely emphasizing the unlimited sufficiency of Christ's death for all affected by the Fall as a number of traditional evangelicals do. No, Kruger is not speaking about the sufficiency of Jesus for all. He is speaking about the efficiency of Jesus for all. That is to say, all people are actually included in Christ and have eternal life with God when they die whether they realize it or not. He writes (emphasis mine):

> The very essence of the gospel lies right here in Jesus Christ himself, in his humanity, in his incarnate relationship with the Father in the Spirit, and in the mysterious way in which he included us in this relationship. For the great conversion of his humanity to his Father, wrought out through thirty-three years of fire and trial, and decisively accomplished in his death and resurrection, was a vicarious event. The miraculous and wonderful truth is that we were included in his baptism, in his life and death, in his resurrection and ascension. When he died, we died. When he rose, we rose. When he ascended to the Father, he took *the whole human race* with him to the right hand of God the Father almighty—inside the circle of all circles, into the very life of the Triune God. With this, and this alone, the Father is at last thrilled, for our exaltation and adoption in Jesus Christ is the fulfillment of the primal decision made before all worlds began.[19]

The good news then is that you are included in Christ whether you realize it or not.

So what then is the role of believing in Christ? The answer for Kruger is that faith gives us freedom to experience a life relieved of self-centeredness. When we come to believe in Christ, then we have what he calls the "baptism of assurance,"[20] and now reap the results of a life rescued from the anxieties that plague us in our egocentric ignorance of

---

18. Kruger, *Jesus and the Undoing of Adam*, 31.
19. Ibid., 55–56.
20. Ibid., 51–52.

Christ. So faith brings us the felt freedom of life in Christ but is irrelevant to the fact of our inclusion in him.

Christology and soteriology do not stand alone as doctrinal categories where emergents have dislodged themselves from orthodoxy. But, for my purpose, they serve to illustrate the dislocation and to highlight that the Jesus they describe and the Jesus of historic Christian orthodoxy look rather different. Additionally, I need to point out that the appeal of this Jesus is indeed full of flavor, rather tasty to the cultural climate. He is inclusive, he doesn't get hung up on differences but spends his time emphasizing similarities, and he paints an appetizing picture of his Father that isn't angry at personal sin—unless that sin involves judging another person's postmodern sense of autonomy.

## Flavorful Appeal #2: Hermeneutical Suspicion

The postmodern skepticism about language being used as a power play to keep people locked into narratives of restriction, oppression, ignorance, or a combination of all three abounds in the emergent circles. It is no accident that McLaren came into church life from the academic world of English literature. Literature departments overflow with postmodern thought as language gets utilized to persuade and dissuade and as literary forms take artistic license to say more or less than they actually mean. The cynicism about language infiltrates not just the emergent approach to the text of Scripture but also its approach to the narratives of Christian tradition and to the texts about Christian history.

This question of what to do with historical texts looms incredibly large in the divide between the emergent church and those holding to a traditional theology of Christian orthodoxy (a loaded and oppressive term to a postmodern, eliciting thoughts of a coterie of self-intoxicated theological elites). This is only to be expected because of the authoritative role Scripture has taken in the development of Christian theology. The tension that the emergent movement has with the traditional evangelical views about Scripture is not just about what the text actually says but about what role the text ought to play in the formation of theology.

The postmodern/emergent view of texts and historic creeds of the Christian tradition is summed up in the words of postmodern philosopher John Caputo, reflecting on the challenge of understanding Jesus through the ancient text:

There are many interpretations of what he actually said and did, and both the New Testament itself and the "orthodox" Nicene theology of the later churches are just two of them, a point that unsettles the long-robed powers that be (*ta onta!*) all the way down to their episcopal toes. In deconstruction the New Testament is an archive, not the *arche*, and to mix up the two, as the fundamentalists do, is to make an idol out of an icon. Deconstruction saves us from idolatry, while scriptural literalism succumbs to the idolatry of a book.[21]

Caputo's statement may take a little explaining. The term "deconstruction" comes from the philosophical work of Jacques Derrida. Employing the full arsenal of postmodern cynicism, texts are analyzed showing their inconsistencies, their cultural conditionality, and the power plays they employ or are used to employ. This is done in an effort to find alternative meanings to what has traditionally been held. When Caputo talks about deconstruction, he is referring to getting behind the power play of language and the dominating influences of the culture, the church, and tradition to get at what he sees as the egalitarian heart of the ethos of the kingdom of God. He makes an important and indicting statement when he says that the hermeneutic he is employing when he comes to the text, "deconstruction," makes the written record of Jesus in the New Testament an "archive" and not an "arche." The term "arche" is used in the phrase "arche-writing" by Derrida, which referred to an original form of language that is above deconstruction. Caputo is saying that the New Testament is an archive of history that must be uncluttered by the interpreter. It needs to lose the baggage that has collected on it throughout history and that is part of its original context. He is saying that the New Testament, however, is not a text that stands static and timeless. It is rather entirely conditioned and must be emptied of the manipulative narratives that have been spun around it throughout church tradition.

Of course it is fascinating that by the time Caputo is done, the kingdom of God that Jesus espouses gets interpreted (read: "deconstructed") to be an egalitarian, homosexuality-approving, liberal morass. Who is spinning the cultural narrative around the text now?

The same approach shows up in the way emergent author Tony Jones talks about theological formation. He sees theological formation possessing three traits: it is local, conversational and temporary. Of the last one he states:

---

21. Caputo, *What Would Jesus Deconstruct*, 104.

> Finally, theology is temporary. Since our conceptions of God are shaped locally and in conversation, we must hold them humbly. We must carry our theologies with an open hand, as it were. To assume that our convictions about God are somehow timeless is the deepest arrogance, and it establishes an imperialistic attitude that has a chilling effect on the honest conversation that's needed for theology to progress.[22]

But what does it mean for "theology to progress"? Is God actually changing? Does the text, rooted in history, actually change its meaning? If we answer yes to the first question, we would be overtly heretical. If we answer yes to the second question, then it seems pointless to assert that the words I am writing actually mean anything, and it would be pointless for any reader to ask what I mean by what I say. Theology can only be temporary if the subject matter itself is changing. So Jones's statement presupposes either a mutable God or an understanding of language that makes even his own statement lack intended meaning.

The deconstructionist approach to the text, coupled with the idea that our interpretation of the text ought to be temporary, leads to some important and crucial questions about hermeneutics. Is the text of Scripture, as it sits, true in everything that it affirms? We have to answer this logically prior to asking about specificities of its content. If we don't, we may well be overcome by one of two propensities: 1) to see in it what isn't there in hopes of redeeming it as an important tool for our spiritual lives; or, 2) reject it as carrying any clout at all because it so radically diverges from the accepted norms of our present culture.

To say that the Bible is true in everything that it affirms is to say that it is inerrant. This term smells like modernism to many. To the emergents this term feels divisive. And in one sense it is—but that doesn't make it wrong. Some emergent thinkers feel like holding to the doctrine of inerrancy is unrealistic and unnecessary. Carlos Bovell opines, "It appears virtually impossible to be a believer and a critical scholar at the same time."[23] I think this is overly pessimistic and exaggerates the divide between scriptural and academic integrity. There are many scholars and pastors holding both in tension just fine. I am not trying to oversimplify the issues surrounding inerrancy, and I think it is safe to say that not enough has been clarified concerning the term's elasticity. There is no question that the term needs some good explaining, and room needs

22. Jones, *The New Christians*, 114.
23. Bovell, *Inerrancy and the Spiritual Formation of Younger Evangelicals*, 29.

to be made for the breadth of genres, as well as careful thought made concerning authorial intent. But the real problem with emergents and inerrancy is how ready they are to give it up.

The implications of the Bible serving as an archive and not an authority are unsettling to traditional evangelicals. Emergents, on the other hand, are ready to level the playing field on Wesley's famous interpretive quadrilateral consisting of revelation (primarily Scripture), reason, tradition, and experience. Historically, evangelicalism has exalted revelation over the other three while recognizing that they function as an inevitable interpretive milieu for it. Emergent theology seems content to give them an equal say, and if any one of them gets to be the lead partner in the hermeneutical dance it undoubtedly gets to be *experience*. But why? Why does experience consistently seem to lead the hermeneutical process in emergent thought? This issue will be addressed in the next chapter, where I hope to propose some means of correcting this drift.

## Flavorful Appeal #3: Individual Spiritual Expression

Postmodernism dodges definition with full intent. It is a reaction to systems and forms, so it gravitates to the chaotic and amorphous. This is part of its appeal to those who have been burned out and burned over by the church. They want something new without losing God. This is not inherently bad, but it is rather adolescent and puerile. The problem is not about just wanting something new, it is about what you are discarding to make this neoteric shift. The title of Dan Kimball's book, *They Like Jesus but Not the Church: Insights from Emerging Generations*, sort of tells the story. Jesus gets high marks so emergent Christians want to hold onto him. But the church has disappointed and disaffected them so now it is time to move on. The church may have its flaws, but it remains the Bride of Christ. The analogy of a husband and wife to Christ and the church in Paul's letter to the Ephesians is instructive. If someone rejects, turns their back on, talks down about, or generally dishonors my wife, they have done so to me. The parallel is obvious when it comes to Christ and his church. She may be battered and stained, but she should not be abandoned. In short, we need the church. Postmodernism's rejection of the church and efforts at reformulating communities to be as "unchurchified" as possible smack of an underlying idea that helps postmodernism stay afloat: individualism.

## Individualism

An emergent reader of this is likely to object to my inclusion of individualism as a trait exuded by the postmodern reaction since community is such a prized concept. As I mentioned earlier in the chapter, Sartre's existentialism had its roots deep in the idea of individual freedom and responsibility. As the cultural wave of the 1960s came, personal expression was glorified. Music was charged with angsty themes rejecting oppression and violence. Protests ballooned on the streets, letting those in positions of power know that the days of manipulation were over. Art forms took on displays of personal expression that meandered toward the absurd.

Individualism sets up the self as the ultimate authority. One of the great paradoxes of the postmodern Christian is that he longs for community but shuns accountability. In other words he wants all the benefits of living in relationships, but he wants them on his terms. Social action makes him feel good, but being told he is out of line makes him feel bad. I personally find that postmodern community is actually a hidden form of individualism. Genuine community means that I connect in meaningful relationship with people who are very different from me. It means that I employ the thirty-five *one anothers* of Scripture to help me create long-lasting, impactful relationships. But all too often postmoderns break off into groups based on affinity. In fact, rallying points are created that revolve around subcultural and mutually shared interests. These groups tend to be far from eclectic and far from stretching. In that sense they are more individualistic than communal.

Perhaps individualism can help explain the extraordinary thin skin of the postmodern community. Today we live in a culture too sensitive to the slightest invasion of our rights or to the most menial social offense. Individuals are radically convinced that they need no one to tell them what to do, nor do they want or regard opinions of others who may be a bit further down the road in life. The ultimate judge and jury of wrongs or being wronged is the individual himself. "In other words if I am the center of my reality and know that reality better than anyone else, a corollary belief is that others have no right to criticize how I live."[24]

---

24. Wilkes and Sanford, *Hidden Worldviews*, 32.

## Tolerance

The sensitivity mentioned above turns up another trait of postmodernity that shows up in the emergent movement, that of tolerance. To be tolerant in its most rudimentary form just means to permit or to endure the actions or attitudes of another. In this sense tolerance is a virtue every Christian would readily celebrate. But tolerance in the postmodern mind looks more like acceptance than endurance. And this distinction is a big one.

Reflecting on postmodernism in general, D. A. Carson observes:

> Religions that speak of being right or wrong on certain matters or that support any form of exclusive claim or that uphold rigorous standards of personal and public morality will be dismissed as "intolerant," even if they vigorously support the right of all religions to defend their own patch and seek new converts.[25]

Carson's prophetic words find a fulfillment in McLaren's own prescription for an evangelism that would seem to have tolerance in view:

> This kind of evangelism would celebrate the good in the Christian religion and lament the bad, just as it would in every other religion, calling people to a way of life in a kingdom (or beautiful whole) that transcends and includes all religions. Yes, it would welcome people into communities of faith in which they would experience formation in the way of Jesus, and yes, you could call these communities Christian churches if you'd like, although you could call them other things too. But whatever you call these communities, they would be interested in breaking out of the cocoons of Christianity that were spun within the Greco-Roman narrative, governed by a constitutional reading of Scripture, oriented around violent and tribal views of God, and so on.[26]

Tolerance, as presented by both the secular postmodern culture and the emergent church's adaptation, rules out a robust theological exclusivism.

Individual spiritual expression is prized in the practice of the emergent church. Responses in public worship range from tactile acts like painting and making pottery to contemplative meditation. Interaction and conversation are valued, as opposed to more classic didactic methods like formal instruction and sermonizing.

---

25. Carson, *Becoming Conversant with the Emerging Church*, 100.
26. McLaren, *A New Kind of Christianity*, 216.

### Flavorful Appeal #4: Egalitarian Culture

On the face of it, the most appealing piece of the emergent church to the present culture is its strong penchant for egalitarianism. It is too simple to define egalitarianism as the desire for equality. The manner in which it enters into the discourse of sociology and theology is more nuanced. An egalitarian holds that people are seen on an equal plane in terms of their ontology and their capacity or opportunity for particular functions. The contrasting perspective can be called hierarchicalism. The hierarchical perspective typically sees people as ontologically equal but is very comfortable with functional distinctions that may entail roles of authority.

### Why Egalitarianism?

There are a number of reasons why the emergent church, buttressed by postmodern philosophy, embraces egalitarianism. In fact, "embrace" may not be strong enough. Egalitarianism is being thrust on the church by both our present secular culture and by emergent church leaders and writers. Reasons for the affinity between the emergents and egalitarians include a desire for social acceptance, an impulse that values individual expression, a longing for less structure, a resistance to personal accountability, and a rejection of the expectation of others. But two larger ideas rise above these points of affinity and are worth mentioning.

I have already touched on the concept of cynicism toward people and language earlier in the chapter. This is the first of the two larger ideas fueling the connection of egalitarianism with emergent theology. Social structures are seen as tools of manipulation and oppression. But what does it mean to view a "structure" cynically? The cynicism is not really resting on the mechanism or idea, but on the people that stand for, behind, and in the mechanism. We have witnessed global horrors at the expense of carnal hearts in positions of power. We have also seen thousands, nay, millions cared for because of the benevolent hearts of people in power. But only one gets the reaction. Only one colors and jades the mechanism. I find this intriguing and disturbing. It seems that the issue has less to do with social structures and language and more to do with cynicism toward people.

The second idea is a theological one that deals with the Trinity. Trinitarianism is a foundational Christian doctrine. The classic definition of the Trinity goes something like this: *God is one in essence, eternally subsisting in three equal persons.* There is a phrase that is sometimes added and really sits at the heart of the distinction between egalitarianism and hierachicalism. When this phrase is added to the definition of the Trinity it would be articulated this way: God is one in essence, eternally subsisting in three equal persons *who operate with subordinating functions.*

This addition plays an important role because of a particular facet of trinitarian doctrine that has found a significant resurgence in theological literature—general and postmodern theology in particular. This facet deals with the intra-trinitarian relationships of the three persons of the Trinity. This gets into some fairly rarified theological air, but it is wildly important to some very practical and important differences among evangelicals themselves and specifically between traditional evangelicals and emergents.

A little-known theological term that is growing in the frequency of its use in theological literature is the term *perichoresis*. Perichoresis refers to the mutual indwelling of the persons of the Trinity in one another. Postmodernism's emphasis on organic community, its value of individual expression, and its sensitivity to any form of personal criticism or judgmentalism meld together and establish a deep affection for the notion of perichoresis. The connection goes like this. The Trinity is the ultimate community. It consists of three persons sharing one essence and relating to each other with a mutual concern driven by a devoted and entirely pure self-giving love. Stanley Grenz and John Franke, in an important philosophical book supportive to the framework of emergent theology, write: "Perhaps the single most significant development in the contemporary renaissance of trinitarian theology has been the emphasis on relationality."[27] This development is no doubt the result of the principal postmodern concept of community. For the postmodern, this trinitarian relational prototype seems inimical to any sense of hierarchy and structure. Mutual love and self-effacement seem to fit egalitarian notions of personal equity. If this is true there seems to be little room for a hierarchical understanding of community.

At the popular level this is seen clearly in William Paul Young's fictional best seller *The Shack*. The book deals with human difficulty and explores how God relates to us in the midst of personal tragedy and loss. In so doing, Young works from a commitment to trinitarian theology with a postmodern bent. Young's main character, Mack, finds himself in

---

27. Grenz and Franke, *Beyond Foundationalism*, 193.

a cabin in the woods with three personages who relate to him and to each other as Trinity. As Young tells the story, he is deep into the immanent and economic facets of the Trinity. In one portion of the characters' interaction in the cabin, Mack asks if one of the three is in charge. The question seems odd to the Godhead but is noted as something they do discuss. The comments that follow are too lengthy to cite here, but a few will do. Young writes:

> Mack nodded, relieved and a little chagrined that he had again allowed himself to lose his composure. "Mackenzie, we have no concept of final authority among us, only unity. We are in a circle of relationship, not a chain of command or 'great chain of being' as your ancestors termed it. What you're seeing here is relationship without any overlay of power. We don't need power over the other because we are always looking out for the best. Hierarchy would make no sense among us. Actually, this is your problem, not ours."[28]

The dialogue continues between them and more light is shed on humans and their penchant for functioning in roles of authority and their acceptance of hierarchy:

> "But every human institution that I can think of, from political to business, even down to marriage, is governed by this kind of thinking; it is the web of our social fabric," Mack asserted. "Such a waste!" said Papa, picking up the empty dish and heading for the kitchen. "It's one reason why experiencing true relationship is so difficult for you," Jesus added. "Once you have a hierarchy you need rules to protect and administer it, and then you need law and the enforcement of the rules, and you end up with some kind of chain of command or a system of order that destroys relationship rather than promotes it. You rarely see or experience relationship apart from power. Hierarchy imposes laws and rules and you end up missing the wonder of relationship that we intended for you."[29]

The imposition of laws and rules seems adverse to real relationship. But what does this say about the New Testament structure of local church ecclesiology in 1 Timothy? How does it account for the author of Hebrews telling his readers to "obey your leaders and submit to them" (Heb. 13:17a)? How does it fit with domestic structure articulated by Paul and

28. Young, *The Shack*, 122.
29. Ibid,. 122–23.

Peter? Are these all just contextualizations to the fallen system of human life? That would seem like a surprising conclusion.

What Young then puts in the mouths of the characters depicting the Father and Jesus is particularly insightful:

> "It is the human paradigm," added Papa, having returned with more food. "It *is* like water to fish, so prevalent that it goes unseen and unquestioned. It *is* the matrix; a diabolical scheme in which you are hopelessly trapped even while completely unaware of its existence." Jesus picked up the conversation. "As the crowning glory of creation, you were made in our image, unencumbered by structure and free to simply 'be' in relationship with me and one another. If you had truly learned to regard each other's concerns as significant as your own, there would be no need for hierarchy."[30]

Young represents the postmodern/emergent idea that hierarchy is a problem created by humanity. It is thus not part of the original design. So the only way to reflect the beauty of the intra-trinitarian perichoresis is by shunning authority and hierarchy in an effort to maintain a level playing field. The operating (and in my view faulty) assumption here is that this is simply what real love does, because love is inimical to power over another. I will now bite my theological tongue and refrain from a response until the next chapter. Right now we just need to be clear about where the egalitarian emphasis comes from. This takes us a little deeper into some theological waters.

One of the great trinitarian theologies of note comes to life in Wolfhart Pannenburg's *Systematic Theology*. Pannenburg gives detailed analysis throughout his work to the social aspect of trinitarian theology. He focuses on the monarchy of the Father, which stands out in an assessment of the varied operations of the persons of the Trinity.[31] He then makes the following concise statement, "The Son is not subordinate to

---

30. Ibid,. 124.

31. "The mutuality and mutual dependence of the persons of the Trinity, not merely as regards their personal identity but also as regards their deity, do not mean that the monarchy of the Father is destroyed. On the contrary, through the work of the Son the kingdom or monarchy of the Father is established in creation, and through the work of the Spirit, who glorifies the Son as the plenipotentiary of the Father, and in so doing glorifies the Father himself, the kingdom or monarchy of the Father in creation is consummated. By their work the Son and Spirit serve the monarchy of the Father. Yet the Father does not have his kingdom or monarchy without the Son and Spirit, but only through them." Pannenburg, *Systematic Theology*, Vol. 1, 324.

the Father in the sense of ontological inferiority, but he subjects himself to the Father."[32] Pannenburg is making the distinction between ontology (essence, being) and function (role, operation). Later, in his section on Christology, he burrows deeper regarding functional subordination:

> In his form of life as Jesus, on the path of his obedience to God, the eternal Son appeared as a human being. The relation of the Son to the Father is characterized in eternity by the subordination to the Father, by the self-distinction from the majesty of the Father, which took historical form in the human relation of Jesus to God. This self-distinction of the eternal Son from the Father may be understood as the basis of all creaturely existence in its distinction from God, and therefore as the basis of the human existence of Jesus, which gave adequate embodiment in its course to the self-emptying of the Son in service to the rule of the Father.[33]

This distinction of ontology and function, persons and ideas, being and acting is minimized in postmodernism. In fact, sometimes, it is all but erased.

Pannenburg is countered by his contemporary Jürgen Moltmann. Moltmann seems driven by the fact that sociologically, patriarchy is repulsive to him, and he sees its abuse as the cause of deep social evils. In fact, in the introduction to one of his works, he is perplexed as to why Pannenburg insists on holding onto a monarchichal aspect to the Father's role in the Trinity.[34] Moltmann seems bent on explaining away patriarchy by perceiving the Father's role as only defined in relationship to Jesus. It is this that keeps fatherliness from being loaded with patriarchalism. And it is patriarchy that has led to domination and abuse. Moltmann asserts:

> The visions are there in concrete promises: a community of human solidarity, communication free of domination, an open society. This future is only betrayed in patriarchy and only hindered in a 'fatherless' bureaucratic society. Women and men, mothers and fathers, will only enter into a 'just, participatory and responsible' human society if first patriarchy and then also

32. Ibid.
33. Pannenburg, *Systematic Theology*, Vol. 2, 377.
34. "Because Pannenberg maintains the 'monarchy of the Father', he dispenses with the idea of communion or fellowship in the divine *perichoresis* and instead of this takes up the monarchy into the relationships within the Trinity. It is not completely clear to me why he has to maintain the idea of monarchy." Moltmann, *History and the Triune God*, xix.

the fatherless society have been done away with. In principle that already happens in the motherly love which Jesus manifested in the Father and put into practice through his own behavior towards the poor, the sick and the sinners.[35]

Moltmann's argument sounds pretty postmodern:[36] an egalitarian view of the Trinity will lead to loving others well and to the fulfillment of social-justice concerns. In contrast, a hierarchical view of the Trinity only feeds the fallen proclivity for power and domination of others.

Emergent Egalitarian Issues

In our present culture, the outflow of the cynicism about people and language along with the egalitarian perspective of the economic Trinity have led the emergent church to conclusions about two important social and ecclesiological issues.

First, issues of gender roles both at home and in church are being thrown aside. Distinctions in domestic or ecclesial roles are seen as archaic and discriminatory. Virtually all emergent leaders and thinkers are egalitarians. To be otherwise would be seen as a power play and inimical to intra-trinitarian love. Much is layered in a discussion of this issue, but it is enough now to say that hermeneutics, the interplay of Christ and culture, and the ontology/function distinction make up the heart of the matter. These will be discussed in more detail in the next chapter.

The second issue is fast becoming the most significant social issue in North America: *homosexuality*. From Supreme Court cases to state laws to high school bullying, the issue has kept the political arena of the

---

35. Ibid., 17. This statement comes at the close of his chapter entitled, "I Believe in God the Father: Patriarchal or Non-Patriarchal Talk of God?".

36. The notion that postmodernity is driving Moltmann is brought into question by Colin Greene, who states: "Similarly, one wonders at times whether or not Moltmann really has the perspectives of postmodernity in view. One searches in vain for much evidence of radical engagement with postmodern thinkers and, of course, universal soteriological contexts of expectation and meaning, and other totalizing systems of discourse are inherently vulnerable to the claim that there is a semiotic plasticity of meaning to the representational content of language that defies such categorization. In this regard, it is hardly conceivable that a messianic Christology, which looks forward to Christ's universal rule, would have so little to say about the particular context of religious pluralism and the competing truth claims among the religions that some have claimed is one of the dominating horizons of postmodernity." Greene, *Christology in Cultural Perspective*, 343–44. But he seems to miss the point that Moltmann is writing as a man of his time. He is not a theologian necessarily in interaction with postmodernity but rather a theologian who is himself influenced by the postmodern *weltenschauung*.

United States absolutely buzzing. But politics is not alone. The issue is now reverberating through the aisles of churches all over the United States and Canada. The emergent church is helping shape not only the discussion but ultimately the theology and ethics of Christianity. Rob Bell has now endorsed same-sex marriage.[37] Brian McLaren participated in a ceremony celebrating his son's same-sex union.[38] Popular blogger and author Rachel Held Evans now endorses same sex unions. In fact, she wrote an opinion piece for CNN about why millennials (those born from the early 1980s to about 2000) are leaving the church. Her words are insightful . . . and scary (emphasis mine):

> What millennials really want from the church is not a change in style but a change in substance. We want an end to the culture wars. We want a truce between science and faith. We want to be known for what we stand for, not what we are against. We want to ask questions that don't have predetermined answers. We want churches that emphasize an allegiance to the kingdom of God over an allegiance to a single political party or a single nation. *We want our LGBT friends to feel truly welcome in our faith communities.* We want to be challenged to live lives of holiness, not only when it comes to sex, but also when it comes to living simply, caring for the poor and oppressed, pursuing reconciliation, engaging in creation care and becoming peacemakers.[39]

The placement of an acceptance of homosexuality right before an expressed desire "to be challenged to live lives of holiness" is indicative of the embrace same-sex relationships are receiving by the emergent church. It has ceased to be a question in the emergent church. Instead, it has now become a point of rebuke used by emergent leaders against those "ignorant" church leaders who seem bent on repelling today's generation.

## Conclusion

I began the chapter with the thesis that Christian postmodernism has parallels to the liberalism that emerged in the late nineteenth and twentieth centuries. However, its underbelly, as we have seen, is formed by some different—but not entirely unrelated—philosophies. The carnage

37. Carey, "Rob Bell Endorses Marriage Equality."

38. Steffan, "Brian McLaren Leads Commitment Ceremony at Son's Same-Sex Wedding."

39. Rachel Held Evans, "Why Millennials Are Leaving the Church."

produced by the two World Wars of the first half of the twentieth century produced some societal insecurities. Those insecurities led to a cynicism about governmental and social structures that leaked into the church in the form of the emergent church movement.

The movement's cultural appeal has made it influential and a major player in the formation of theology, church life, and ethics moving forward. Christ will be getting a pretty significant makeover if we do not assess where the emergent church has come from and where it is very rapidly moving. If you are concerned about the future of the Bride of Christ and how she sees the Groom, then read on. Smorgasbord Jesus is on the move.

# 6

## Giving Jesus the Freedom to Form His Own Menu

*At what point does an "orthodoxy" that is more "generous" than God's become heterodoxy?*

D. A. CARSON

IT HAS BEEN SAID that perception is reality, but in reality it is not so. Instead we know that sometimes things really are not what they seem. The intentional or even the often unintentional consequences of the disconnection between perception and reality can be a very painful thing. This is illustrated in a scene in the movie *Falling Down* starring Michael Douglas as William "D-Fens" Foster, a middle-aged, unemployed defense contractor who has simply had enough of life in society. He leaves his vehicle amidst a Los Angeles traffic jam and wanders throughout the city, getting into altercations with people who are themselves on edge. The movie depicts a culture filled with angst, and Foster seems to be the most combustible of all. In a scene drenched in black comedy, he makes his way into a fast-food restaurant and wants to order breakfast only to find out that he is three minutes too late, and is told at the counter that he can't get breakfast. This does not sit well. He gets in an argument with the manager, insisting that he get his breakfast. The manager will not back down. As the dispute moves on, Foster puts a bag on the counter and asks the manager "Rick, have you ever heard the expression, 'the customer is always right'?" The manager ends up informing him that their policy is that after 11:30 a.m. customers must order something from the lunch menu, not the breakfast menu. Frustrated by this news, Foster pulls out an automatic weapon from the bag and everyone in the place goes into a panic. After a moment (and an accidental firing of the gun) things quiet down and he realizes that he does, in fact, want lunch and not breakfast any longer.

The scene continues with Foster getting his order of a double-Whammy burger with cheese, an order of Whammy fries, and a choco-Wham shake. The patrons of the fast-food joint are sitting in silent fear as he waits for his order. When it comes he opens the box and registers a disappointment I and many others have personally felt in fast-food establishments all over these great United States . . . the burger looks nothing like the one on the menu. He is not happy. He tosses it down on the counter saying:

> "See this is what I'm talkin' about! Turn around, look at that (as he points to the picture of the burger on the menu). You see what I mean? It's plump, it's juicy, it's three inches thick . . . Now look at this sorry, miserable, squashed thing (as he holds up the burger he received, half-hanging out of its wrapper)." He then adds, "Can anybody tell me what's wrong with this picture? . . . anybody . . . anybody at all?"

It is dramatic and comedic. It is part spoof on life and part psychotic rambling. While his reaction is absurd and the tension he produces in the restaurant is criminal, his observation is right on.

There is a disjunction between what is advertised and what is; between the seduction of the image and the reality of the object. This severance between the apparent and the actual, between the purported and the palpable, is a divide that produces disappointment, confusion, calamity, mistrust, and destabilization. Fast-food mis-advertisement is one thing—worldview mis-advertisement is another. I believe one of the central issues in the emergent church movement is this mis-advertisement. The gap between what is opined for and what actually comes to fruition is wide and, in my opinion, dangerous. This is no more evident than in the prized emergent-church, postmodern value of authentic community.

## So You Want Community . . . ?

The buzzwords and phrases of the postmodern individual's search for a local church to plug into are slogans like: "A place where people can be real," "Real relationships," and "Come as you are." These all speak of authenticity and relationships that are rooted in shunning hypocrisy. I don't think there is any question that hypocrisy ought to be shunned and that authenticity ought to be an important value for the local church. In fact, at the church I lead, our second core passion is "authentic spirituality." The problem isn't the advertisement. It isn't the picture on the menu behind the counter. It is whether or not the chef and the appliances in the kitchen can in fact produce what the picture purports. It is my contention that four facets of postmodern culture keep the emergent church from producing the very thing it advertises as one of its primary stated values.

### Deterrent #1—Hypersensitivity

In almost every area of our postmodern culture, interpersonal sensitivities are on display. This is seen in our culture's obsession with politically correct language. Now people object to referring to a group of people as "guys" because it lacks the gender nuance necessary to refer to a group that may include females. Some Indians hear oppression in the term Native American but others don't. In an ironic twist, women now compliment each other by calling one another "bitches," and it is accepted for young homosexuals to refer to other homosexuals as a "fag"—whereas if an outsider to the homosexual community uses the same term, they are rightly seen as condescending and discriminatory.[1] This penchant for political correctness is apparent in the media's obsession with every movement of public figures. Politicians and athletes have never had their lives and movements so scrutinized and so reacted to. Our hypersensitivity itself is seen in the constant stream of literally hundreds of millions of Tweets that hit cyberspace every day, tuning us in to the emotional landscape of individual lives on an hourly and sometimes minute-by-minute basis. We want everyone to know how we feel, and we want to find out how everyone feels. We want people to "Like" our Facebook status, and if not enough people do, we feel unnoticed and even rejected.

---

1. These and other interesting terminological insights can be culled in Bleifuss, "A Politically Correct Lexicon."

So why is sensitivity a challenge to real community? The answer rests in the fact that people simply cannot be "real" when they have to filter all of their language through an ever-changing grid of cultural acceptance. Certainly culture changes, and certainly some terms are pejorative and condescending and are so loaded with an oppressive history that they cannot nor should they ever be redeemed. However, the rapidity at which the communicative appropriateness changes in our culture is absurd. People cannot relax on eggshells. Additionally, the norm in our culture is to place our thoughts out for everyone to see and observe in any number of online forums. So we live in a world where my feelings or thoughts are constantly receiving a thumbs-up or a thumbs-down by someone else. We "friend" (Facebook made it a verb!), unfriend, and refriend. The entire enterprise makes people self-conscious and makes the language of friendship extremely tenuous and shallow. Hypersensitivity does not stand alone. The next two deterrents really explain in more detail why sensitivity is such a crucial component of postmodernism.

## Deterrent #2—False Equivalence

I was teaching at a Bible school on the Oregon coast a few years ago. In one of my lectures I reflected on some leaders in the emergent church who have, in error, stated that the doctrine of substitutionary atonement portrays divine child abuse. As I criticized this notion, I took umbrage with Brian McLaren's writings, ideas, and his endorsement of others' (namely Steve Chalke) works. As the week of teaching was drawing to a close, I was approached by a student who was very angry with me. She was in tears. She proceeded to tell me that I had offended her because I had criticized Brian McLaren, and she wanted me to know that her father and Brian McLaren were best friends. I felt genuinely bad that she was hurt. But as we talked I realized that the reason she was hurt had more to do with her postmodern perception than with the actual context and content of my words. She felt I had attacked Brian McLaren without knowing him personally, and because of that she deemed my statements to be inappropriate.

But what had I actually criticized? His person? His character? His essence? His being? Or his ideas? My remarks were about ideas. Did I need to know him personally to criticize his ideas? She did not know me personally but seemed fine criticizing my statements to the class. This inequity never seemed to occur to her. But her criticism of my ideas, while misguided and poorly informed, was fair game because I am more than my ideas. My person and my ideas are not to be equated. But this false equivalence plagued her emotions and clouded her assessment. I am not picking on her. She is prototypical of a postmodern person. If you look closely, you will see the same inability to separate the two shows up throughout the blogosphere, printed media, and major news outlets. This ideological hiccup plagues us.

The very thought that ideas are separate from persons is foreign to the postmodern mind. This has some roots in the Kantian notion that we all experience the phenomenal world of the categories of our mind. Maybe it is inferred because of postmodernism's sensitivity to this subjective Kantian idea that was carried forward in the romantics and later the twentieth-century existentialists. In any event the bifurcation of person and idea is, in my opinion, essential for the formation of genuine community. In fact, its neglect the single greatest inhibitor for the emergent church's capacity to possess the very thing it claims to want: *community*. The church simply can't have community where people and ideas are not separated. What emerges in place of community consists of affinity groups—people who share the same ideas, the same convictions, and the same cultural tastes. Amazingly, these groups get patted on the back in our postmodern culture. They are said to have "organic community." But what is "organic community" but an oxymoron? It ends up consisting of a monolithic strand of mutual interests and banal ideas. It turns into a group inundated with insulated relationships and myopic perceptions. "Organic" means that it comes naturally. But real community is formed any way but naturally. This longing for it to be natural actually leads to hurt and segregation. It locks people into cycles of immaturity because they aren't with others who press for them to change.

For community to be "authentic" it must permit the real me with all of my ideas to meet the real you with all of your ideas. It must permit the real me with my communication patterns to meet the real you with your communication patterns. It must keep the real me with my ideas and communication patterns from running away from the real you with your ideas and communication patterns. If neither of us can separate the other person from their ideas, it will make our happy coexistence impossible. We will be too offended at every turn to remain. We will take wounds where none were intended. And this is precisely the case. Just think of it. To combine the natural (organic) desires, ways of communicating, and commitments of people with others who do not have the same patterns or passions in a postmodern context—characterized by high levels of personal sensitivity and autonomy—can only produce tribalism (and in some cases alienation). The very thing that drives the emergent church ends up remaining outside of its grasp.

Supreme Court Justice Antonin Scalia was interviewed a number of years ago on the show *60 Minutes*. One of their avenues of inquiry probed his personal life and unusual friendship with one of the most liberal justices on the bench with him, Ruth Bader Ginsburg. Scalia and Ginsburg are known to hang out together quite a bit in Washington social life. They pressed Scalia about how he could be so scathing toward her in some of the opinions he had written for the court and at the same time be such marvelous friends. I loved his response to the question: "I attack ideas; I don't attack people. And some very good people have some very bad ideas, and if you can't separate the two you gotta get another day job; you don't want to be a judge, at least not a judge on a multi-member panel."[2] All of us have some bad ideas—this alone doesn't make us bad people. So if someone says "That's a bad idea," that doesn't mean he is really saying "You are a bad person." Only someone who is immersed in cynicism would think so. And that is the nagging plight of the postmodern person.

## Deterrent #3—Cynicism

Postmodernism is by definition a reaction of some kind to modernism. Its basic ideas were born from a subtext of cynicism. Its hermeneutic of deconstruction is entirely suspicious. The postmodern person needs to get behind what the language says. It needs to get behind the locution (the actual words that are spoken) and expose the illocution (what was meant by those words). Postmodernism views all of society the way an unruly marital couple perceives each other's words. They are sure there is a hidden agenda somewhere. There is some manipulation lying underneath the surface. They live convinced that linguistic power plays are abounding. Tragically, this distrust never lets genuine relationship emerge. It stagnates real community and imprisons people into patterns of suspicion that drive them into either individualism or tribalism.

2. Scalia, Interviewed by Leslie Stahl, *60 Minutes*.

### Deterrent #4—Techno-Relationships

In the section above about "hypersensitivity," I touched on Facebook and status updates. I want to go a little further with this. The manner in which relationships in our world are cultivated has completely changed in the last thirty years. Business relationships are now maintained using virtual offices and teleconferences. A business person can stay connected to professional relationships via LinkedIn. Dating relationships are formed, at times for months, in cyberspace. In fact, a whole method of deception known as "catfishing"[3] has developed wherein someone creates a false profile and envelopes someone else in an emotional or romantic relationship usually over prolonged periods. Match.com, eHarmony, and Christian Mingle provide people with services to peruse profiles of others like one would look at nutritional information on a jar of peanut butter. From the perusals one can send a note of interest to another, and off goes cyberspace's version of *Love Connection* (minus Chuck Woolery).

Friendships are now mediated over Facebook, Google+, Myspace, MyLife, Foursquare, and many other social media sites. As I mentioned earlier, friends are dropped and added by the click of a button, opinions are shared about everything from what a person is eating tonight to whether a couple ought to have another child. People get fired because they gripe about their job and marriages end because people include their feelings about their partner in their "status update." As a pastor I have watched social media be used to bless others in meaningful ways as they walked through difficulty and even personal tragedy. I have also watched it destroy people's lives by untimely words, arguments, and private things made public at another's expense. In one sense social media is a neutral tool, but in another, and I think more profound sense, it diminishes community by technologizing relationships. It ends up with at least a few pitfalls:

1. It fosters our propensity to hide from others and only put our best foot (or face) forward.
2. It plays with our sense of self-worth by enabling too many people to have a voice in our lives.

---

3. The term comes from the title of a 2010 American documentary film called *Catfish* that exposed a Michigan woman caught falsely representing herself on Facebook.

3. It feeds the pervasive demon of comparison and invites us to feel dissatisfied with ourselves.
4. It leads to prejudice: Our profiles pre-define us before we ever say or write a word.
5. It mistakes selective transparency for genuine vulnerability.

I think this last pitfall is of particular concern.

In an intelligent cultural critique written in 1979, Christopher Lasch surmised that narcissism was both ruling his day and setting the course for the future. His critique of literary figures in his day was a scathing review of their narcissistic tendencies. I wonder what he would say now, over thirty years later. He wrote when home computing was just getting started. The Commodore 64 wasn't even around yet, but his critique sounds like someone who has been watching the Internet social-media cafés of today with a keen eye:

> Undertaken in this evasive mood, confessional writing degenerates into anticonfession. The record of the inner life becomes an unintentional parody of inner life. A literary genre that appears to affirm inwardness actually tells us that the inner life is precisely what can no longer be taken seriously... In recording his "inner" experiences, he seeks not to provide an objective account of a representative piece of reality but to seduce others into giving him their attention, acclaim, or sympathy and thus to shore up his faltering sense of self.[4]

Two parts of Lasch's observation stand out. First, he notes, "to affirm inwardness actually tells us that the inner life is precisely what can no longer be taken seriously." Facebook and Twitter have both become forums where inwardness is turned outward with little discrimination. Privacy made public ceases to be private. Social media is not the place for confidants and personal accountability; it is a place for the soul to garner a billboard. This is not to say it has to be this way, but in a fallen world that highly values autonomous self-expression, a sort of moral entropy tends to take over and propriety is often sacrificed for a few more followers or a handful of "likes."

Second, the last half of Lasch's remarks is important for our techno-relationships. "He seeks not to provide an objective account of a representative piece of reality but to seduce others into giving him their

---

4. Lasch, *The Culture of Narcissism*, 20–21.

attention, acclaim, or sympathy and thus to shore up his faltering sense of self." Social media screams of insecurity on a minute-by-minute basis. Every day, thirty-five million people update their Facebook status for others to see.[5] People want to be known, and they are letting the world know it on a daily basis. Reports abound with information and analysis of depression and envy enhanced by Facebook.[6] I am not trying to pooh-pooh Facebook, or social media in general for that matter. I think it is just natural for people who are given to crafting socially convenient relationships because of self-autonomy, cynicism, and hypersensitivity to leverage technology toward those ends. And when this happens, real community takes a hit.

## Real Community

As a pastor, I have an honorary doctorate in conflict and conflict management. I spend much of my time talking to people about their attitude toward others. I regularly talk individuals and families down from the ledge of abandoning the local church in search of another or from abandoning it altogether. I battle with people over their insecurities, misunderstandings, sensitivities, and manipulation. All of which drive wedges between them and others in the body. If there are two things that I can say with complete and utter confidence about community they are:

1. It is not organic.
2. It must be fought for.

But people rarely want to fight for something that needs cultivation. It is too much work and the reward is not often immediate.

## Escaping Community

To have "community" is to have unity together with others. If community is not organic then it must be cultivated. Since we are cultivating people, we cannot program our way into community. Churches have escaped the daunting task of forging real community in one of two ways: they have not permitted any dissenting voices and been dictatorially controlled; or,

---

5. Leonard, "This is What an Average User Does on Facebook."
6. Van Pelt, "Is Facebook Depression For Real?"; Jimenez, "Social Envy—Study Finds Facebook Causes Depression and Isolation."

they have released themselves from the typical ecclesiological confines of "church" and opted for the feel of a "missional" community.

Regarding the first escape, I would hope that any reader of this would realize that a dictatorial rule over people in the name of Christ is on the face of it hypocritical. The stifling that often happens in these churches pours out in what was identified a few chapters ago as No Carb Jesus. Fundamentalism's proclivity for control and its "safe" but freedom-limiting approach to community ends up pushing love aside altogether.

The second escape is more nuanced and intriguing. It is nuanced because many approaches to missional community are healthy and great expressions of the body of Christ rallying together for a gospel-centered purpose. It is intriguing because some of those promoting missional communities seem to me to be hearkening at something very seriously lost in the mega-church bonanza. Missional communities look to live out the gospel all week. The point of emphasis for them is less on the gathering Sunday morning, though it is still important, and more on living together with small groups of others in a way that will draw men and women formally and informally to the gospel life. It would be hard to see this as anything but helpful. In contrast, the mega-church, seeker approach to Sunday mornings ended up turning the church into an event rather than a community. It is this distortion of the church from community to event that missional communities long to restore. As a pastor, every impulse in me cheers on this holy response to a model that, in my view, commodified Sunday morning worship and made it into a talent show in the name of Jesus. My fear is not that the church will adopt the concept of missional communities. I would enthusiastically encourage the church to do just that. Instead my fear is with adopting the concept of missional communities as *a replacement* for the church.

It is in vogue to trash the church. It is in vogue to find some alternate option. People do church in their homes with just their family. People do church by watching an online or televised preacher. People do church by gathering with some neighbors in an informal format and call it a house church. And people find others dissatisfied with the way the church treated them and form their own missional community. And what is really so wrong with this? Why would anyone who loves Jesus speak negatively about people wanting to gather and worship? Aren't objections to non-traditional forms just people trying to maintain the status quo or keep ministry jobs for themselves? Well, I think there are some problems, and I think the propensity in the emergent church is to upend everything with little regard for the theological problems it creates. Missional communities cannot function as a replacement for the church any more than the Loyal Order of Water Buffaloes can (for all you *Flintstones* fans). So before we go any further, we have to get clear on our ecclesiology.

The Church as Community

The name of our church is Lifeline Community, but to my chagrin, everyone calls it Lifeline Community Church. When I speak somewhere I am introduced as the Lead Pastor of Lifeline Community Church. When I hear people in our body talk to others they say, "I attend Lifeline Community Church." When people call the office they ask, "Is this Lifeline Community Church?" I used to correct everyone, now I have just given up. There is actually a reason why "church" isn't in our name. Believe it or not, the explanation is actually theological.

In the sixteenth century William Tyndale brought the Bible into English. He was a master linguist whose work and wording actually ended up forming a lot of the phraseology of the King James Bible translated some seventy-five years after his death. When Tyndale translated, he was very conscious of the theological language and politics of his day. So he chose to use certain English words instead of others to translate Greek terms. For example, the Greek term *homologeo* is commonly translated "confess." Tyndale, however, at times would translate the term "acknowledge." The Greek term *charis* is usually translated "grace." But Tyndale would often translate it as "favor." He did so because he wanted to stay within the justifiable semantic rendering of the word while at the same time steering clear of the loaded Roman Catholic baggage that the term had been endowed with. In similar fashion to the above examples Tyndale also translated the Greek word *ekklesia* a bit differently. The term is usually rendered "church," but Tyndale chose the term congregation. He was trying to get clear of the institutionalism of sixteenth-century Romanism and yet retain the heart of the term. *Ekklesia* is used in the New Testament for gatherings associated with the organized local church, the church universal, and for gatherings of secular assemblies.[7] The *ekklesia* is at its bottom the gathering or assembly of God's people. In that sense it is a community of people set apart to God.

When I started Lifeline it seemed redundant to call the church Lifeline Community Church. The last two terms were saying the same thing:

---

7. Acts 19:32 and 39 are examples. In Acts 7:38 *ekklesia* is used to speak of the children of Israel gathered in the wilderness. Additionally, some would read the use of it in Matt. 18:17, while applied later to the church, as anachronistically rendered "church."

*A people gathered in union together.* To call a church a community is like calling a tornado a twister. They are the same thing. However, the word "community" has a sense about it that the term "church" lacks. Community encases the idea of togetherness, of unity around something, of individuals losing themselves in something larger. "Church" is a fine term, but it has come to be a label for so many counterfeits from worship contexts that focus on Mother Earth to robed prelates charging money to touch relics. In my context, I minister in a valley of over one million people, over 50 percent of whom are part of what they deem as the "one, true church," The Church of Jesus Christ of Latter-day Saints.[8] Church can be a loaded term. But I think it gets most loaded when it loses its attachment and identification with the concept of *community*. If you lose real community you still have something, maybe an organization, maybe a group of friends feeding the homeless, maybe a Bible study, but you no longer have a New Testament church.

Having identified that the church is a group of people gathered together in union around a gospel purpose, it is important to mention a brief and very non-generous (all winks to Brian McLaren) ecclesiology. My primary concerns here are the marks, not the purposes, of the church. The church is marked by a specific structure. It is comprised of a multiplicity (Acts 14:23) of qualified (1 Tim. 3:1–7) men chosen to give it spiritual leadership. These men are referred to most commonly as elders or overseers but are also commonly called pastors. It also contains individuals chosen to lead in service (1 Tim. 3:8–13).[9] The church is a community that is marked by the regular celebration of the Lord's Supper (Acts 2:42; 20:7; 1 Cor. 11:17–34) and the regular initiatory practice of the ancient symbol of baptism as a rehearsal of the gospel and a statement of personal faith in Christ (Matt. 28:19; Acts 2:38, 41). The church is marked as a community whose qualified leadership hold people accountable even to the point of releasing them from the community itself (1 Cor. 5). The church is also marked by the regular dissemination of doctrine through teaching and preaching (Acts 2:42; 2 Tim. 4:2). The

---

8. Canham, "Census: Share of Utah's Mormon Residents Holds Steady."

9. After issuing the qualifications for the office of elder and deacon, Paul immediately tells Timothy, "I hope to come to you soon, but I am writing these things to you so that, if I delay, you may know how one ought to behave in the household of God, which is the church of the living God, a pillar and buttress of the truth" (1 Tim. 3:14–15). Clearly Paul's purpose in writing is to show a local pastor, Timothy, the order and structure of the local church.

church is marked by worship which includes prayer (Acts 2:42; 1 Tim. 2:1–8), song (1 Cor. 14:26; Col. 3:16), the public reading of Scripture (1 Tim. 4:13), and giving (1 Cor. 16:1–2, 2 Cor. 8–9). All of these marks are undergirded by healthy fellowship (Acts 2:42) of different people (1 Cor. 12:12–30) bound together by love (1 Cor. 13) and focused on a mission (Matt. 28:18–20) to the glory of God (Col. 3:17, 24).

This definition is important because if we take these essential elements away, we may have something, but it cannot be called a church. So a missional group of people feeding the poor has its own merit, but without these defining marks set out in the New Testament they cannot be said to be functioning as a church. The church alone is the Bride of Christ and is "the pillar and buttress of the truth" (1 Tim. 3:15). And the Bride carries all of the above marks tattooed on her as tenets of identification. We are not permitted to freelance on our ecclesiology.

## Cultivating Community

If the church is a community, and as community it contains the marks mentioned above, then it seems that certain things have to be cultivated if real community (aka "churchness") is to be found. Rather than suggest what tons of other literature already does in terms of how to have lasting relationships, how to be real, how to be honest, and how to form a sense of mission and purpose, let me point out some concepts that need to be plumbed deeper in the form of rows that need hoeing if we are going to cultivate community.

### Row #1—Embracing Conflict

Anyone who really enjoys conflict should probably not be in ministry. Conflict is no fun. But it is inevitable, it can be healthy, and it should be fruitful. Pastorally, I most often find people wanting to run from conflict. Yes, there is always that man or woman who prides themselves on how "tell-it-like-it-is" that they are, but they fortunately are the anomaly and not the norm. People usually disengage from the body when there is an issue, and my job often is coaxing them to stay and face the problem with another member of the body instead of bailing.

I value conflict. In fact, it is one of the main reasons why segregated life-affinity ministries are often counterproductive to the very thing they are attempting to provide . . . community. Conflict arises when I am with people that I would not naturally choose to be with. If our missional teams and our small groups only possess people who have a natural affinity for one another and are all in the same life situation, it appears that we could easily mistake organic connection for genuine community. *Community comes about as the result of the one anothers of Scripture being applied to the gospel rhythms of the heart.* When someone is broken and those who either contributed to that brokenness or were observers in the breaking now lay hold of the *one another* tools and apply those with gospel receptivity and grace, the church finds itself really being the church.

I love and respect the emergent church's longing for community. I think their gift to the body of Christ collectively has been raising an awareness of our need to meet postmodern culture with community. Their emphasis on shunning our modernistic, programmatic concept of church has been helpful. I may sound like a downer about the emergent church, but I really do appreciate their prodding on these issues. I just think the solution they are offering mistakes the sweetness of natural intimacy with robust community. I am suspicious that their faulty solution is really accidental. The emergent church largely appeals to a specific age segment of white suburbanites. Their appeal has been pretty mono-cultural. So community for them has largely been accomplished by reaching out to people in the same life situations as those doing the reaching. My point isn't to say that they somehow don't have real relationships or that they are purposely counterfeiting community. I am just trying to pull back the curtain a bit and make the point that real community is not typically an organic enterprise, nor should it be, because we all need the growth steps of what it means to love the other when we just don't click and where no mutual inclination draws us together.

Peter wrote his first letter and spent the first portion of it talking about hope and holiness. As a bridge to the next section of his epistle, in which he described the people of God, he touches on the gospel and relationships, wedding them together (emphasis mine):

> . . . knowing that you were ransomed from the futile ways inherited from your forefathers, not with perishable things such as silver or gold, but with the precious blood of Christ, like that of a lamb without blemish or spot. He was foreknown before the foundation of the world but was made manifest in the last times for the sake of you who through him are believers in God, who raised him from the dead and gave him glory, so that your faith

and hope are in God. Having purified your souls by your obedience to the truth for a sincere brotherly love, *love one another earnestly* from a pure heart, since you have been born again, not of perishable seed but of imperishable, through the living and abiding word of God. (1 Pet. 1:18–23)

The gospel is the ground or basis of believers' ability to love each other. Peter's adverbial nuance in his exhortation shows up again in 1 Peter 4:8 with the same basic phrase: "keep loving one another earnestly." To love "earnestly" in the Greek means to love "at full stretch." It is to love outside the comfort zone. It is to love unnaturally. The gospel is about loving people who are enemies, not merely those with whom we have organic connection. C. S. Lewis saw friendship as organic. He wrote:

> Friendship arises out of mere [C]ompanionship when two or more of the companions discover that they have in common some insight or interest or even taste which the others do not share and which, till that moment, each believed to be his own unique treasure (or burden).[10]

But Peter is after something beyond the organic and is moving into heart of real gospel community. Community calls for stretching. It calls for a fruit of the non-natural life of the Spirit. It may take conflict and interpersonal tumult, but community demands love and a love that is anything but natural.

### Row # 2—Applying a Forgotten Proverb

If you are in the market for a good Christian tattoo, Proverbs 19:11 is as good as any to get inked on the body. It is so easily forgotten and yet so invaluable to life with others. It reads, "Good sense makes one slow to anger, and it is his glory to overlook an offense." Some readers might be surprised that after extolling the importance and value of conflict that I would now say that some things ought to be overlooked. Well, rest assured, there are a number of things that need to be dealt with, but we are often not the best at choosing which ones to let slide. My favorite Christian author is Mark Buchanan. I remember reading in one of his books something that has always stuck with me as a good rule of thumb. He essentially said that when we feel a strong urge to speak up and say something to someone it is likely a good indication that we should remain

---

10. Lewis, *The Four Loves*, 248. "[C]" was part of quoted published text.

quiet, and when we really just as soon not say anything, maybe then we should speak up and let our voice be heard. I like that. I like it because it reminds me that my natural impulses are too natural.

The term for "glory" in the proverb is also translated as "beauty" in a number of its other Old Testament uses. The beauty of a man or woman's character is put on display when they move past someone's offense against them. Community often gets robbed of its luster by little offenses—molehills that become mountains—instead of serious violations and transgressions against one another. Can you imagine what our relationships would look like if we consistently overlooked indignities and wrong tones and thoughtless comments? Applying this forgotten proverb could be a gem that, in and of itself, goes a long way to restoring the value of sweet communion.

## Row #3—Caring for the Least

Mistreatment of the poor within the body is no small issue in the New Testament. Perhaps no text shows its incongruity with the heart of Jesus as clearly as 1 Corinthians 11. Communion was the centerpiece of local church worship for nearly 1500 years. It is the time in corporate worship when the church rehearses the gospel and is reminded of the sacrifice of Jesus that reconfigured repentant man's relationship with God. When this practice of spiritual worship through symbol took place in the early church, they ate entire meals around its remembrance. Not unlike our potluck (or if you are a Calvinist, "pot-providence") dinner, people brought their food to eat together. In Corinth something drastically opposed to the gospel was taking place during the very meal that was intended to commemorate it. The wealthy were coming and bringing their abundance, eating it and offering none to the poor who showed up with little or no food. Think of it. The church's enduring symbol of selfless grace and love poured out for broken people was being polluted by self-indulgence and marginalization. Paul rebuked them:

> When you come together, it is not the Lord's supper that you eat. For in eating, each one goes ahead with his own meal. One goes hungry, another gets drunk. What! Do you not have houses to eat and drink in? Or do you despise the church of God and humiliate those who have nothing? What shall I say to you? Shall I commend you in this? No, I will not. (1 Cor. 11:20–22)

The apostle's strong words for them did not stop there. He went on to identify their sin against one another as a sin against the body—the whole local church—and the result was that some were judged with sickness and some with death. He wrote, "For anyone who eats and drinks without discerning the body eats and drinks judgment on himself. That is why many of you are weak and ill, and some have died" (1 Cor. 11:29–30).

As Paul concluded that section, one of the most subtle *one anothers* of Scripture flowed from him. He told the Corinthians, "So then, my brothers, when you come together to eat, wait for one another" (1 Cor. 11:33). What a great exhortation: "*wait for one another.*" Indulgence, lack of consideration, flaunting abundance, hoarding goods, playing into social stigmas—none of these constitute waiting. To wait is to think of the other; it is to move in the space of the other. It is to let their life situation set our pace. People who live in real community learn to wait. They learn that the world they have entered into is the world of the other and not the realm of the self. They find the Crucified there, in the land of the other. As Brennan Manning has beautifully written:

> Because of the mysterious substitution of Christ for the Christian, each encounter with a brother or sister is a real encounter with the risen Lord, an opportunity to respond creatively to the gospel and mature in the wisdom of tenderness. Time has been given to us to cause love to grow, and the success of our lives will be measured by how delicately and sensitively we have loved. There's no escaping the Gospel logic that all our thoughts, words, and deeds addressed to others are in a real way addressed to Christ himself.[11]

Real community cannot escape this "gospel logic."

## Row # 4—Staying

One of the great influential leaders and shapers of men for ministry was Howard Hendricks. I had the privilege of meeting with Prof, as we called him, and eleven other seminary students at 6:00 a.m. once a week for a full semester as he taught us how to disciple. Needless to say, his commitment to discipleship bled into my life and convinced me that the long, arduous process of discipling men is well worth the effort. Prof was known to say that the people who make the difference in other people's

11. Manning, *The Wisdom of Tenderness*, 68.

lives for God are the people who stay. That sounds so simplistic. But it really is profound. Depending on the study you read, the tenure of senior or lead pastors is anywhere from two to seven years. That is a wide range, but I contend no matter what the real number, it is still too short. Staying matters because community takes time. Earning a voice in a community of people takes years, not days.

Staying is not an idea reserved for pastors. Lay people need to be reminded that staying matters because community matters. I stand amazed at the things Christians will attempt to defend. I read an article put out by *Christianity Today* that made a miserably failed attempt to defend church-hopping. Michelle Van Loon wrote that while some move around from church to church out of shallow immaturity, others do so looking for community and their love for the church is what keeps them looking rather than just giving up. She highlights three scenarios where people long to find a place and stay put, but their life situations keep them looking because the ideal or even acceptable place is hard to find. She concludes her article this way:

> Despite a negative experience with a toxic church, despite loneliness, despite facing a lack of hospitality or ministry resources, each of these friends continues their hop with the hope of finding a church home. They have not "given up on meeting together." Their persistent and prolonged church searches fully capture the spirit of those words penned to the dispersed Hebrew believers in the first century. Martin Luther said, "Anyone who is to find Christ must first find the church. How could anyone know where Christ is and what faith is in him unless he knew where his believers are?" Sometimes it takes a marathon of church hopping to find them.[12]

Seriously?! It is no wonder that real community comes at such a premium in the church. With articles like this written in leading magazines and on leading Christian websites, is it any wonder that the church and Jesus himself continue to be smorgasbords? It doesn't take a marathon to find community. It takes staying put to create it.

---

12. Van Loon, "In Defense of Church Hoppers," 2.

## Responding to the Flavorful Appeals

The rest of the chapter will focus on responding to the "flavorful appeals" mentioned in chapter 5. I will respond to three of the four below. The third flavorful appeal I mentioned in the previous chapter was termed "Individual Spiritual Expression." All that I have written up to this point in the chapter regarding the nature of real community and how to cultivate it comprises my response to that "appeal." What follows is an effort to deal with the other three.

## The Case for an Ungenerous Orthodoxy

In chapter 4, I proposed a possible template for a theological hierarchy. My intention in that chapter was to define areas that are both more important and/or more clearly articulated in the text for the purpose of resisting the fundamentalist tendency to relate to others as though every doctrine matters to an equal degree. But having a theological hierarchy also performs another function. It lets us know which doctrines are essential for eternal life, which are crucial for the practice and function of the church, and which doctrines stand as nonessential components of debate and speculation within our theological framework. In doing this it reminds us that some things are worth fighting for.

Jim Belcher wrote in his book *Deep Church* about a third way of conceiving church that navigated in between the emergent church, and what he called the "traditionalists." The book has much to merit as Belcher writes irenically about both camps and yet offers some very helpful critique. He is careful not to demonize people but consistently assumes the best. He follows C. S. Lewis and Robert Greer in proposing two levels to doctrinal discussion. These two levels separate "the essentials of orthodoxy from the particularities of differing traditions within the boundaries of orthodoxy."[13] I appreciate that he wants to separate essentials from non-essentials. This is helpful. I also really like that he goes on later to point out that differences do matter, and that his real purpose in proposing this two-tiered approach is to keep the diverse and distinct members of the universal church focused on the common essentials they agree on—and so enable them to be one people worshiping one Lord.

13. Belcher, *Deep Church*, 60. Belcher mentions both Lewis's writing in *The Screwtape Letters* and Greer's work in *Mapping Postmodernism* regarding a two-tiered or two compartment perspective in how believers ought to view theology.

But I want to clarify two parts of his approach to this that make me a bit uncomfortable and relate it directly to this issue of the emergent church's dislocation from orthodoxy.

First, one of the problems with the emerging church is that some of the second-tier "differing traditions" are not within orthodoxy. Their views on same-sex marriage for example may not keep you out of heaven because you still subscribe to the essentials of orthodoxy, but this issue matters significantly for pastoral ministry, parenting, Christian ethics, our theology of common grace, and many other areas of our life and doctrine. To endorse same-sex marriage is outside historic orthodoxy. It is not within the parameters of historic confessional faith and does not fit with historically accepted textual interpretations. I find it interesting that Belcher wrote his book in 2009 and articulated one of the traditional church's problems with Brian McLaren regarding his de-emphasis of substitutionary atonement. He noted:

> The traditional church doesn't believe Brian is trying to correct a tragic reduction of the gospel; they see in him and the emerging church a wholesale abandonment of the gospel. They contend that once the church loses the hard edges of the cross, which judge as well as forgive, it is a short step to going soft on hell, eternal judgment, homosexuality, and other religions. Without the doctrine of atonement at the center of Christianity, the hub of the wheel, it is easy to abandon the King of the kingdom.[14]

And now, four years later, this is precisely what has happened. In the time since Belcher wrote those words, Brian McLaren has commemorated the same-sex union of his own son by taking part in its celebration. Rob Bell has endorsed same-sex unions. Bell has also written *Love Wins* and rejected the idea of a conscious eternal hell. Others of a new emergent ilk, like Baxter Kruger, have, in the name of trinitarian theology, embraced "Christian" universalism as I demonstrated in the last chapter. All of the above concerns of the traditional church have come home to roost.

This leads right to my second concern. The emergent church has, in my view, actually been pressing the bounds of the first level or tier of essentials. As I noted in the last chapter, several of their authors genuinely feel like everything is up for grabs. I understand first-level doctrines to include, at least: the Trinity, the deity of Christ, the clear presence of a substitutionary atonement, the reliability of the Bible, the bodily

14. Ibid., 111–12.

resurrection of Christ, the exclusivity of trust in Christ for salvation, and the reality of a second coming.

As the experiment continues of watching the emerging church emerge, some of what Belcher was concerned about in *Deep Church* is now fully out of the pipeline and on display. In Brian McLaren's book *A Generous Orthodoxy*, he writes that experience or praxis is prior to theology. This means that theology is formed from experience, not experience from theology. In the fourth chapter of that book he states: "I have become convinced that a generous orthodoxy appropriate for our postmodern world will have to grow out of the experience of the post-Christian, post secular people of the cities."[15] For McLaren there seems to be a theologically generous orthodoxy that is uniquely appropriate for our postmodern world. Don't miss the subtleties here. Theology is not being shaped by the text; the text is being shaped by the experience of postmodern citified hipsters to be wider and broader than our myopic forbears had envisioned.

### Exhibit A: The Atonement

In the same chapter—which is titled, "Jesus: Savior of What?"—McLaren is obviously out to summarize what it means for Jesus to be "Savior." This is the focus of the chapter, and yet penal substitution is completely absent. He does flirt a bit with it as he talks about salvation:

> The good news of salvation is that God sent Jesus not to condemn but to save: to save by bringing justice with mercy, true judgment with true forgiveness, first by exposing our wrong (judging) so we can face our wrong and turn from it . . . and then by forgiving our wrong, God intervenes and breaks the chain of cause and effect, of offense and alienation, so we're truly saved—liberated, rescued—from the vicious cycle (a.k.a., mess) we created.[16]

But he seems to mistake the work of the Holy Spirit convicting us of sin (cf. John 16:7–11) with the act of sin being judged. Because of this confusion, substitution is astonishingly neither here nor there in a chapter about Jesus' role as savior.

---

15. Mclaren, *A Generous Orthodoxy*, 92. Apparently traditional rural folk are so theo-culturally redneck that only the hipsters in the city can now move the meter.

16. Ibid., 95.

As McLaren—the movement's leading light—has "emerged," his flirtation with a notion of Jesus as the means of forgiveness of sins through his work on the cross has grown weaker and weaker. Two years after he wrote *A Generous Orthodoxy* he wrote *The Secret Message of Jesus*. It is a book focused on the good news of the kingdom of God. In the work's first footnote he throws a bone to would-be objectors, presumably since Jesus' "secret message" has nothing to do with substitution. He states:

> The theological meaning of Jesus' death is central to all streams of Christian thought and life, but since this is a book on Jesus' message, I limit my reflections on his death here to how it relates to his primary teaching theme. Emphasizing one theme is not meant to minimize the other.[17]

He is conscious that his message about Jesus' secret message could be misunderstood as a sweeping gospel claim, but he is careful to preempt that with this caveat.

This is important because it seems that times have changed for McLaren (and if we are to believe him, other emergents as well). In 2010 McLaren wrote *A New Kind of Christianity*. In it his tone about the gospel has morphed. He uses reformist language as he speaks of the role of the new approach he and others represent. He says that they, "being peace-loving people," thought among other things that they might have been able to "simply add this kingdom-of-God stuff as fine print on the bottom of our existing theological contracts."[18] But he notes that he can no longer do this. He declares, "This is good work, I suppose, and must be done for a generation or two, but it is not the work to which I feel called."[19] So to what then does he feel called? Pay close attention to his words:

> At some point, though, more and more of us will finally decide that it would make more sense to go back and *revise the contract from scratch*. And that process has begun. It is nowhere near complete, but the cat is out of the bag; imaginations are sizzling, and exciting theological work is being done—by theologians, yes, but, equally important, by pastors, teachers, songwriters, screenwriters, producers, poets, dramatists, sculptors,

17. McLaren, *The Secret Message of Jesus*, 226.
18. McLaren, *A New Kind of Christianity*, 141.
19. Ibid., 142.

photographers, painters, architects, youth leaders, community organizers, moms and dads, and thoughtful readers like you.[20]

He has progressed in his thinking from adding an emphasis about the kingdom onto the picture of the "existing theological contract" to feeling it is time to "revise the contract from scratch." I guess he really does think "everything must change."

I share the analysis of McLaren on his doctrine of the gospel because I think it gives an important example that orthodox essentials are now on their way out of leading emergent thought. As time goes by, this "emergent" lab seems to be putting out more and more heterodox fumes. These fumes include the Christian universalism that decimates historic Christology and soteriology. If you can release a hold on substitutionary atonement, then you can fairly easily slip away from the exclusivity of trust in Jesus for salvation altogether.

### Exhibit B: The Scope of Salvation

In the last chapter I mentioned Baxter Kruger and his perspective of Christian universalism, which also seems to be shared by William Paul Young, the author of the bestseller *The Shack*. As Kruger builds his foundation for Christian universalism, he makes an assertion regarding historical theology that must be addressed. He asserts that the church is held in a type of "Augustinian captivity."[21] We are children of Augustine and our theological orientation is so baptized in his thinking that we can't see the text in any other way. His proposal is that we should read it in the manner that he understands Athanasius interpreting it. But does the idea of the exclusivity of Christ and the need to orient oneself in belief to him as the only hope for salvation stem from Augustine alone or is there a pre-Augustinian tradition for this doctrine? And so what if it is within the Augustinian tradition? Does this somehow militate against it?

Three brief responses are in order. First, Baxter so aligns himself with his interpretation of Athanasius that he pits himself against Augustine and in so doing commits a type of genetic fallacy. Genetic fallacies serve as regular anecdotal ammunition for emergent writers. A common objection to aspects of systematic theology and substance-dualist philosophy is to throw around the idea that traditional Christianity is too

20. Ibid. [emphasis added]
21. Kruger, *Jesus and The Undoing of Adam*, 10.

"platonic" or "neo-platonic." These terms amount to emergent church cuss words. But they don't actually tell us anything about the content of the theology or philosophy objected to. Similarly, when Kruger throws historic Christology and soteriology under his Athanasian bus and runs it over by passing it off as an "Augustinian captivity," he hasn't helped his case. He has only fallaciously said functionally "something is wrong because I think the ideological genes of this idea started in Augustine." He is wrong about that, but even if he isn't, his point still isn't proven.

Second is a piece of evidence regarding the Athanasian Creed. While the creed certainly wasn't written by Athanasius,[22] it is at least curious that the church throughout about a thousand years of history attributed its statements to him. I note this because the creed is seen to have Augustinian influence but apparently the church for a thousand years—until the seventeenth century—did not see it as incompatible with Athanasius. Additionally, the opening line of the creed absolutely contradicts Kruger's interpretation of Athanasius. It states, "Whoever desires to be saved must above all things hold the Catholic faith. Unless a man keeps it in its entirety inviolate, he will assuredly perish eternally. Now this is the Catholic faith . . ."[23] It then gives clear, orthodox doctrinal affirmations of the Trinity, deity of Christ, and the work of Christ. Its concluding line bookends the opening statement: "This is the Catholic faith. Unless a man believes it faithfully and steadfastly, he will not be able to be saved."[24] This sure sounds exclusionary. If he doesn't believe it he won't be saved. It doesn't fit with Christian universalism. This doesn't prove that all of it is Athanasian theology, but it at least tells us that for a thousand years the church was comfortable with it being considered so. I think this is significant.

Third, pre-Augustinian church fathers on the whole rejected Christian universalism. It is difficult to get chronologically closer to the New Testament itself than citing Clement of Rome (AD 30–100). Does this statement of his sound like everyone is included in Christ irrespective of whether they believe?

> Let us look steadfastly to the blood of Christ, and see how precious that blood is to God, which having been shed for our

---

22. It was likely written in France in the early sixth century and reflects an orthodox trinitarianism and a Chalcedonian Christology. Cf. Allison, *Historical Theology*, 737.
23. Leith, *Creeds of the Churches*, 705.
24. Ibid., 706.

salvation, has set the grace of repentance before the whole world. Let us turn to every age that has passed, and learn that, from generation to generation, the Lord has granted a place of repentance *to all such as would be converted unto Him.* Noah preached repentance, and as many as listened to him were saved. Jonah proclaimed destruction to the Ninevites; but *they, repenting of their sins, propitiated God by prayer, and obtained salvation, although they were aliens [to the covenant] of God.*[25]

God is "propitiated" by repentance, and without it Clement understands people to be "alienated" from God. Clement is not alone in the early church. Rather, he is joined by a grand chorus.

Justin Martyr (AD 110–65) wrote of the exclusivism of Christ and the need for repentance:

> By reason, therefore, of this laver of repentance and knowledge of God, which has been ordained on account of the transgression at God's people, as Isaiah cries, we have believed, and testify that that very baptism which he announced *is alone able to purify those who have repented*; and this is the water of life.[26]

Irenaeus (AD 120–202) wrote of the need to receive Christ and the dire consequences of of not doing so:

> The elders pointed out that those men are devoid of sense, who, [arguing] from what happened to those who formerly did not obey God, do endeavour to bring in another Father, setting over against [these punishments] what great things the Lord had done at His coming *to save those who received Him,* taking compassion upon them; while they keep silence with regard to His judgment, and all those things which shall come upon such as have heard His words, but done them not, and that it were better for them if they had not been born, and that *it shall be more tolerable for Sodom and Gomorrah in the judgment than for that city which did not receive the word of His disciples.*[27]

Tertullian (AD 145–220) wrote emphatically, "It would suffice to say, indeed, that there is not a soul that can at all procure salvation. Except it believe whilst it is in the flesh, so true is it that the flesh is the very

---

25. Clement, 1. 7. [emphasis added]
26. Justin Martyr, 1. 217. [emphasis added]
27. Irenaeus, 1. 501. [emphasis added]

*giving jesus the freedom to form his own menu* 171

condition on which salvation hinges."²⁸ For Tertullian, what you do with Christ in this life matters for eternity. To all of these I could add Cyprian and even Cyprian's critics in *A Treatise on Re-Baptism*, both from the third century; the Epistle to Diognetes (AD 130); Ignatius (AD 30–107); Lactantius (AD 260–330); and others still . . . but hopefully by now you get the point.

All of this should show us that for Kruger and others to say that we are held in "Augustinian captivity" is to pay too little attention to the words of church fathers before Augustine. Now I want to be careful to note that I am not attempting to refute him by invoking a genetic fallacy like his own. I simply want to show that the wealth of theological continuity prior to Athanasius and Augustine understood there to be an eternal judgment for those who did not repent and believe. There wasn't a wide adherence to an idea of Christian universalism.²⁹ Consequently, the line of continuity from the New Testament authors to the early church and on into Augustine seems very credible.

Whether it regards the atonement or the broader contours of soteriology, we cannot go where these postmodernism-intoxicated teachers want to take us. The church must not yield on essential tenets of orthodoxy. We cannot dispose of it for the sake of unity, for then our unity ceases to be Christian in nature. So what are we to do?

## Staying Moored to Orthodoxy

First, *we have to acknowledge that the necessary hierarchy of theology we need must contain more than two compartments.* It must be graded to keep us from the theological ethos of fundamentalism. But that gradation must take into account that if things within "the particularities of differing traditions" fall outside orthodoxy, we might not be able to gather around the fire, hold hands, and sing "Kumbaya" together. For us to do that with "brothers" who, for example, call homosexuality righteous when the apostle Paul blatantly and unambiguously called it unrighteous is to pollute the corporate expression of worship with the toleration of known sin. Analogously, it is the very error rebuked

---

28. Tertullian, 3. 551.

29. Two possible adherents to a purgatorial finite version of hell are Origen and Clement of Alexandria. The wealth of literature in the early church goes against this understanding.

at the celebration of the Eucharist mentioned in 1 Corinthians 11 and referred to earlier in this chapter, namely, corporate worship tainted by the acceptance of known sin.

So the taxonomy I proposed in chapter 4 takes into account that there are doctrines that strongly affect the life and health of the local church and consequently the fellowship of local churches. This is true both in terms of principles and pragmatics. This does not make us fundamentalists. This does not make us isolationists. This makes us people longing for unity, embracing flexibility and freedom but unwilling to make orthodoxy malleable. This tension has been fought throughout the history of the church. Luther sat at a table and could agree on everything with Zwingli except for specificities regarding the nature of the eucharistic elements, and that tragically kept him from uniting the German and Swiss reformations when he should have. Whitefield and Wesley both accomplished amazing things for God but stood askance from one another. Billy Graham created dividing points in evangelical history by his choice to associate with Catholics in crusade evangelism. The tensions of when to associate and when not to have been and always will be with us. The essential point is not creating a rule about when and when not to. It is to have a template that identifies what is up for grabs and what is not. It is to keep ancient boundary stones while not overstating the boundaries. It is to embrace the humility necessitated by our finitude and to respect the limits of orthodoxy.

Second, *we need to be reminded of our role in theologizing.* When McLaren talks about the new theological enterprise and says "imaginations are sizzling," I get nervous. Theology is not about creativity and innovation. It is about faithfulness and clear, relevant articulation. What changes is not the truth, but how truthful ideas are presented in new cultural languages while retaining their substance. Pastors and church leaders need to remember this. Our job is not to say something new. It is to say something old, tested, and tried in a way that connects the present and often chaotic rhythms of the human heart to the static reality of divine revelation. It is, in the words of the great John Stott, to stand "between two worlds." It is not the recreation of an old world to look like the new one.

Third, *we must remember that we stand confidently as part of a historical community of orthodox faith.* All you need to do is pick up a good text on historical theology where sound scholarship has combed the pages of theological writing throughout the ages. You will quickly see that a consistent theme of core doctrines flows throughout the varied cultural and political grounds of western history. I would recommend reading John Hannah's *Our Legacy: The History of Christian Doctrine*, Gregg Allison's *Historical Theology*, *The History of Christian Doctrines* by Louis Berkhof, and *The History of Christian Thought* by Jonathan Hill. You will find that the doctrines I mentioned as first-level issues are represented and accepted consistently throughout the history of the church. And yes, contrary to many emergent writers, the same holds for substitutionary atonement. It is not merely a Reformation idea.

Finally, *our teaching must reflect both freedom within orthodoxy and rabid fidelity to it*. We are to move up the hierarchy of chapter 4, from the foundational doctrines, releasing our grip a bit. We are to move down, from the speculative notions to the essential precepts at the bottom, tightening our grip. This theological move of squeeze and release needs to be clarified in what we say about theology, and how we say it. It is the only way to pass between the errors of fundamentalism on one side and emergent neo-liberalism on the other.

## The Case for Honoring Authorial Intent

The nature of Scripture is a pretty hot subject in evangelicalism these days. At the very least, historic orthodoxy has asserted that the Scriptures are utterly reliable. To say that the Bible is completely true is to ultimately say that it is inerrant. But as soon as the word inerrancy gets thrown around, people tend to get either defensive or nervous. The issues we face in inerrancy today are real and need to be discussed (and quite possibly clarified). However, I am troubled by the emergent approach to dealing with the text of Scripture. They seem ready to jump ship on issues of inerrancy, and at bottom I think their approach is hermeneutically wrong-headed.

The basic problem I see is that the postmodern hermeneutic treats the text like a piece of modern art. I recall years ago going to an art exhibit where the works of Salvador Dali were being put on display. I remember looking at painting after painting and found myself flummoxed at the meaning of his works. When engaging modern art, the aesthetic hermeneutic is viewer-centered. We are told that the answer to the question "What does it mean?" is in the eyes of the beholder. But as I look at art, it seems logically impossible to detach the art from the artist. Didn't Dali have a purpose in painting? Didn't he have a formal cause in his mind? Of course he did. He himself was an amateur philosopher of sorts and had reasons to go with his colorful rhymes. Yet the postmodern cultural savant would have us believe that there are many interpretations to Dali's work. While there no doubt are many and varied responses and feelings elicited by his art, those remain something altogether different than the assertion that there are many viable meanings or interpretations of it. I can make a statement to my wife in the presence of others and everyone may have a different response to it; however, I am the one who ascribes its meaning.

Textual hermeneutics should not fall into the same quagmire as its sister discipline in aesthetics. And this is precisely the wrench that postmodernity has thrown into the machinery of biblical interpretation. As a young seminary student I was surprised to read in *Who Needs Theology?*, written by the late Stanley Grenz and Roger Olson (both very capable thinkers regarding postmodern hermeneutics), the idea that we should look through the lens of our culture when doing theology because the Bible is a trans-cultural text. They see a matrix of three tools that work together to help yield our understanding of the text. They write:

> The theological art involves an interplay among three tools, which in their differing ways function as sources and norms: the Bible message, the theological heritage of the church and contemporary culture. We have discussed these three tools in isolation from each other, but they are in fact inseparable. We do not first get our understanding of the Bible straight, then look to our common heritage to make sure we are orthodox, before finally seeking to talk about these matters in our social context. Rather, we draw from all three simultaneously. We read the Bible through eyes conditioned by our culture. And we read it as those who stand at this specific point in the twisting and turning trajectory of theological history.[30]

While I agree with the premise that more than the Bible informs our interpretation, I don't agree that *the goal is to have it* inform our interpretation. I would argue that I need to know what traditional and cultural baggage I bring to the text so I don't let it lead me so much that I mess with the original intent of it as revealed in its own given context. My culture is a lens that is relevant for the process of applying the text, but I need to be sure that my twenty-first-century American suburban culture

30. Grenz and Olson, *Who Needs Theology?*, 101.

*giving Jesus the freedom to form his own menu* 175

doesn't get a say in what Moses, Jeremiah, Jesus, or Paul meant. To get my culture involved too early in the hermeneutical process ultimately devolves into me ascribing meaning. And once that happens, there is no confident place to stand when it comes to the biblical text but only an array of equally valid and often conflicting interpretations. See the figure below for a depiction of the two differing hermeneutical approaches. The first looks to place meaning with the author's intent. The second looks to leave it up for grabs depending upon the reader's vantage point. The first puts our cultural lens after we have already defined the theological principle evidencing itself from the historical text. The second puts our cultural lens in a posture of deconstructing the historical text to find a present theological meaning.

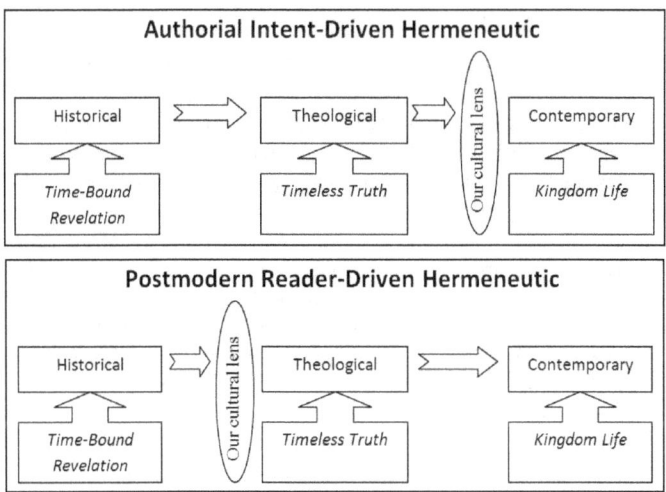

Are we trapped inside a culture construct with no hope of getting out? The answer is yes and no. Yes, I am a creature of my culture more than I realize. And yet this does not mean that I must be unaware of the cultural goggles I have on. No, just the opposite is true. My job is to know what the goggles are and from whence they come. Knowing this keeps me from unwittingly importing my culture into that of the biblical text.

But there is another issue altogether that postmoderns are raising, and that is the idea that the biblical text is a sort of living document that takes on differing interpretations to differing cultural movements. So the emergents are always speaking of "re-imaging" theology or "re-defining" doctrine. These are not tweaks of application, these are reconfigurations of the content of truth.

In the last chapter I wrote about John Caputo's thesis of applying deconstructionism as the hermeneutic of God's kingdom. He is looking to get behind what is said, to what he, from his cultural viewpoint, assumes must be meant. I also mentioned Tony Jones's view that theology is in constant flux because of the changing cultural tide. It seems that present experience of socio-cultural life gets a trump card at the table of hermeneutics. Theology is left to bow to culture. While this hermeneutical approach can be dressed up in Derrida's deconstructionism, it ends up running parallel to the principles of late-nineteenth-century-liberal hermeneutics. Postmodern hermeneutics are driven by a reader-centered approach rooted in contemporary communal ethical, social, and religious constructs, and nineteenth-century-liberal hermeneutics were driven by a reader-centered approach rooted in naturalism.[31] Pick your

31. In *Beyond Foundationalism*, Stanley Grenz and John Franke attempt to separate the postmodern hermeneutic from the liberal approach. It seems they feel compelled to do so because mistaking the two for parallel thoughts is pretty easy to do. They offer three delineations why their postmodern approach to theologizing is different than the classic liberal approach. In their own words:
"First, as we noted earlier, liberalism transformed experience into a new foundationalism. . . . The Christian ethos as we understand it asserts that the various religions mediate religious experiences that are categorically different from each other. The encounter with the God of the Bible through Jesus, which is foundational to Christian identity, is shared only by those who participate in the Christian community. . . . Second (and providing the theoretical basis for the first), our understanding of the Christian ethos takes seriously the experience-forming dimension of interpretive frameworks. As Lindbeck has pointed out, the older liberal project tended to give primacy to experience and to view theological statements as expressions of religious experience. But this approach misunderstands the nature of experience. Experience does not precede interpretation. Rather experiences are always filtered by an interpretive framework—a grid—that facilitates their occurrence . . ." Grenz and Franke, *Beyond Foundationalism*, 48–49.
Thirdly, they attempt to push further away from classic liberalism by rejecting any sense of "generic religious experience"; instead, religious experience is specific to particular religious traditions. All of this leads them to state the following:
"Christian theology, in turn, is an intellectual enterprise by and for the Christian community. Through theological reflection, the community of those whom the God of the Bible has encountered in Jesus Christ seeks to understand, clarify, and delineate its interpretive framework informed by the narrative of God's actions on behalf of all creation as revealed in the Bible. In this sense, we might say that the specifically Christian-experience-facilitating interpretative framework, arising as it does out of the biblical narrative, is "basic" for Christian theology. As the intellectual engagement with what is "basic," theology is a second-order enterprise, and in this sense theological statements constitute second-order language." Ibid., 49
I mentioned all of this simply to show that while attempting to distance itself from classic liberalism, all that the postmodern enterprise has done is taken experience and

poison, but both place a form of experience before arriving at theological interpretation.

As pastors, teachers, and church leaders we need to make sure that our people learn hermeneutics. We need to teach a common-sense approach to language. People, in their space/time context, get to define what they meant when they said what they said. The only way we can get to that meaning is to get out of our world and into theirs. Pastors, let me exhort you: teach Bible history; study what words meant in their context; be informed about biblical social matters, political contexts, geographic issues, surrounding cultures that permeated the ancient Near-East. The teacher of the Bible must be a student of the biblical world in order to reconstruct the authorial intent to the best degree possible rather than deconstruct the text from a present vantage point. The Bible is dynamic revelation through divinely orchestrated history passed down through divinely directed human authors who wrote as men of their times because God had a message for all time. Our job is to find out what it *was* and teach people how it relates to what *is*.

## The Case for a Non-Sexist, Non-Homophobic Hierarchicalism

It is possible to reject egalitarianism and not be a closet sexist or homophobe. It is possible to reject egalitarianism and not secretly long for white heterosexual male-dominated power structures to rule the world. It is possible to reject egalitarianism and believe in a vibrant trinitarian perichoresis. But if you read the emergent church literature, you would never know it. I used to think that the complementarian/egalitarian question regarding church leadership was moderately important. I now see that the broader issues standing behind this question are paramount and fundamental to the health and well-being of the church and society. I now also believe they are crucial to understanding even Jesus himself.

---

placed it inside socio-religious communities. While Grenz and Franke insist that experience is not prior to interpretation, it seems they cannot escape it. Their framework for defining theology is described as a "Christian-experience-facilitating interpretative framework" which arises "out of the biblical narrative." At best they have stepped in a Barthian direction where an experience of Christ in reading the text brings it alive. But they have placed even that in a communal context, and it seems to me, have simply swapped in the collective experience of particular socio-religious communities for the generalized naturalistic experience of liberalism. But I do not think they have shaken free at all of the primary role experience plays in their formation of theology.

Was Jesus an egalitarian? No. Jesus lived in functional subordination to his Father. He repeatedly appealed to the Father throughout his earthly life (e.g. John 17). He was appointed to his role by the Father (Heb. 1:2). He submitted his will to the Father's (Luke 22:42). He looked to the Father for rescue (Heb. 5:7). He learned obedience as the Father permitted him to suffer hardship (Heb. 5:8). He acknowledged the Father's role in giving him people for eternal life (John 10:29). His exaltation came at the behest of the Father with the goal of glorifying the Father (Phil. 2:9–11). Jesus wasn't an egalitarian because he functioned in a hierarchical structure of relationship to his Father.

## New Testament Hierarchicalism

Does the New Testament teach egalitarianism? No. The New Testament repeatedly embraces functional hierarchicalism as part of God's design for the operations of the cosmos. This is demonstrated in the *civil sphere*. Romans 13:1 clearly demonstrates that government structure and authority comes only by God's ordination. It says, "Let every person be subject to the governing authorities. For there is no authority except from God, and those that exist have been instituted by God." Additionally, God's will is that humans would live in willing functional subordination to governing authorities. 1 Peter 2:13–17 states:

> Be subject for the Lord's sake to every human institution, whether it be to the emperor as supreme, or to governors as sent by him to punish those who do evil and to praise those who do good. For this is the will of God, that by doing good you should put to silence the ignorance of foolish people. Live as people who are free, not using your freedom as a cover-up for evil, but living as servants of God. Honor everyone. Love the brotherhood. Fear God. Honor the emperor.

The New Testament also shows that the *domestic sphere* embraces functional subordination as a God-designed normality. Paul chooses to use the church's subjection to Christ as his analogy for a wife's relationship to her husband in Ephesians 5:22–24. This functional hierarchy is not negated by the fact that verse 21 exhorts us to submit to one another. That verse acts as a segue into the subject matter of Ephesians 5:22—26:9 that shows three different domestic and social relationships entailing subordination. The church is subordinate to Christ, and wives are to submit to their husbands *as the church submits to Christ*. If functional subordination is ignored, the analogy is meaningless. God's will is that we embrace his created order in civil society and not buck against it.

The New Testament also shows that the *ecclesial sphere* embraces functional subordination. The position that sees a God-ordained functional hierarchy in both the family and the local church is called complementarianism. It teaches that men and women are designed by God to complement one another in life and ministry. They therefore honor God best and reflect the ethos of his kingdom most when they live out of that design rather than ignoring or rejecting it. Biblically speaking, complementarianism is taught in Ephesians 5:22–33, 1 Peter 3:1–7, 1 Timothy 2:8—3:7, and Titus 1:5–6. The first two texts are domestic and the last two are ecclesial. The most crucial of these is the 1 Timothy passage. The heart of the textual discussion centers on 1 Timothy 2:11—13:2. It says:

> Let a woman learn quietly with all submissiveness. I do not permit a woman to teach or to exercise authority over a man; rather, she is to remain quiet. For Adam was formed first, then Eve; and Adam was not deceived, but the woman was deceived and became a transgressor. Yet she will be saved through childbearing—if they continue in faith and love and holiness, with self-control. The saying is trustworthy: If anyone aspires to the office of overseer, he desires a noble task. Therefore an overseer must be above reproach, the husband of one wife, sober-minded, self-controlled, respectable, hospitable, able to teach, . . .

In keeping with each of the other two social spheres mentioned above, Paul appeals to the created order as evidence for his role distinction. He said, "For Adam was formed first, then Eve." This creative, pre-Fall order is noted as one of the groundings for the distinction of roles between men and women in the local church. Appeals to interpretively sidestep Paul's distinction have come in many forms, but almost all resort to one of the following errors:

1. Special pleading by grammatical over-analysis. This comes in the form of reinterpreting the Greek word for women to read "wife" instead. But this is not the direction basically every major translation goes, and practically it renders the text almost pointless. If the text were only to prohibit wives from teaching their husbands, we would

have the odd experience of women teaching mixed adults but they would need to cease if their husbands entered the room.

2. Special pleading by an appeal to a specious re-creation of cultural background material. This comes in the form of interpreting the prohibition as a rebuke against dominant women who were not showing propriety or women who were deceived by false teachers. Streams of assumptions and speculations show up in commentaries with very little data to support the assumptions.[32]

3. Trumping up another text in an effort to say a woman's role must not be limited. This often involves an appeal to Priscilla's role in correcting Apollos (Acts 18:26) or an appeal to the fact that women in Corinth prayed and prophesied in the local church. (1 Cor. 11:5). But none of these texts are in conflict with the normative prohibition Paul is articulating to Timothy. Teaching and exercising authority in the assembly are not the same as privately correcting another or even as publicly prophesying in the assembly.

4. A false bifurcation of the two infinitives in verse 12 ("to teach" and "to exercise authority over"). Some who are willing to modify egalitarianism or take a very soft form of complementarianism will say

---

32. An example of this is highly regarded New Testament scholar and egalitarian Gordon Fee. In commenting on the infinitive "to teach," he says, "Part of the problem from this distance is to know what 'teaching' involved. The evidence from 1 Corinthians 12–14 indicates that teaching" may be presented as a spiritual gift (14: 6, 26); at the same time, some in the community are specifically known as teachers (cf. Rom. 12:7), while more private instruction is also given (Acts 18:26; here by a woman). Given that evidence and what can be gleaned from the present Epistles, teaching most likely had to do with instruction in Scripture, that is: Scripture as pointing to salvation in Christ (cf. 2 Tim. 3:15–17). If that is what is being forbidden (and certainty eludes us here), *then it is probably because some of them have been so terribly deceived by the false teachers*, who are specifically abusing the OT (cf. 1:7; Titus 3:9). At least that is the point Paul will pick up in verses 14 and 15." Fee, *New International Biblical Commentary, 1 and 2 Timothy, Titus*, 73. He goes on to talk about the next infinitive "to exercise authority over," and the speculation about background continues. "The word translated authority, which occurs only here in the NT, has the connotation 'to domineer': In context it probably reflects again in the role the women were playing in advancing the errors—or speculations—of the false teachers and therefore is to be understood very closely with the prohibition against teaching." Ibid.

Fee's commentary on these infinitives amounts to an assertion about theologically deceived women with almost nothing given to buttress the claim. This is a typical way to get around the plain sense of the text when it doesn't cohere naturally with our culture. Paul's appeal to the created order as one of the groundings for the prohibition doesn't fit well with Fee's thesis.

that a woman cannot serve in the office of elder in the local church because she cannot fit in 1 Timothy 3:2, but if the elders give her permission she can teach men in the local church because she is operating under their authority. But this splits an issue into two that Paul treats as one. He is not permitting either of them. There is no indication that he is subjecting the first infinitive to the second and in some way making the real issue about authority and not about authority *and* teaching.

On the face of it, Paul's words to Timothy are not confusing, and the text is not riddled with mystery. It reads pretty straightforward. It just doesn't sit well with our cultural sensibilities.

## The Failure of Other Egalitarian Arguments

Three other attempts to support egalitarianism are worth noting. Both also deal with issues in hermeneutics. The first employs an approach known as a redemptive-movement Hermeneutic. This has been most cogently expounded by William Webb in his book, *Slaves, Women and Homosexuals*. The hermeneutic basically teaches that we need to sense the ethical trajectory of the text of Scripture and carry that ethic forward in our application of Scripture. So, for example, the Bible's version of slavery is quite a bit softer than the cultural backgrounds of the institution in the ancient Near-East and later in the Greco-Roman world. So we see a discontinuity between the Bible and culture and a progressive ethical trajectory from the Old to the New Testament. As a result, a redemptive-movement Hermeneutic says we should carry forward the trajectory of the Bible's softening of this institution and stay in the lead, redeeming culture's captivity to oppressive institutions like it. The basic approach is then laid over the issue of women in civil, domestic, and church life. The conclusion becomes the same. The Bible is softer in its ethic and so we ought to follow this trajectory further than the text goes, because the Bible is relating to culture in a consistent way by correcting its ethic. Interestingly the opposite holds true, as Webb notes, regarding homosexuality. The Bible is restrictive and harder in its condemnation of that lifestyle and so we ought to hold the line as the text does in this regard.

I will say that this hermeneutic has appeal and Bill Webb is genuinely a good scholar and has put great thought into his approach. But I do think it suffers from an irreparable flaw. It tries to ground the hermeneutic in the Bible by describing its appeal to an ultimate ethic as that which is "reflected in the spirit of the biblical text,"[33] but this ends up being arbitrary. I would argue that the trajectory of the biblical text as it relates to a woman's role is definitively complementarian. I see no evidence of it being otherwise. What happens in a redemptive-movement Hermeneutic is that a place out beyond the biblical text, a supposed ethical ideal—usually driven by culture, gets marked as the ultimate landing place and then biblical data back feeds the pre-conceived conclusion. At least this seems to be the case on the gender issue.

Another attempt to support egalitarianism is the hermeneutical approach referenced both in the previous chapter and earlier in this one: deconstructionism. It is easy to arrive at egalitarianism simply by putting our present cultural lens up front in the process of interpretation and working to get behind the words to upend the power structures that be. Of course, egalitarianism is the only game in town for the deconstructionist because their very hermeneutic comes from a rejection of hierarchical power. The discussion in the previous section suffices in response to this deconstructionist approach.

The third attempt is rooted in the idea that mutual love, as exhibited in the intra-trinitarian perichoresis (mutual indwelling of persons by one another), can only be accounted for by an egalitarian view of the Trinity wherein any sense of functional hierarchy is rejected. But is this really the case? Two questions need to be answered. First, *is the social Trinity egalitarian or hierarchical?* And second, *can the hierarchical view of the social Trinity account for mutual self-giving love?*

In answer to the first question I would assert that the Trinity is a functionally hierarchical relationship of three persons consisting of one essence or being. The postmodern inability to distinguish the categories of being and function trap people in egalitarian notions of the Trinity. In the last chapter I showed this to be the case with William Paul Young and *The Shack*. The sense I get from him and others is that for God to have real mutual self-giving love, then hierarchy must be out. But why?

I have already shown that the three main spheres that govern human life—civil, domestic, and ecclesial—are described as functionally hierarchical structures in the New Testament. They function in this order because God designed them to. Does it not seem reasonable that

---

33. Webb, *Slaves, Women and Homosexuals*, 32.

their communal structure would be indicative of his nature? I would think it odd of his creation's functionality to have no resemblance to his own. So theologically, it seems that we can argue backward from the created to the Creator, since we know that he approves of functional subordination in human mechanisms and even attributes its origins to his own creative enterprise.

Additionally, I began this section responding to egalitarianism by looking at Jesus and his relationship to the Father. The contours of their relationship clearly take into account functional subordination. But just as clearly, this does not mean that the Bible affirms that the Son is any less God than the Father. To see him is to see the Father (John 14:9). The Son and the Father are one (John 10:30). In Christ all that makes God "God" subsists in a bodily form (Col. 2:9). So the way the Bible talks about the Father and Son shows precisely a distinction between ontological attributes and functional roles.

In answer to the second question I would absolutely affirm that a hierarchical view of the social Trinity can account for mutual self-giving love. I actually would go a step farther and say that roles are to love what a pipe is to water. Without pipes, water doesn't know where to go. It takes constriction to empower its full force. A pipe makes water effective. It takes it places. It channels it to areas of need. Roles in the interaction between persons do much the same. This is true whether we are speaking of human interpersonal action within society or divine interpersonal action within the Trinity. Family roles give shape to expressions of love and they define what service in the name of love demands. This is true in church ministry as well. Gifted women relate to church leadership and vice versa in a love appropriate as brothers and sisters in Christ with a mutual appreciation and value for the other. The roles that each of them fill don't diminish their contributions or the contributions of the other. Instead, the roles themselves channel the nature of how love expresses itself so God's glory gets put on full display through their mutual sacrifice and respect for the vulnerabilities and authorities of one another.

## Exhortations: Cherish Structure in the Local Church

As caretakers of the Body of Christ we need to embrace structures that resemble God's design. As of the writing of this book, I have yet to turn forty and many would see me as antiquated in my ecclesiology because

I simply cannot get around the common-sense, *prima facie* reading of Scripture regarding roles. My encouragement to you as a reader is to join me and remain stuck in the mud. Family is a timeless modality, church is a timeless modality, government is a timeless modality. The future will be government of grace by God for his glory, but it will be orderly. These timeless modalities call for normalized structure and roles. And this is precisely what we find in the Word of God. So teach it. When people accuse you of being a sexist, don't let it slide. Ideologies matter and rhetoric like that only wounds. When people accuse you of homophobia, show them through your love of mercy and grace toward the homosexual community that their accusations are lies. But in the process, don't bend on the moral imperatives of the Bible. Stand firm on ideas and love people well.

If you are a pastor, teacher, ministry leader, or discipler in the local church, consider these following exhortations. They will help you say no to Smorgasbord Jesus. They will help your church capture and transform culture instead of sitting by and watching it shape Christ. They will help you be a part of letting the historical Jesus say what gets served on his menu rather than letting the masses tailor-make it for their tastes.

- *Teach people to treat each other with self-giving love that embraces roles within community, not as restrictive, but as constrictive for the effectiveness of their expressions of that deep compassion.*
- *Continually remind people of the need to separate people and ideas.* This false equivoalence is so embedded in our cultural subconscious and the subtext of our shared language that we have to keep beating the drum on this one again and again.
- *Show the connection between hermeneutics and practice.* People need to see that interpretive method is not an issue for academics; it is an issue for believers.
- *Remind people that the abuse of something is never a good reason to ignore the proper use of something.* Just because patriarchy has been abused doesn't mean structure and authority should be thrown aside. Reactions that swing the pendulum in the other direction like that are typically very unhelpful.
- *Teach in such a way that your church sees the need to capture and transform culture, not primarily for the moral well-being of culture but so the gospel can be put on display as God's order is celebrated.*

## Conclusion

This chapter sought to respond to the four "flavorful appeals" of the emergent church movement mentioned in chapter 5. The first portion of the chapter exposed the largest pragmatic flaw I see in the movement and at the same time addressed one of the four flavorful appeals. *The emergent church yearns for community but does not have the currency of relational virtues to cash it out.* This leaves those of us outside the emergent stream with the opportunity to put real community on display as we do the hard work of cultivating it. In this sense, we can give a postmodern culture what it really needs without condescending to immature or puerile pathways of getting there.

The last portion of the chapter focused on the three other flavorful appeals. We must reject the idea that orthodoxy itself is malleable. We must teach a hermeneutical approach that holds strong to authorial intent. We must not capitulate to egalitarian social norms regarding gender and sexuality. We are presently at the brink. Smorgasbord Jesus is franchising himself all over, and if we do not get a handle on it, we will find the culture dictating all the items that go on the Christian menu. It is already happening, both wittingly and unwittingly. We can't afford to let Christ get co-opted by this fickle culture.

7

# Gourmet Jesus

## The Christ of Prosperity Theology

*In the story of the camel and the needle's eye, the disciples recognized, all men stand condemned—not because we are all rich, but because almost all of us desire to be so and too often organize our lives around that desire.*

ROSS DOUTHAT

WHILE I WAS A young seminary student my wife worked in the office of a civil engineering firm in Fort Worth, Texas. Every year the firm had a Christmas party held at a high-end club in a wealthy suburb. One year Jennifer and I attended. We had gotten word that the firm would be giving away a number of gifts—ranging in value—to their employees and, as a couple barely managing our way through my education on a shoestring budget, we thought maybe we would strike it lucky.

The room at the club had a classy décor that typified the success of the firm. We were seated at tables ranging from six to eight people, none of whom I knew. As the night began we were invited to go get our meal in an adjacent room where we would be served delicious food buffet style. The room was dimly lit, and I made my way through the buffet line in relatively short order. As I zipped through, I came to a bowl filled with heaps of what appeared to be mashed potatoes. The serving size was fairly small, but the one thing I knew about gourmet food in high-class establishments is that the portions, while tasty, are disappointingly small. So the last thing I wanted to do was ask one of the attendants what the deal was with the potatoes. After all, there is nothing worse than attending a highfalutin affair and not knowing how to play the part. So I spooned out a rather manly portion and made my way back to my seat. As I sat down my wife was to my right, and a man I did not know was sitting at the end of the table to my left. Ever conscious of the rules of formal dining, I placed my napkin on my lap and began to partake of this epicurean delight. My first indulgence was the potatoes. I heaped up a hefty spoonful and transported them to my mouth only to have a sensate experience that remains visceral to this day. After the spoon entered and then left my mouth, my eyes began to water, my nostrils fumed as though a fire-breathing dragon now inhabited them, and my throat felt like fiery demons were hollowing out residences in the side walls of my esophagus. Guess what . . . they weren't potatoes after all . . . nope, instead every passage in my cranium was being roto-rooted by the largest spoonful of horseradish known to man. Needless to say, my attempt to fit into society's upper crust came crashing down. With tears in my eyes I looked at the man to my left and muttered, "I bet you're wondering why I just ate a big spoonful of horseradish." He looked astonished, and I looked embarrassed.

Why didn't I just ask the attendant what was in the bowl? Why didn't I pay more attention in the dimly lit elegance of the buffet room? The truth is I liked feeling like I had left the bourgeois behind for just one night. I liked the perception that I was a man of means and not just a grad-school student with hardly two nickels to rub together. It was good being gourmet. But I found out that being gourmet has its downside too. Sometimes you can want a piece of the pie so much that you don't pay much attention to the pie itself. You can long for the foppery and frippery and lose the substance of the matter altogether. Such has been the case with a large segment of evangelicalism, particularly over the last thirty years, in what has become known as the prosperity gospel, prosperity theology, or the health and wealth gospel.

The evangelical world has been infected with a hunger for a Christianity that sees God as a grand gift-giver in search of faithful people just naïve and bold enough to ask him for his bounty. Certainly I recognize that this is indeed "my Father's world" as the hymn writer declared, and I realize that as my Father, he longs to "give good things to those that ask him" (Matt. 7:11). However, he is not a celestial investment broker and the prosperity gospel and its teachers are guilty of treating him as such. They have been painting a christological cameo of a Gourmet Jesus whose real hope is that we can join him in the "Finer Things Club." This sophomoric propensity dressed in theological garb is a natural fit for an individualistic culture driven by a subtext of materialism. However, its popularity and labeling power presents followers of Jesus with a very serious distraction that has contributed to an unhealthy caricature of evangelicals—as though we needed more data points to form the public pastiche.

There is something latent within the fallen human soul that gets called up into materialistic service by temporal enticements. We not only want the "good life" (whatever that is), but we would like our "best life now." And this pull, this desire for more, this sense that we are tired of getting the raw deal in the realm of hard knocks, heightens our sense of longing for something that would take us to the land of the blessed and out of the land of the broken. In one sense there is a holy impulse at the front of this discontent. Perhaps no one has said it better than C. S. Lewis in his famous work *Mere Christianity*. He noted that "If I find in myself a desire which no experience in this world can satisfy, the most probable explanation is that I was made for another world."[1] For Lewis, unmet "desire" pointed (with the texture of a Platonic metaphysic) to an ultimate satiation of that desire. One might represent his sentiment by saying we are thirsty for a reason, but we are thirsty in a land of sand and rocks. His sense was that we live in a world that is simply incapable of slaking the thirst of our most essential desires, and so we are left in a land of discontent by God's crafting to forge within us a longing for our heavenly destiny. So our best life is yet to be.

But the perversion of this holy desire is that heaven gets preempted by earth and our essential cravings find their contentment in the temporal realm rather than the eternal. Our best life is now rather than yet to come. One of the most significant modern proponents of a Gourmet Jesus bringing a prosperity gospel is Joel Osteen, who leads the largest church in America, Lakewood Church, in Houston, Texas. Osteen's first book and multi-million-copy best seller was titled *Your Best Life Now*. Osteen has an incredible mass appeal, and it is no accident. On the one hand he speaks to the felt desires of thousands upon thousands in a western climate filled with the clouds of individualism and materialism. On

1. Lewis, *Mere Christianity*, 136–37.

the other hand, his message strikes a chord with the discontent that is endemic to a fallen world no matter what the cultural aroma. And this may be its most insidious aspect. Discontent is not new to the human condition. The desire for something different or something more has been with us since the garden. In the early seventeenth century the Puritan Jeremiah Burroughs penned a timeless work titled *The Rare Jewel of Christian Contentment*. While the book is almost four hundred years old, its relevance to our culture cannot be overstated. Burroughs, in classic Puritan style, works with the biblical text like a surgeon with a scalpel, cutting away the flesh to get to the heart of the problem. He then systematically creates a theology of Christian contentment. In the next chapter we will need to come back to this book in an effort to help this rare "jewel" of contentment shine. But for now it is enough to note that our present culture and our sinful desires work together to keep us always wanting and never satisfied. Osteen's message is both a twisted type of balm for the soul and a provocation for the proclivities of the flesh shared by the mass of humanity, from the wealthy in suburban America to the poor in sub-saharan Africa.

But how did we get to the ubiquitous acceptance of Joel Osteen's happy message of a gourmet Jesus? As with each of these piquant portraits, there is a lineage of ideas that gave rise to it. If we are to have any idea how to change the church's appetite, we need to know from whence this Jesus has come. What went into the recipe of Gourmet Jesus?

## Gnosticism

We need to start in the ancient world with something the church fathers warred against, known as gnosticism. Gnosticism has recently been in vogue in academic and popular circles. But what on earth is it? Gnosticism had no stated creed or code. In fact, the gnostic label did not emerge until the seventeenth century. But it wasn't until after the discovery of gnostic texts at a place called Nag Hammadi in 1945 more information about the teachings of various groups in the second century emerged. These texts helped fill in some of the gaps in our understanding of the "heretical" beliefs that were primarily understood through the apologetic responses of second-and third-century figures like Justin Martyr and Irenaeus (among others). With all of the collected data but no creed, the best way to identify gnosticism is by noting certain ideas and beliefs that are common to many of the texts. Gnosticism then, as we talk about it today, is basically a label placed upon heterodox teachings from primarily the second and third centuries that, while distinct in many ways, share particularly common themes. New Testament expert Darrell Bock reflects similarly on the Nag Hammadi texts, observing that, ". . . these texts reflect a set of religious ideas within the same family of concerns."[2]

In one sense each of the themes can be traced back to one foundational idea known as dualism. The dualist conceives of reality consisting of two concepts or entities that exist in antithetical or at the very least non-intersecting polarities. For the gnostic thinker, God is thought of in dualistic terms. This is the case when thinking about key doctrines like God, creation, and salvation. The God of the Old Testament, the creator God, and the ideal unknowable God are not the same. Creation itself is thought of in dualistic terms. Matter and mind are separated in such a way that matter is sullied and inherently bad, while mind is in the ineffable realm of the ideal God. This ideal God exists untainted by creation and therefore is known only when we transcend our material existence through a special endowed knowledge (*gnosis*). So gnostic salvation then is really the story of our enlightenment by a uniquely endowed knowledge. In fact the eminent Yale scholar Jaroslav Pelikan has defined gnosticism itself in terms of its salvific theme: "Gnosticism may be defined as a system which taught the cosmic redemption of the spirit through knowledge."[3] The focus is on the redemption of the immaterial from the inherent, sullied burden of the material. Even ultimate salvation in gnostic eschatology is had by divorcing the spiritual from the material. So in the meta-narrative of theology, gnostic Christian thought and orthodox Christian thought diverge on the most central of issues: God, creation, salvation, and eschatology. So whom we worship, from whence we come, how we are made whole, and where we are headed all find different expression between the two ancient ideas. These are not insignificant starting points and signposts on the road of understanding God and our purpose in life.

Complementing gnosticism's divergence from the orthodox understanding of the redemptive history is its heretical Christology, specifically as it relates to the essence or ontology of Jesus Christ. The gnostic typically held to one of two explanations for the person of Jesus. One option

---

2. Bock, *The Missing Gospels*, 18.
3. Pelikan, *The Christian Tradition: The Emergence of the Catholic Tradition*, 82.

was that Christ, in coming to earth, only appeared as a man but did not actually take on flesh and bone. This is known as a docetic Christology. The apostle John referred in one of his letters to precisely this ontological error when he said, "For many deceivers have gone out into the world, those who do not confess the coming of Jesus Christ in the flesh. Such a one is the deceiver and the antichrist" (2 John 7). John sees a dangerous deception in the docetic idea that Jesus did not perform his earthly ministry, culminating in his death and resurrection, in real physical flesh.

The other version of the gnostic error regarding Jesus' ontology is seen in Irenaeus's writings as he discusses one gnostic sect's views on Jesus. He observes:

> They also hold that Jesus was the son of Joseph, and was just like other men, with the exception that he differed from them in this respect, that inasmuch as his soul was steadfast and pure, he perfectly remembered those things which he had witnessed within the sphere of the unbegotten God. On this account a power descended upon him from the Father, that by means of it he might escape from the creators of the world.[4]

This gnostic approach to Jesus' ontology is the opposite of the former. In the first version Jesus does not actually come in true physicality, and so his purity is preserved because he never fully partakes in the stained realm of matter. In this latter version, his pure state is maintained because his uniquely endowed knowledge (gnosis) enables him to transcend the flesh. This latter theology forms an important link to the problems that emerge in the nineteenth and twentieth centuries where the ontological distance between Jesus and us was shrunk in an effort to permit us to tap into the divine mind and live in a manner that surpassed the physical debilitation of disease and the fiscal limitations of poverty.

These two perspectives are illustrated in the following figure:

**The Material Malady:**
**Two Gnostic Views of Christology**

| Docetism | Enlightenment |
|---|---|
| *Real Divinity* | *Divine Enlightenment* |
| *Faux Humanity* | *Real Humanity* |

---

4. Irenaeus, *Against Heresies*, 25. 1.

Our awareness of this gnostic divergence on Jesus is crucial because this dualism is reflected in later thought that eventually gave rise to a Jesus zeroed in on the prosperity of his devotees in their material existence. But to get from ancient gnostic Christian thought to modern prosperity teachers, a couple of additional elements need to be added to the recipe. Our next link is found in the cultural fireworks of the nineteenth century, through the rise of divine metaphysics in a diverse movement that became known as New Thought.

## New Thought

The New Thought movement usually traces its origin to a Maine watchmaker named Phineas Quimby (1802–1866). Quimby was influenced by a Frenchman named Charles Poyen who brought the metaphysical teaching of an Austrian named Franz Mesmer (1734–1815) to America. Mesmer believed that the body could be healed through accessing energy, which he termed "universal fluid," and that it could be transferred through the body with the use of magnets.[5] The manipulation of this "fluid" became the foundation for the practice of hypnotism. Thus when we say someone is "mesmerized" we are using a term whose etymology is from the man who became known as the "father of hypnotism." While Quimby did not fully adopt "mesmerism," as it was known, the foundational idea that the body could be healed through the power of the mind was important for Quimby. And this idea was foundational to what flowed out of others influenced by his ideas in the eclectic waters eventually known as New Thought.

New Thought had a number of teachers and movements that fit underneath its metaphysical umbrella. What is important for this study is to note that New Thought carried forward a dualism reminiscent of the early Christian gnostics. The movement operated in the ideological corridors of Christian thought and served as an unorthodox complement

---

5. For Mesmer "there was an agent, which he called 'universal fluid' that being subject to an eternal ebb and flow, affected planetary and human bodies alike. This 'universal fluid' was alleged to have a 'tidal effect' within the human body, the movements of the flow in a healthy body in synchrony with the universe. Mesmer went further, adding that the above fluid was the 'material cause of gravitation' or the 'cause of material gravitation,' which led to a force he termed 'animal gravity.'" Oon, "A Critical Presentation of the Life and Work of Franz Anton Mesmer MD and Its Influence on the Development of Hypnosis," 33.

to the growing naturalism of mainline theologians. While Strauss and Ritschl were busy taking all of the mystery out of the text, the divine metaphysicians were, like their gnostic forbears, separating mind from matter and developing what they called their own version of "science." However, it was very removed from the garden-variety views of the material world provided by Newtonian physics and of Darwinian naturalism. Instead, this "science" sought the control of the material through the immaterial mind and in some cases eliminated the material altogether.

The best and most appropriate example for our purposes is the thought of Mary Baker Eddy and her branch of divine metaphysics known as Christian Science.[6] Eddy taught that matter is illusory and inconsequential. In her primary religious revelation, known as *Science and Health* she wrote:

> The realm of the real is Spirit. The unlikeness of Spirit is matter, and the opposite of the real is not divine—it is a human concept. Matter is an error of statement. This error in premise leads to errors in the conclusion in every statement into which it enters. Nothing we can say or believe regarding matter is immortal for matter is temporal and is therefore a mortal phenomenon, a human concept, sometimes beautiful, always erroneous.
>
> Is Spirit the source or creator of matter? Science reveals nothing in Spirit out of which to create matter. Divine metaphysics explains away matter. Spirit is the only substance and consciousness recognized by divine Science. The material senses oppose this, but there are no material senses, for matter has no mind. In Spirit there is no matter, even as in Truth there is no error, and in good no evil. It is a false supposition, the notion that there is real substance-matter, the opposite of Spirit. Spirit, God, is infinite, all. Spirit can have no opposite.[7]

So, for her, matter is not real and the world is a monistic entity of Spirit which is the only "thing" that is real. This concept, rooted in

---

6. While some Christian Science practitioners today might distance themselves from an identification with New Thought, their ideas are moored to it in both a historical and an ideological sense. With few exceptions, New Thought adherents identified as Christians and focused their theology on Christian Scriptures and the life of Jesus. Strangely, New Thought has often been treated by scholars and the public as antithetical to Christianity, a sentiment that has led Christian Scientists to reject the label "New Thought" despite Eddy's prominence as a New Thought thinker and founder of Christian Science. Hladky, "I Double-Dog Dare you in Jesus' Name! Claiming Christian Wealth and the American Prosperity Gospel," 85.

7. Eddy, *Science and Health with Key to the Scriptures*, 277–78.

the gnostic dualism I already mentioned, is a crucial middle step from gnostic thought to the message of modern prosperity preachers. In fact, of the two types of gnostic Christology I cited earlier, Eddy's is closely related to the second that I termed as "enlightenment." She saw Jesus as man who came to the necessary realizations requisite to be absorbed by the divine mind, through the discovery of the spiritually "real" that served as the cause for the "material surface of things."[8] Without specifically stating the term *gnosis*, she was essentially saying the same thing as some of the gnostics with a strong Platonic metaphysic that the spiritual forms and concepts grounded the ultimately unreal illusions of the material world.[9]

Since matter is an illusion, it is thus overcome by mind. It is very easy to see the ground being formed for the modern self-help world and the false notions taught by literature that emphasizes the power of positive thinking and positive confession. Thoughts and words—properties of mind—have the authority to dictate and even create the illusion of matter. Present-day prosperity teaching is a Christianized brand of this positive thought and confession ideology. For Eddy, physical malady and sickness was part of the illusion of matter and could be overcome by the proper appropriation of the powers of mind.[10] She saw that the laws of divine metaphysics operated in a formulaic fashion just like mathematical laws. The divine mind established the rules of how the "real" (read: spiritual or metaphysical) world operates and those rules were as reliable as mathematical formulas. Eddy stated early on in her magnum opus:

> Who would stand before a blackboard, and pray the principles of mathematics to solve the problem? The rule is already

8. Ibid., 313.

9. Consider the entire statement about Jesus' understanding of reality: "Jesus of Nazareth was the most scientific man that ever trod the globe. He plunged beneath the material surface of things, and found the spiritual cause. To accommodate himself to immature ideas of spiritual power,—for spirituality was possessed only in a limited degree even by his disciples,—Jesus called the body, which by spiritual power he raised from the grave, 'flesh and bones.' To show that the substance of himself was Spirit and the body no more perfect because of death and no less material until the ascension (his further spiritual exaltation), Jesus waited until the mortal or fleshly sense had relinquished the belief of substance-matter, and spiritual sense had quenched all earthly yearnings. Thus he found the eternal Ego, and proved that he and the Father were inseparable as God and His reflection or spiritual man. Our Master gained the solution of being, demonstrating the existence of but one Mind without a second or equal." Ibid., 313–14.

10. "All that we term sin, sickness and death is a mortal belief." Ibid., 278.

established, and it is our task to work out the solution. Shall we ask the divine Principle of all goodness to do His own work? His work is done, and we have only to avail ourselves of God's rule in order to receive His blessing, which enables us to work out our own salvation."[11]

God's blessing is just a matter of applying the spiritual rules of the divine mind's economy.

The significance of Eddy as a middling between the gnostics and the prosperity preachers of the twentieth and twenty-first centuries is established in the two main ideas I have mentioned. The first is the carrying-forward of a gnostic Christology that reduces Jesus to an enlightened man. The second is the role of positive thinking and confession grounded in the mind-over-matter notions of her metaphysic. These two tenets are writ large in different strands of prosperity/Word-Faith teaching. The idea that we can have what Jesus had in terms of enlightenment and power, coupled with the idea that the negatives of our physical existence—namely, sickness and poverty[12]—can be overcome by living above the fray, pointed the skis downhill and Gourmet Jesus was set to be savored.

## Two Key Themes

Before continuing to roll down the historical trail, I need to pause and highlight two ideas that form the central issues buttressing Gourmet Jesus. At first their connection may not be completely apparent to the present situation in popular American culture, but hopefully that will become clear as I move along.

The first theme I will call "shrinking the distance." This deals with the ontological distance between God and man. At the heart of Word-Faith theology is the consistent and objectionable tendency to reduce the distance between man and God. Undoubtedly this is influenced by both New Thought and the general theological confusion that poured out of

---

11. Ibid., 3.

12. Hladky noted in her article that New Thought ultimately extended its healing benefits beyond illness to economic woes. "From 1875 to 1905, New Thought primarily focused on mental and bodily healing. But by the turn of the century, healers increasingly targeted poverty as a mental affliction, teaching that God intended all people to be prosperous." Hladky, "I Double-Dog Dare you in Jesus' Name! Claiming Christian Wealth and the American Prosperity Gospel," 85.

the spiritual chaos of the Second Great Awakening, with its ideological pioneerism that spawned such aberrant movements as Mormonism and Millerism, which eventually formed the basis of Seventh-day Adventism. Much of this emerged in the middle of the nineteenth century in upstate New York in an area that history now refers to as the "Burned-over District." It has been observed that "All the spiritual experiments of western New York were alike genuine growths, rooted in a heritage of moral intensity and blossoming in the heat of evangelistic fervor."[13] This is important for understanding the movements in evangelicalism to come because as people zealously searched for God outside of traditional mainline options, they began to be theologically creative. Therefore the mood by the end of the nineteenth century was established and theological innovation was in vogue. Amidst this innovation, a significant development was the propensity to elevate man to a quasi-divine status (as exemplified by the influence of New Thought) and to reduce God—specifically Jesus—to solely human stature (as demonstrated by the development of theological liberalism discussed in chapter 1). And so effectively the table was set to shrink the distance.

The second theme was the evolution of positive confession. Here New Thought's influence was felt strongly. Since mind could move the illusory state of matter, things could be thought and said which could re-create real existence. If sickness was an illusion and poverty a state of mind, it was now just a matter of changing thought patterns to get past such chimerical concepts. With the distance between God and man effectively shrinking (both were identified as spirit beings) and since God created the world through his words, then it seemed only natural to conclude that man could speak things into being just like God did.

These two themes are the essential conceptual ingredients in the delicacy that became Gourmet Jesus. With these two identified, it is important to reengage the ideological narrative to clearly understand from whence this Christ came to us.

## A Marriage of New Thought and the Evangelical Church

It has been well established that the progenitor of the Word-Faith movement was a man named E. W. Kenyon. Kenyon served as the next step

---

13. Cross, *The Burned-over District: The Social and Intellectual History of Enthusiastic Religion in Western New York, 1800–1850*, 144.

in bridging the gap between the principles of New Thought and the Christian church of the twentieth century. By the turn of the century, the New Thought pump had been primed to not only discuss overcoming sickness, but also poverty.

Kenyon was born in 1867 in the southeast corner of the Adirondacks in upstate New York. He was converted at the age of seventeen and spent some of his theologically formative years in the Boston area during the 1890s. It was here that he was exposed to New Thought. No one questions that New Thought seriously impacted Kenyon's ideas; however, there is great disagreement as to just how much it formed some of his subsequent doctrines.[14] His influence was felt in the Boston area as a clergyman and founder of a Bible school. Eventually he rose to prominence as a radio evangelist in Seattle during his later years. He clearly was part of an evangelical tradition—converted as a Methodist, he later became a Baptist pastor in 1893—but some of his ideas were heterodox to say the least. Where precisely these ideas came from, and what percentage of influence is to be granted New Thought as opposed to theological movements within the pre-Pentecostal faith-healing evangelicalism of the nineteenth century, is very questionable. My purpose is not to delve into this discussion of ideological genetics, but rather simply to show that Kenyon was an absolutely paramount figure in what was to become known as the Word-Faith movement and that his doctrine (resembling facets of both incipient Pentecostalism and New Thought) formed a legacy of thought still felt today.

Kenyon was crucial to throwing together the two ingredients vital to the formation of a Gourmet Jesus that I mentioned earlier. It will be worth it to note several subthemes in Kenyon's thought that fit underneath the umbrella of the two themes I have already mentioned ("shrinking the distance" and positive confession). First, we should note the *role of faith* in Kenyon's theology. In this he follows the pre-Pentecostals and Higher-Life teachers like Christian Missionary Alliance founder A. B. Simpson, among others.[15] Simpson reflects on Jesus' miracle of healing the woman

14. For two different perspectives from evangelicals rejecting the health/wealth tradition spawned by Kenyon, see D. R. McConnell, *A Different Gospel* in favor of the idea that Kenyon was primarily influenced by New Thought; and Robert Bowman Jr., *The Word-Faith Controversy* for the view that Kenyon was primarily influenced by Higher-Life and Keswick Theology within the evangelical tradition.

15. Simpson was not alone in this era. He was joined by men like pastor and speaker William Boardmen (1810–1886), the Episcopalian physician Charles Cullis (1833–1892), and Baptist pastor A. J. Gordon (1836–1895), who was also the founder of Gordon College and Gordon-Conwell Theological Seminary.

with a blood issue that touched his garment (Mark 5:25–34), exhorting, "Our faith must be in tune with God, and when it is, there is no limit to the blessing we may claim."[16] This statement is indicative of the trajectory of the nineteenth-century Higher-Life movement. Faith is the means by which we "claim" what is ours. This idea, while not intended by Simpson to be abused, is basic to the health and wealth gospel.

The sense that, if we are in tune with God, the sky is the limit and the world is our oyster is expressed strongly by Kenyon. In fact, the two ingredients of God and man being not that far apart and the power of positive faith confessions merge in a short work by Kenyon entitled *Claiming our Rights*. The following quote illustrates this convergence about as vividly as any:

> God's hands are tied until He can use ours. Angels are our servants. They cannot do our work. God is limited to our Faith, our obedience. God is as small in the world as we make Him. God is big only where some man makes Him big, by using this divinely given authority. We are the body of Christ; the Head is powerless without our hands and feet. Oh men, can't you see how helpless God is until we let Him live omnipotently in our acts? A sin in the heart binds the arms of God that would embrace a multitude. Our fear to be used binds God's omnipotence. Men of God, be God's men and use the authority delegated to you."[17]

While the world may be our oyster, God is apparently locked, albeit by his own choosing, in the shell. For Kenyon, "our Faith" takes on such a life of its own that it controls the scope of God's expression of his own power.

In another section of the same work, Kenyon shows a possible connection to the metaphysical cults that influenced him during his time in Boston when he studied at the Emerson College of Oratory. Here I will lump together two issues into one since they share a common "on-demand" characteristic. The two issues are *spiritual laws* and *rights*, but together let's just call them "God on demand."

I mentioned earlier in the chapter that Christian Science founder Mary Baker Eddy saw metaphysical laws operating akin to mathematical ones. But the New Thought teachers were not alone in appealing to spiritual laws. Robert Bowman shows that A.B. Simpson exhorted followers, writing:

16. Simpson, *The Christ in the Bible Commentary*, Vol 4, 205
17. Kenyon, *Claiming Our Rights*, 6

> Now, get to work and study the laws of the Holy Ghost; find out all the modes of his operation, the things that help to bring Him, and then adjust yourself to Him, and you will find out that the Spirit of God will fit into your life as the power fits into our machinery.

This mechanistic view of modernity where the movement of God's power could be commodified was adopted by Kenyon. In *Claiming Our Rights* he states, "You have as much right to demand healing as you have to demand the cashing of a check at a bank where you have a deposit."[18]

For Kenyon, as for faith teachers subsequent to him all the way to our present situation, God is at our beck and call. He operates according to metaphysical laws and he has granted us legal rights to lay claim upon his power. As he states in *A New Type of Christianity*:

> We are exercising our rights and privileges in the Name of Jesus. Disease and sickness have lost their dominion. We are masters over them. Poverty and want no longer challenge us. We know our Father.[19]

It is important to the development of Gourmet Jesus that we notice Kenyon extends the legal right afforded us as sons and the power of privilege presented by invoking the name of Jesus to the issue of money. I don't want to read too much into this as Kenyon was only seeking deliverance from poverty and not a divine right to opulence. However, it is important to note that the history of the Word-Faith movement is rooted in perceiving financial means as both a spiritual right of sonship to be claimed and a spiritual law to be invoked.

There are lots of aberrant doctrines that we could discuss in terms of the theology of the Word-Faith movement (e.g. Jesus' spiritual death, his satanic nature on the cross, and God in a body to name a few), but I want to be particular and stay focused on those things that pertain to Gourmet Jesus. The subthemes I have highlighted so far: 1) the role of faith, and 2) the role of spiritual laws and spiritual rights both combine to make God someone who is at our bidding. The two big ingredients contributing to a Christ of prosperity that I started this recipe with—"shrinking the distance" and positive confession—are evident in the seminal stages of the Word-Faith movement. The problems are clearly emerging. It subjects God to our notions of what we need or desire and reduces theology to

---

18. Ibid., 4
19. Kenyon, *A New Type of Christianity*, 38.

a sort of genie-ology. God is on demand. God is in a lamp waiting to be rubbed by faith and summoned by spiritual laws and then emerge bound by the ones who invoked him. While Word-Faith doctrine is bigger than its prosperity component, its theology formed the fertile ground for the weeds to grow.

## Every Family Needs a Dad

Kenneth Hagin (1917–2003) was known as "Dad Hagin." He was responsible for bringing the Word-Faith teaching that came from Kenyon (with contributions from others) into the heart of full-fledged Pentecostalism. Hagin was an Assemblies of God minister who trained people extensively through his Rhema Bible Training College, centered smack in the middle of the Bible Belt in a suburb of Tulsa, Oklahoma. Hagin spoke to the culture with simplicity and clarity, and he spoke of the accessibility of God's power with such surety that people latched on. He is considered by most to be the "Father" of the movement. As critic D. R. McConnell noted in 1988, "All of the major ministers in the Faith movement readily admit Hagin's tutelage."[20]

In the late 1980s, the first published edition of McConnell's scathing critique of the Word-Faith movement came out. In 1982 McConnell first surfaced his thesis in the master's program at Oral Roberts University that the Word-Faith movement had its origins in E. W. Kenyon, who had his origins in late-nineteenth-century New Thought. McConnell's work is important because of its controversial ideas about the beginnings of the movement, but also because he showed without much doubt that Hagin fairly extensively plagiarized Kenyon. It wasn't that Hagin never admitted that he used Kenyon as a source, but McConnell exposed the degree to which Hagin's ideas in general and language in particular were directly Kenyon's.[21] The significance of this is that Hagin often passed off most things as revelatory knowledge (a doctrine that ironically he picked up largely from Kenyon) from God when in fact his sources were likely more human than he admitted.

Hagin's doctrine then often resembled things from Kenyon and from other early Pentecostals as well. For our purpose I want to note specifically his role in carrying forward the trajectories of the key ingredients

---

20. McConnell, *A Different Gospel*, 55.
21. Cf. Ibid., 6–11.

contributing to Gourmet Jesus that I have already mentioned were in Kenyon. I showed earlier that Kenyon had a low view of God that tied him to the rope of human faith and rendered him "helpless" without being unleashed by our words and faithful proclamations. In one sense, Hagin brought God even lower than Kenyon because he espoused a doctrine that is not found in Kenyon, but is indicative of the low view of God we have already seen.

Hagin taught that God has a body. He wrote, "Even though God is a Spirit, we know that He has a face and hands, a form of some kind. He is no less real because He is a Spirit than He would be if He had a physical body."[22] In the context of the quote Hagin seems to be likening God's "body" to how he perceives angelic beings to exist, possessing some type of "spirit" body. Regardless of the particular nature of the body, Hagin sees God as limited in his eternal nature in some sense. The seeds of this are important because the devolution of God's ontology meets its lowest point in the Word-Faith movement in a follower of Hagin's named Kenneth Copeland. But for now it is enough to note that the distance continued to shrink between God and man as the Gourmet Jesus evolved. Kenyon saw God limited to our beck and call. Hagin saw God limited ontologically. Both were different than historic Christian orthodoxy.

The second key ingredient, the doctrine of positive confession, is vigorously carried forward from Kenyon into Hagin. Here Hagin's homey sense of telling a good tale operates at its rhetorical best. Spiritual laws and our spiritual rights as children of God clearly merge into the same strain of thought in Hagin's teaching. In his short work titled *In Him*, Hagin begins, "A spiritual law too few of us realize is: Our confessions rule us."[23] Just a little later in the same work, Hagin transitions to the relationship of this law of positive confession to our legal position in Christ. He declares:

> Faith's confessions create realities. As far as God is concerned everything you have or are "in Christ" is so. He has done it. Everything the Bible says is ours, is ours legally. The Bible is a legal document, sealed by the blood of Jesus. However, it is your believing it and your confessing it which makes it a reality to you.[24]

---

22. As cited in Bowman, *The Word-Faith Controversy*, 116.
23. Hagin, *In Him*, 14.
24. Ibid, 87.

In this area of practical theology he reaches beyond Kenyon. It is here that the ideas behind prosperity really start gaining momentum. While Kenyon laid claim to God pulling us out of poverty, Hagin saw that wealth was within the purview of our confessional rights as God's children. In his booklet *How God Taught Me about Prosperity*, Hagin recounted one of the Lord's conversations with him and wrote:

> He replied, "In the first place—and this will help you—don't pray about money anymore; that is, the way you've been praying. Claim whatever you need." I never had heard anybody say that about money. That came as a shock to me. I guess my mouth fell open and my eyes bugged out . . .
>
> People will argue, "Well, I can believe that God will meet our needs, but that's getting too far out when you start talking about wants!" That's just what I said to the Lord. "Now, Lord, I can believe that you want to meet our needs—but our wants?"
>
> He replied, "You claim to be a stickler for the Word. In the 23rd Psalm that you quote so many times, it says, 'The Lord is my shepherd; I shall not WANT' [v. 1]. "It says in the 34th Psalm, 'The young lions do lack, and suffer hunger: but they that seek the Lord shall not WANT any good thing' [v. 10].
>
> "Claim whatever you need or want. Say, 'Satan, take your hands off my finances.' Then say 'Go, ministering spirits, and cause the money to come.'"[25]

Hagin egregiously misrepresents the psalmist in utilizing these texts to go beyond necessities into the land of wishes. Psalm 23 is all about the comfort we get from knowing that God is our caretaker and will not leave us abandoned, but instead will lead us and provide for us. Provision and prosperity are not the same. Psalm 34:10 is an antithetical parallelism that shows that while young lions—representative of nature's strongest animals—go hungry at times, God is gracious in that he will not allow his people to endure that same struggle of hunger. Consider the ESV rendering of Psalm 34:10, which says, "The young lions suffer want and hunger; but those who seek the Lord lack no good thing." The intent of the Psalmist in both texts is not to promise wish fulfillment accessed by a faith that claims what one *wants*. Instead the Hebrew term for "lack" is the same

---

25. Hagin, *How God Taught Me about Prosperity*, 114–29.

one used in both Psalm 23:1 where the Psalmist declares, "The Lord is my shepherd; I shall not *want*" and in Psalm 34:10. The term is used to describe the fact that the wilderness generation had their provisions met (Deut. 2:7 and Neh. 9:21). The issue in these Psalms is sufficiency, not splendor. Hagin's misrepresentation of the text is typical of the prosperity teachers that would follow him, each committed to genie-ology, attempting to rub the lamp of God with the hand of faith to extract the genie of abundance.

## Oklahoma Seeds for a Texas-Sized Faith

I lived in Texas for six and a half years and knew the saying well: "Everything is bigger in Texas." In the panhandle you can stop in at a local Amarillo restaurant known as The Big Texan and try your mouth and stomach capacity on a steak that is seventy-two ounces. If you finish it and all the sides in under an hour, it is yours for free. If you tour the state you will see some of the largest privately-owned ranches in the world numbering well over 500,000 acres. You can take in a football game at AT&T stadium in Arlington, Texas and watch one of the largest jumbo screens in the world, measuring seventy-two feet high by one hundred sixty feet long. If you are looking for a place to worship you could go to three of the ten largest churches in America according to a 2012 study.[26] This list includes *the* largest church in America by far, Lakewood Church in Houston, pastored by prolific author Joel Osteen, that is made up of a congregation over 43,000 strong. I will come back to Osteen in a bit because of his influence and popularity but before getting to his more innocuous (but no less dangerous) message I must mention Hagin's contemporary in Oklahoma, Oral Roberts.

Roberts thematically paralleled Hagin. Both men eventually set up shop in the Tulsa, Oklahoma area. Hagin established his ministry there in 1967; Roberts founded Oral Roberts University there in 1963. Roberts came up through the Pentecostal Holiness tradition. He cut his teeth as an evangelist apprenticed to his father Ellis until he split from him as a young man in 1937. After experiencing relatively short pastoral stints in North Carolina, Georgia, and Oklahoma, he embarked on an evangelistic endeavor based on the ministry of healing in 1947. One of the key events that turned his world upside down occurred that year when he

---

26. "10 Largest Churches in America." Christculturenews.com.

flipped open his Bible at a time in life where he was filled with frustration, lamenting both his own fiscal challenges and his church's apathy—two things familiar to most local-church pastors. When he opened the text it landed on 3 John 2, which in the King James Version read: "I wish above all things that thou mayest prosper and be in health, even as thy soul prospereth." This opened up a new world to Roberts, who now concluded that God was good and wanted to directly bless people. His wife would later look on this event as the beginning of their worldwide ministry.[27]

Roberts's prosperity message developed throughout his ministry, beginning in the 1950s with his fundraising campaign idea known as the "Blessing Pact." In this agreement, supporters of the ministry would agree to send in their money and Roberts, for his part, would pray that their money would be miraculously returned to them, and if God did not provide their return from an unexpected source then the donor's money would be given back to them by the ministry.[28] His prosperity theme continued to develop and found its full flowering in the 1970s with the introduction of a theology of New Testament giving based on the idea of "seed-faith." This term became essential to the lexicon of Gourmet Jesus. "Seed-faith" was built on three New Testament principles that Roberts thought replaced the Old Testament concept of tithing. They functioned as spiritual laws that governed the way God relates to his creatures. First, God was the source of blessing. As Harrell notes:

> The promise meant that God would supply "abundantly" the "material" needs of his children, not just the "bare essentials of existence." There were no limits to the riches of God. More important, however, one depended not on man but on God to supply his needs.[29]

Second was a principle drawn from Luke 6:38, which in the KJV reads, "Give, and it shall be given unto you; good measure, pressed down, and shaken together, and running over, shall men give into your bosom. For with the same measure that ye mete withal it shall be measured to you again." In other words, give and it will be given back to you. Third, Oral instructed people to "expect a miracle." The oft-cited text of

---

27. Harrell, *Oral Roberts: An American Life*, 65–66. The account is set in the context of Robert's life challenges and emotional disposition at this crucial point in his life in 1947.
28. Ibid., 141–42.
29. Ibid., 461.

*gourmet jesus* 205

prosperity teachers found in Mark 11:24 is used as evidence for this principle: "Therefore I tell you, whatever you ask in prayer, believe that you have received it, and it will be yours." This third concept heightened the anticipation of the second principle. God would give back, but you don't know how or when, so live with expectation. This third principle forms one of the hooks of prosperity teachers, "Just hang on—your blessing is somewhere around the corner!" If you have the faith to hang on, you will reap, but the longer it takes to reap, the more your faith is called up—and so you have a dilemma: Do you stop expecting and lose the opportunity to reap, or do you continue to trust? The further down the rabbit hole you get, the harder it is to come out, because you have put too many chips on the table so you can't back out now. How insidious!

## Prosperity South of the Red River

In 1979 Oral Roberts was facing fiscal disaster, and his friend and fellow minister Kenneth Hagin came to his aid. At a camp meeting held annually by Hagin, Roberts was the recipient of one evening's offering. This surprise gift on this particular evening boosted Roberts's spirits but more important than the money were two friends sitting alongside Roberts: Kenneth Copeland and John Osteen.[30] The heart of the prosperity movement was moving south across the Red River, and its first stop was Fort Worth, TX.

Kenneth Copeland and his wife Gloria are indicative of the low-hanging fruit of those subscribing to Gourmet Jesus. The statements of overt modern-day prosperity teachers like them are at times so preposterous, so outlandish, that it seems implausible that otherwise rational people would be able to sit under their teaching. But the pull of personal prosperity, and the idea that the God of the universe just might have a desire that would mean a personal windfall, provokes an emotional intoxication that dulls our senses to truth, rendering us vulnerable to the love of money.

Gloria Copeland recounted her and her husband's early years together by noting the Oklahomans' influence on them:

> After we moved to Tulsa and Ken became a student at Oral Roberts University, we began hearing the Word of God from Oral Roberts and Kenneth E. Hagin. We learned that faith comes by

30. Ibid., 423–24.

hearing, believing and saying the Word. We learned this same faith made us overcomers.[31]

Hagin and Roberts's legacy of a faith formula that yielded personal prosperity was on full display in Copeland.

No one exemplifies the convergence of the two key ingredients in the recipe of Gourmet Jesus quite like Copeland. His commitment to carry forward a doctrine of positive confession is apparent. In a short pamphlet he wrote, he observed a canonical theme of the preeminent role of confession and its timeless role in the order of cosmic operations:

> Like it or not, this is a word-created, word-controlled universe. God established it that way from the very beginning. He made everything by calling "things which be not as though they were" (Romans 4:17). He set this whole system in motion by speaking into the darkness and saying, "Light be!" and light was (Genesis 1:3). The whole Bible, from Genesis to Revelation, makes it clear that we live under a word-activated system. It's always been that way and it always will be. We can, however, choose the words under which we live. We can change our environment by what we say.[32]

Notice what Copeland is saying. God creates everything by the power of his word, and in doing so, models for us how the system (read: "spiritual laws") operates. He concludes with an assumption that is bridged by a doctrinal commitment of his that is not obvious in the quote itself. He jumps from God's creative capacity to ours . . . but why does he feel the liberty to do so? What makes him think that we have the creative potency to "change our environment by what we say"? The answer is found in his commitment to an ontology of God and man that shrinks the distance between the two.

Two theological observations by Copeland assist him in shrinking the distance. First is his high view of man as expressed in his understanding of the creation of Adam. Copeland preached:

> Adam is as much like God as you could get—just the same as Jesus when He came into the earth. He [Jesus] said, "If you've seen Me, you've seen the Father." He wasn't a lot like God; He's God manifested in the flesh! And I want you to know something— Adam in the Garden of Eden was God manifested in the flesh! He

---

31. Copeland, "Seeing the Unseen."
32. Copeland, *How You Call It Is How It Will Be*, 23–41.

was God's very image, the very likeness. Everything he did, everything he said, every move he made was the very image of almighty God.... You see, Adam was walking as a god. Adam walked in the gods class. Adam did things in the gods class. Hallelujah.[33]

With man operating in a class of gods, he pointed his ideological shrinking ray at the ontology of God and man, pulled the trigger, and went even further than his predecessors. In truth there is a litany of statements Copeland has made that are just plain heretical along these lines. But putting his hyperbole aside, he is emblematic of a low theology of God and a high anthropology that had been on simmer for decades going back to Kenyon, Hagin, Roberts, and others.

The second observation that helps Copeland shrink the distance is his Christology. Part of the Word-Faith Christology that Copeland advances is that Jesus took on Satan's nature in becoming sin for us on the cross and so went to hell. Through this process he was "born again." It goes beyond my purpose to refute this view, and there are other works that I have already cited that do just that.[34] However, the fact that Copeland holds to this view establishes the ground for him to liken our capacities with Jesus' power. In the next chapter I will make clear that we do have power, but the manner in which Copeland and others see us entitled to it is wrong. It is wrong because the premise is that since Jesus was born again and since I can be too, then we can share the same potency. Copeland testifies:

> God spoke to me and he said "Son, realize this, now follow me in this, don't let your tradition trip you up." He said, "Now think this way, a twice-born man whipped Satan in his own domain."... I said, "What?" He said, "A born-again man defeated Satan, the firstborn of many brethren defeated him," he said. "You are the very image and the very copy of that one," and I said "Goodness gracious sakes."... I said "Well now you don't mean, you couldn't dare mean, that I could have done the same thing?" He said "Oh yeah, if you'd had the knowledge of the Word of God that he did you could've done the same thing, cause you're a reborn man too."[35]

Man's capacities mirror Jesus Christ's because of our ontological similarity as born-again persons. This low Christology and exalted anthropology

33. As cited in Bowman, *The Word-Faith Controversy*, 126.
34. Cf. McConnell, *A Different Gospel* and Bowman, *The Word-Faith Controversy*.
35. Thompson, *Word of Faith Teachers: Origins and Errors of Their Teaching*. Online documentary.

contribute yet another bullet point to Copeland's theses: that we can call things into being and co-opt the power of God because we have an absolute right to those powers.

It is important now to return to the notion of prosperity. Since Copeland shrinks the distance between God and man, and since he sees that minimization expressing itself in a human creative capacity via positive confession, it is natural for him to embrace personal prosperity as the manifestation of man's divine right. Following, probably unknowingly, in the tradition of his metaphysical forbears, Copeland draws parallels reminiscent of Mary Baker Eddy. In his book *Laws of Prosperity*, he draws upon natural scientific laws as an analogy for spiritual laws, one of which is the "Law of Prosperity." He states:

> We must understand that there are laws governing every single thing in existence. Nothing is by accident. There are laws of the world of the spirit and there are laws of the world of the natural... We need to realize that the spiritual world and its laws are more powerful than the physical world and its laws. Spiritual law gave birth to physical law. The world and the physical forces governing it were created by the power of faith—a spiritual force... Faith is a spiritual force, a spiritual energy, a spiritual power. It is this force of faith which makes the laws of the spirit world function. When the force of faith is put to work, these laws of the spirit function according to the way God says they will... There are certain laws governing prosperity revealed in God's word. Faith causes them to function. They will work when they are put to work, and they will stop working when the force of faith is stopped.[36]

By faith the world is at his fingertips. Copeland's commitment to prosperity has led to his own excessive lifestyle, including an 18,000-square-foot home in Texas and a personal top-of-the-line jet, along with a collection of other aircraft. Apparently this is all in the moral will of God, as he has exercised the spiritual law of prosperity. It seems appropriate to ask why there seems to be no sense of conflict for Copeland between his affluence and the abject poverty of the "fifty-four countries in sub-Saharan Africa"[37] that his organization states they minister to.

---

36. Copeland, *The Laws of Prosperity*. 121–36.

37. "About KCM," kcm.org. This must be an indication of data exaggeration since sub-Saharan Africa contains only fifty nations at present. Cf. "List of Sub-Saharan African Countries," loc.gov.

Sitting in that same row of seats at Hagin's camp meeting with Oral Roberts in 1979 was John Osteen. He was the pastor of a mega-church in Houston that he founded in the late 1950s. I remember watching him on television when I was a teenager as he preached from Lakewood Church, which was coined as the "Oasis of Love." Osteen obviously ran in the Word-Faith teaching circles and built a very successful and wide-reaching ministry of his own. But his greatest contribution to the legacy of the movement furthering a Gourmet Jesus was fathering his oldest son Joel. In January of 1999, John Osteen died of a heart attack and later that year his son Joel took over the ministry. In the last fourteen years, Lakewood church has grown to be the largest church in America, six to seven times larger than when Joel assumed the helm. They now meet in an arena that they own which was formerly home to the NBA's Houston Rockets. Osteen is widely regarded as the most influential and recognizable pastor in America. He has written bestselling self-help books, traveled the talk-show circuit, and been consulted by many media outlets. His high profile makes his theological perspective deeply important to the kind of Jesus that mainstream society sees the church holding forth.

We have seen the two ingredients in this recipe of Gourmet Jesus put on display to varying degrees in the theology of some of the key figures in the development of prosperity doctrine. While Osteen is not overt by any measure concerning God and man being ontologically similar, he is overt in his endorsement of positive confession. It seems clear to me, as I have demonstrated in this chapter, that the heart of positive confession is grounded on the idea of an insufficient sense of God being Wholly Other and completely distinct from man. I think this insufficient view of the transcendence of God is to blame for the self-help veneer that lies over the top of Osteen's statements and the entire thrust of his ministry. To the public he is seen as a self-help guru, encouraging the power of positive thinking and the importance of verbal confession as a means of moving life's mountains. In his recent book *I Declare: 31 Promises to Speak Over Your Life*, he counsels those facing challenges by stating:

> A lot of times we pray about mountains: God please help me. God, please make my child straighten up. God, please take away this fear. And yes, it's good to pray. It's good to ask God to help you. But when you face a mountain, it's not enough to pray. It's not enough to just believe. It's not enough to just think good thoughts. Here's the key: you have to speak to your mountains. Jesus said in Mark 11:23 (KJV): "Whoever will say to this

mountain, be removed, and does not doubt in his heart, he will have whatever he says."[38]

Talking to God is insufficient? We must talk to the mountains? He goes on to couch his call to "declare" with the proviso that you are doing it "in the authority of the Son of the Living God."[39] However, in the same chapter he says that "your mountain will respond only to your voice."[40] Does our "mountain" have a mental center with which to respond to our rebukes? This seems to devolve into nonsense.

Osteen clearly falls in line with the old guard of Hagin, Roberts, and his father when it comes to the role of positive confession:

> Get in agreement with God. Say what He says about you. Speaking His words is one of the most powerful things you can do. Remember, it's not enough to think it. It's not enough to believe it. Give life to your faith. Speak it out. Once you make a habit of declaring favor and speaking faith-filled words, you will see negative situations turn around.[41]

"Negative things will turn around." Here is the self-help speak, the Oprah-like veneer, Chopra with a glaze of faith, glossing old-school Word-Faith theology. But let's face it, he speaks to today's cultural niche that brings together the therapeutic egoism of postmodernity and the modernistic drive to achieve the "American Dream." In this sense his message stands between two worlds and pulls them both together with a privatized, divinely-permitted materialism and a positive religious outlook. As religion scholar Stephen Prothero observes, "The tragedy is that Christianity has become a yes-man for the culture."[42] And it is this, more than anything else, which strikes at the heart of my present concern. At some point the church has to take a firm stand against this self-help religion that Osteen and others[43] are polluting our already materialistically

---

38. Osteen, *I Declare: 31 Promises to Speak Over Your Life*, 161.
39. Ibid., 163.
40. Ibid., 165.
41. Osteen, *It's Your Time*, 128.
42. Biema and Chu, "Does God Want You to be Rich?," Time.com.
43. I want to note that, in addition to Osteen, Joyce Meyer deserves much attention in regard to the doctrine of positive confession. I would encourage the reader to note her book *Change Your Words, Change Your Life*. She speaks about things coming into reality with what amounts to an unwitting Platonic metaphysic. I would point the reader specifically to her statements and line of argument in chapter 5 entitled "What Do You Want in the Future?"

infected streams with. I hope to help us do that in the next chapter. But before we leave this assessment behind, there are two other brief observations that I need to make.

## A Gourmet Export

Unfortunately, America is exporting a toxic substance in this Gourmet Jesus to the rest of the world. We exist as the most prosperous nation in the history of the world with an insatiable urge for more. Our national debt sits at an incomprehensible sixteen trillion dollars and it is evident that our lust for more has not made us better stewards. On this issue, large pockets of the American church have been little help as we export a theologically buttressed greed.

The prosperity gospel creates a theological penumbra of sorts, as the light of the gospel that could be put on display from the West to the rest of the world is obfuscated by consumerism, materialism, and their companion vice, good old-fashioned greed. In a concise discussion of prosperity theology and the fertile ground it has found in the third world, Philip Jenkins makes the following observation of prosperity teachers:

> At its worst, the gospel of prosperity permits corrupt clergy to get away with virtually anything. Not only can they coerce the faithful to pay their obligations through a kind of spiritual terrorism, but the belief system allows them to excuse malpractice. If the pastor drives a limousine, this is only just recompense for his outstanding faith. And critics must either be lacking in faith, or else they serve as agents of evil.[44]

Jenkins's observations about the global South and its third-world poverty are insightful. In a balanced manner, he also acknowledges that aspects of the prosperity gospel shun debt and advocate fiscal responsibility, and these certainly are good ideas to import into the second and third worlds; however, the theological damage done alongside these ideas seems to me like giving away bags of grain with grenades inside.

What we find in these areas of deprivation is that a pragmatic of need and an existential longing for hope have produced fertile ground for prosperity theology. Of course this creates a sense of repulsion when we observe those at the top of the food chain in these third-world

---

44. Jenkins, *The New Faces of Christianity: Believing the Bible in the Global South*, 92–93.

cultures espousing doctrines of greed. However, it is easy to understand the propensity for the masses to embrace such hope in the shadow of such pervasive squalor. In my mind, this makes the prosperity theology in North America all the more repulsive. We live in a nation that has eight states, according to a compilation of statistics from 2011, that all have a gross domestic product greater than any country in Africa.[45] As Jenkins rightly notes, "The average Christian in the world today is a poor person, very poor indeed by the standards of the white worlds of North America and Western Europe."[46] So one of the theological products that North America has been exporting preys upon many whose only hope is hope itself. And when that hope comes in the form of a God who blesses with money and goods, it is a pretty easy (and diabolical) sell to physically desperate people.

## Conclusion

The seeds of Gourmet Jesus began developing all the way back in the Christian gnostic tradition. The dualism established there set the table for those within and those without orthodoxy in the mid- to late nineteenth century to begin rethinking theology and metaphysics in a manner that carried forward key dualistic presuppositions. The role of faith within the church and the role of positive thinking in divine metaphysics both took on certain characteristics of this early dualism. As thought progressed through the philosophical and theological innovation for the late nineteenth and early twentieth centuries, American pentecostalism ended up becoming enchanted with a theology birthed from the seeds of both the Higher Life movement within orthodoxy and the New Thought (divine metaphysical) movement on the fringe of the church (and in some sense completely outside of it).

This new found Word-Faith theology formed the base for the stew of prosperity theology. Two of the main ingredients that flavored this soup were the minimization of distinctions between God and man and the

---

45. Compare statistical analysis on the gross domestic product of individual US states from the data found at the Bureau of Economic Analysis, "Widespread Growth Across States in 2011," http://www.bea.gov/newsreleases/regional/gdp_state/2012/pdf/gsp0612.pdf and data found on the GDP of nations at International Monetary Fund, "World Economic Outlook," imf.org.

46. Jenkins, *The New Faces of Christianity: Believing the Bible in the Global South*, 68.

formation of the dogma of positive confession. It has been my contention that the former ontological error fed the emergence of the practical missteps of positive confession. In our present context, prosperity theology has taken the modernized notion of mechanistic spirituality and combined that with the postmodern egoism of the self-help industry, and has tragically opted to export it to the world. My hope is two-fold. First, that as the church of a homeless savior, we can somehow reject the materialism of the American Dream and find our fulfillment in a kingdom life that is concerned with righteousness, peace, and joy in the Holy Spirit. And second, that our commitment to the Word of God will keep us from manipulating it to sanctify our carnal urges to find our "Best Life Now."

8

## Feasting on the Rations of a Simple Savior

*What prosperity theology has forgotten is that God does not exist to make us happy. Our righteous God has no truck with the rising tide of appetite that brooks no restraint nor with our increasing unwillingness to defer gratification.*

DAVID LARSEN

*Listen, my beloved brothers, has not God chosen those who are poor in the world to be rich in faith and heirs of the kingdom, which he has promised to those who love him?*

JAMES 2:5

WHO KNEW THAT MAYTAG made more than just large household appliances? The Maytag family, now several generations removed from their roots in the appliance industry, has also been a player in the high-end bleu cheese market. Who would have known? I would never have suspected that the same company responsible for making sure my underwear gets washed would also be a gourmet bleu cheese maker.

Similarly, all I ever knew about Michelin is that they made good tires. In fact, a while back I got a pair of experimental Michelins that worked fantastically on our Subaru. But who would have thought that the world's most coveted award for culinary prowess was doled out by a tire company? That's right . . . a tire company! There's not exactly an organic connection between tire shops and auto mechanics and the world's finest culinary arts. But the most coveted recognition by restaurateurs around the world is to receive one of the Michelin Stars. A three-star rating from Michelin's food critics is given only to a select few eateries on an annual basis. But the notoriety is more than just a feather in the cap. It is an important career-defining award. The world-renowned chef and television personality Gordon Ramsay, known for his bombastic antics in the kitchen, holds fourteen stars at present.

Being gourmet brings with it popularity and a following. There are reasons people pay lots of money for small food quantities to eat in austere atmospheres. And unfortunately, there are reasons Joel Osteen has sold millions of books, has over 43,000 people attending his church, and a television ministry that reaches millions of viewers. There are reasons that his book, *Your Best Life Now*, has spawned at least seven other books from a study guide to a journal to a devotional book to one geared toward moms. There are reasons why people continue to give thousands and thousands of dollars to Kenneth Copeland Ministries as he boasts about its receipts since its inception totaling 1.3 billion dollars (incidentally that was in 2008), all the while living in excess. There are reasons why flamboyant televangelist Robert Tilton can be publicly exposed by reputable news agencies, but still receive dollar upon dollar in annual donations today, some twenty-plus years since he was exposed. There are reasons why Christians live by financial slogans like, "Live like no one else so you can live like no one else," and call it stewardship instead of promissory greed.

The question is: What are the reasons? I think there are a few, and I think these ought to be addressed for the local church to be able to keep Jesus and his gospel from being intentionally and often unintentionally manipulated. The first parable of Jesus that Mark—the first evangelist—records, was told to a crowd on the north shore of the Sea of Galilee in the town of Capernaum. His parable sets the tone for the rest of his ministry. Jesus was God incarnate, and he gave his life to satisfy God's righteous wrath, enabling people to enter life under God's rule in his kingdom. As he went about sharing the good news of the kingdom, he talked in parables and used word pictures to teach pithy lessons as a rabbinic figure. The first parable he told was about seed sown on four different types of soil. The first three sets of seed thrown onto three different soils failed to come to fruition for particular reasons. Only the fourth soil permitted the seed to flower out its full capacity and become productive grain. For the purpose of this chapter, I am concerned with the third set of seed and where it landed. This is what Jesus said about it. "Other seed fell among thorns, and the thorns grew up and choked it, and it yielded no grain" (Mark 4:7). According to Jesus' description, it looks like the seed found some promising ground, but the environment wasn't conducive to its development because there were thorns growing along with it which prevented it from flourishing.

Later, when Jesus was alone with the disciples, he explained the spiritual relevance of the parable of the seeds and soils. He unpacked the meaning of the third set of seed landing among the thorns by saying, "And others are the ones sown among thorns. They are those who hear the word, but the cares of the world and the deceitfulness of riches and the desires for other things enter in and choke the word, and it proves unfruitful" (Mark 4:18–19). Interestingly, Mark gives voice to Jesus identifying three items that "enter in and choke the word" that has been sown. Matthew only recounts two items, and Luke, while lacking Mark's explanatory phrases and verbiage, thematically mirrors Mark's three items.[1]

Jesus identifies the thorns first as anxiety over the age in which they live. The term is translated "world" by the ESV, but it is not the Greek term "cosmos" that is used here, but instead it is the word "aionos." It is from this term's root word that we get our English term "aeon." Jesus is telling the disciples that if their ideas and values are consumed with those of their present cultural zeitgeist, they will lose sight of what God's Word could be doing to make their worldview resemble his kingdom.

Second, Jesus sees the intoxicating deception induced by abundance as a threat to the implanted Word. The term used for "riches" here is a term that speaks of wealth and abundance. It is used repeatedly in the New Testament to speak of the riches of God's character.[2] Perhaps the most insightful use of the term relating to Jesus' use of it in Mark is found in 1 Timothy 6:17, which reads, "As for the *rich* in this present age, charge them not to be haughty, nor to set their hopes on the uncertainty of *riches*, but on God, who *richly* provides us with everything to enjoy." Here Paul actually uses three words related to the same root referring to riches. Certainly God does provide "us with everything to enjoy." I am

---

1. "As for what was sown among thorns, this is the one who hears the word, but the cares of the world and the deceitfulness of riches choke the word, and it proves unfruitful" (Matt. 13:22); "And as for what fell among the thorns, they are those who hear, but as they go on their way they are choked by the cares and riches and pleasures of life, and their fruit does not mature." (Luke 8:14).

2. Rom. 2:4; 9:23; 11:33; Eph. 1:7; 2:7; 3:16.

not trying to replace Gourmet Jesus with an ascetic Jesus. However, the error of prosperity theology is highlighted by this verse because it moves people to "set their hopes on the uncertainty of riches." This is precisely what Jesus warns his disciples about. Wealth can too easily and too often become a distraction from the Word of God.

The final description of the thorns is rather general. This is where Mark goes beyond Matthew. He notes Jesus' warning about the "desires for other things." Individual commitments to Christ regularly get sacrificed on the altar of relationships that people want more than God and on the altar of recreation, which tends to be more exhilarating than the study of the Word and the life of prayer. Today the spiritual disciplines seem little match for RVs, ATVs, MTV, and sitting around all hours of the day playing video games in our BVDs. Desire is at the heart of discipleship. It is the engine that makes it go. But when desire gets misdirected, it is destined to produce destruction. C. S. Lewis had a famous statement, "The great (and toothsome) sinners are made out of the very same material as those horrible phenomena, the great Saints."[3] We are creatures of desire, plain and simple, and the story of our lives is told, in one sense, by which desires win out.

Jesus identified those thorns that keep the plant from being fruitful. Those thorns contribute to the reasons why prosperity teachers garner such a following regardless of whether they are overt and intentional or subtle and unwitting. In the rest of the chapter, I would like to highlight several ideas that the church needs to get right in its discipleship of people if we are to forfeit capitulating to the intoxications of Gourmet Jesus. How do we keep from getting choked by the thorns?

## The Heart of God

We must return to an accurate vision of the heart of God. The reason Gourmet Jesus is so deeply flawed is that he misses the heart of God. If God's heart is misidentified, then with good hearts we can be pursuing the wrong passions and feel entirely righteous. This sets us up for serious destruction.

My real concern for the church is less on the flamboyant professors of the Christ of prosperity, and more on the subtle Jesus of self-help prosperity who woos us to himself because he sets before us felt

3. Lewis, *The Screwtape Letters*, 193.

happiness through a life of emotional and economic ease. There is a reason I termed the Kenneth Copelands of the world the "low-hanging fruit" of prosperity doctrine. Most readers of this book will not have to be convinced that something seems a bit catawampus about these swindlers of the gospel. However, when it comes to more subtle forms of prosperity and when those forms presuppose certain passions at the center of God's heart, then the issue gets complicated. Life is difficult, and the more mileage we put on the more we realize just how true that is. It is tempting for us to cast God in the vein of a warm-hearted, philanthropic uncle whose focus is our felt happiness (one might even say our "Best Life Now") rather than a virtuous parent whose goal is characterological maturity in his or her children.

This faulty presupposition about God's goal for humanity seems to drive Joel Osteen's theology in particular. In one of his books, Osteen illustrates his "Best Life Now" operating principle by telling the story of when he was pulled over by the police and his wife Victoria's long-lost ring was found in the glove compartment as she searched for the car-insurance card. He then goes on to explain that the officer who pulled him over did not ticket him even though he was caught going ten miles over the speed limit. As he recalled the incident he reflected, "I drove off that night thinking: God, You are so good. I didn't get a ticket and Victoria found her ring."[4] The goodness of God is confirmed by finding a ring and avoiding a ticket. How does one even get his mind around how trivial and anecdotal the grace of God becomes in the slough of self-help sovereignty formed by prosperity teachers? Just a few pages later he goes on to proclaim:

> God promises your payday is on its way. If you'll learn to be a prisoner of hope and get up everyday expecting God's favor, You'll see God do amazing things. You'll overcome every obstacle. You'll defeat every enemy. And I believe and declare you'll see every dream, every promise God has put in your heart, come to pass.[5]

Talk about genie-ology!

Osteen, like other prosperity teachers, creates such an anthropocentric starting point that God's glory and our growth get put on the shelf. They have what Bob Sjogren calls a cat theology rather than a dog

---

4. Osteen, *It's Your Time*, 13.
5. Ibid., 16.

theology. A cat thinks that its master lives for him and a dog thinks he lives for his master. This anthropocentric me-ology colors the prosperity meta-narrative: things that don't feel good are typically from the devil, and things that make us feel good about ourselves are from God. And to this all Job's children said "Amen!" . . . oh wait a second—they died as an object lesson for Job. I mean, all the Israelites in Egypt said "Amen!" . . . oh wait—they actually pined away in slavery for four hundred years and died. Hosea the prophet shouted "Glory, hallelujah!" . . . but his wife's infidelity raged on, fulfilling God's purposes for his prophet and his people. And Stephen the faithful witness sang "Kumbaya," but was pelted with stones as he tirelessly proclaimed the good news and his body lay dead in the dirty Jerusalem street.

It must be nice writing books and telling people weekly stories about God that don't account for innumerable stories throughout the ages of life under God's sovereign care and in God's sovereign will. How does Osteen know that God wants to bring each of his readers through? How does he know that their "tough time" is not, in itself, an affliction from God? How does he know that God wants to give them even more than they had before? And why would more necessarily be better? It seems like faulty presuppositions about God and man abound in his worldview.

Reading Osteen makes me feel like I am watching *Blue's Clues* with my children. My oldest daughter loved the show when she was a kid. The host, along with his animated friends, would sing a catchy song that went something like *"You can be anything that you want to be, you can do anything that you want to do."* Once our egos have been stroked and our potential has been painted as basically limitless, we are now set free to leap and dance. Who doesn't want to believe this? But who really does? Isn't it interesting when the materially and professionally successful imply that all of us could be just like them if we could simply grab the same "keys" or abide by the same "spiritual laws" that they did? I wonder if they used those keys, or just thought up seven cool things that could sell a book that would make them even more materially and professionally successful.

The problem isn't that people like Osteen want others to succeed. It isn't even that they have rightly identified that a poor self-image is a detriment to personal development. It's that they believe God is the one who has made life such that everyone has the seeds of greatness if they only realize it, and God is in his heaven wanting you to be as prosperous in the western sense of prosperity as possible if you can only get your act together. It is this presupposition about God that is the main (but not the only) problem.

So what is the elixir to these diseased presuppositions about the heart of God? First, *the local church must never leave behind the role of the gospel in sanctification.* For too long we have seen the gospel as primarily good news about our justification, but surely it is more. The gospel that justifies is the gospel that sanctifies.

I once jokingly called a class of students at a Bible school that I regularly teach at a bunch of "sinners." One of the students objected to the fact that I would label them as sinners because the New Testament called them saints. I think he was concerned, as are many, that our starting point for our actions is the identity that we have as believers. Certainly Paul argued this way in Romans 6:1–14. However, I think his correction missed something important. Yes, of course, as a believer I am a "saint." I have been set apart or sanctified in my position before God. However, I am not *only* a saint, nor am I *entirely* a saint. Rather, I am a sinner who, as the Greek of Romans 3:23 points out, "continually falls short of the glory of God," and who, as the next verse (again in the Greek) declares, is "continually being justified freely by his grace." So I carry a joint identity. I am a saint who sins, or if you like, a sinner who is a saint. In this sense I am not *only* a saint. Additionally, I am still being set apart for God's glory. Theologically we identify this as the idea of "progressive sanctification." It's the fancy way of saying I am growing to look more like Jesus, or I am being set apart more to God, or (for the sake of this discussion) I am becoming more "saintly." In this sense I am not yet *entirely* a saint.

This dual identity is more than a piece of perceptual minutiae. It is crucial to understanding and living out the heart of God for my life. If I see my identity as solely a "saint" then it makes sense that I will tend to emphasize the benefits that come with my position (and certainly there are many). This has its own merit, but it misses another key part of my identity, namely that I am a sinner. Because I am a sinner, I never outgrow a childlike dependence on Jesus as my Savior. What are the ramifications of this?

Theologically speaking, I am a child of God, and I remain so because the blood of Jesus speaks an eternal message about my identity as a son:

> But when the fullness of time had come, God sent forth his Son, born of woman, born under the law, to redeem those who were under the law, so that we might receive adoption as sons. And because you are sons, God has sent the Spirit of his Son into our hearts, crying, "Abba! Father!" So you are no longer a slave, but a son, and if a son, then an heir through God. (Gal. 4:4–7)

Personally speaking, I will continue to fail and need to be reminded that my identity is rooted in the fact that, in Jesus, God still loves sons who presently sin. So I don't demand rights because of my sonship; instead, I am called to receive whatever my Father sees fit to bestow upon this "less-than-perfect" me, whether it be a blessing or a burden:

> My son, do not despise the LORD's discipline or be weary of his reproof, for the LORD reproves him whom he loves, as a father the son in whom he delights. (Prov. 3:11–12)

Corporately speaking, the gospel establishes the only basic ground I have to love others with any personal security. I can rehearse the process of receiving another's brokenness and blessing them in return because my Father received me that way. Thus it enables me to reach out beyond myself and not worry about what is in it for me:

> Having purified your souls by your obedience to the truth for a sincere brotherly love, love one another earnestly from a pure heart, since you have been born again, not of perishable seed but of imperishable, through the living and abiding word of God. (1 Pet. 1:22–23)

> Beloved, if God so loved us, we also ought to love one another. No one has ever seen God; if we love one another, God abides in us and his love is perfected in us. (1 John 4:11–12)

Missionally speaking, it compels me to seek another's prosperity at my own expense. The gospel does more than set a sacrificial example for me to follow. It actually renovates my life so that I have the capacity to sacrifice for another's good:

> By this we know love: that he laid down his life for us, and we ought to lay down our lives for the brothers. But if anyone has the world's goods and sees his brother in need, yet closes his heart against him, how does God's love abide in him? Little children, let us not love in word or talk but in deed and in truth. (1 John 3:16–18)

The gospel is for sinners and, while it re-creates us, we never outrun our need for it. The way prosperity teachers speak about our spiritual rights and our ability to command God seems to beg the question whether or not our desperate need for the sanctifying gospel is thought much about.

Second, *the local church is a place for dogs.* Our dog is a pug. Pugs were bred to sit on the laps of Chinese emperors. They later became the choice dogs of Tibetan monks. The breed loves to snuggle up to humans. Aside from the fact that every time our pug breathes it sounds like she is dying, her most definitive characteristic is her desire to snuggle. Pugs will remain cuddled up to humans—silently motionless—for hours. Our dog's name is Pixie—such a name emerges in a house with a Disney-intoxicated wife and three girls following suit with mom. But, Pixie lives for *me*. It is made clear by the way she greets me, plays with me, waits for me, comes to me, and sits with me. It is her nature to be this way.

Perhaps the doctrine of what is at the heart of God can be reclaimed by reordering our life to a canine theology that puts us at the master's feet and recalibrates our passions to his desires. In reading Kenyon, Hagin, Copeland, et al., it becomes easy to get drawn in to their God-on-a-leash dogma. We are creatures that naturally glide to felt comfort. This bent becomes a significant issue when it begins to drive the things we seek for our lives from God. When this overtakes us we can be said to have bought into a cat theology. Cats relate to their owners in the opposite manner that dogs do. While a dog lives for her master, a cat thinks that his master lives for him. Dogs meet their owners at the door; cats remain on the couch. Dogs come when you call them, and cats typically stare at their owners and meander where they please. Dogs follow their owners around the house but cats seem to hardly know their owners are alive. Bob Sjogren and Gerald Robinson have written extensively on the analogy of dog/owner relationships and cat/owner relationships as compared to the way that believers relate to God. Sjogren summarizes the distinctions concisely, saying, "Cats think God is a means to an end. Dogs think God is the end."[6] This distinction is huge and impacts every facet of the spiritual life. Particularly poignant to countering prosperity theology are Sjogren's observations about the distinctions between cat and dog prayers. He states:

> Cats are basically saying, "Dear Lord, we come boldly before You and ask You to help us build our kingdom." Cats pray for the things they desire, the things that will make life more comfortable and easy. It sounds like, "Father, please give me . . . , please let me . . . , please bring me. . . ."

---

6. Sjogren and Robinson, *Cat and Dog Theology*, 477.

Dogs boldly come before God as well, but they say, "Lord, we're here with great faith because we need things from You to help advance Your kingdom. We want to make You famous. We know You will answer our prayers."[7]

Cats are concerned with their personal comfort and their machinations; dogs are concerned with their personal character and God's mission.

This leads into a third panacea for the anthropocentric infection produced by prosperity theology's faulty presuppositions about God's heart. *The penultimate of kingdom life is not comfort but character.* I think it is actually true to state that the adherents of Gourmet Jesus actually smuggle in personal comfort as the ultimate in place of even the glory of God. Yet when pressed, I am confident that they would give at least verbal assent to the idea that the glory of God is the ultimate end of man. However, I absolutely am convinced that they see the blessing of God on human life as the penultimate end of all things, and they describe that blessing in terms of personal felt goodness. To say something is "penultimate" is to say that it is next to the end.

John Piper modified the classic Westminster Shorter Catechism's statement that "the chief end of man is to glorify God and enjoy him forever" by switching the "and" to a "by." The significance of this is crucial because it shows that the glory of God and the joy of man are not two separate goals but, when properly understood, they are two sides of the same mountain that converge at the peak. Piper recognized that the framers of the catechism understood this, and that was why they stated that the chief "end"—not "ends"—of man is to glorify God and enjoy him forever. Or as Piper rewords it, "The chief end of man is to glorify God by enjoying Him forever."[8] But we need to ask what it looks like to enjoy him forever.

It seems apparent to me that to enjoy God is to enter into the narrative he is creating with a willing desire to participate in it for his purposes. In this sense it is akin to how I enjoy my wife in our marriage. I enter into the shared space of our union and live with her through blessing and cursing, healing and hardship, love and loss. The events don't define the entire story, but instead the direction and sacredness of the story capture the fantastic and frustrating inexplicabilities of the events. In a smaller way, my marriage forms a narrative that I participate in. Of course, the

---

7. Ibid., 374.
8. Piper, *Desiring God*, 18.

major distinction is that in God's kingdom he is the exclusive storyteller. Another way to express the same thing is to say that we are called to live in his kingdom under his reign in honor of him as the ruler. We must recall that this is indeed a kingdom of "righteousness and peace and joy in the Holy Spirit" (Rom. 14:17b). That same Holy Spirit has drenched us in God's love so that we can "rejoice in our sufferings, knowing that suffering produces endurance, and endurance produces *character*, and *character* produces hope" (Rom. 5:3–4; emphasis added). This means that if God afflicts us so our character grows, then it is his mercy to us and, in this way, some sounds of pain may well be notes in the music of the kingdom. But in Word-Faith theology, *felt good* is from God, but challenges and difficulties are tripwires on the devil's highway. But God's sovereign tools of discipline, hardship, trials, and even tragedy are lost somewhere between being nonessential and nonexistent in the doctrines of those worshiping Gourmet Jesus.

I want to put a bow on this is package of counteracting prosperity theology's faulty notions of what lies at the heart of God's heart with a few practical injunctions for church leaders:

1. The gospel must be preached beyond altar calls and traditional evangelistic appeals. It must be employed as a rehearsed concept for ongoing discipleship. It is to form the basis of not only public appeals to our relationship with God but also sermonic appeals to our relationships with each other in the local body.

2. Our preferences for styles, programs, fundraising, personal development, and personnel development must be subjected to the ultimate goals of ecclesiological mission. That is to say, what God wants where he places us and how he wants us to do it are more important that what we may deem as the most comfortable goals, locations, and methods.

3. It is the job of the local church to disciple, counsel, and shepherd people through life's challenges by telling them how their difficulties find meaning in the grand narrative of God.

## A Theology of Stuff

One of the most understated areas of theological inquiry is that of possessions. Perhaps no area so ignored by theologians has more bearing on the state of our present spiritual crisis. Recently there has been a glut of practical pieces written on what to do with our stuff, how to reprioritize our lives, and how we should reallocate our assets for the sake of God's kingdom.[9] These books have been challenging to the church and very helpful, making us think about our things and exposing just how far off track our materialistic tendencies have taken us. In fact, a good study of one of these books might help us deal with the recalcitrant materialism in our lives.

But I would like to take a step beyond these volumes (or maybe before them) and make my way back to the practical, through the more abstract theological concepts about possessions that are too often ignored. Three facts about the nature and purpose of possessions must be presented.

First, *an abundance of possessions is not a clear indication of God's blessing.* In the Bible, key figures endured relative impoverishment while they clearly had God's blessing. Moses, leading the people out of Egypt, needed to depend upon a daily ration of food miraculously appearing. Elijah needed ravens to come feed him as he hunkered down in fear and depression. David needed to eat bread from the altar to sustain him and his men as he fled from Saul. Jesus made his home in a house apparently owned by Peter in Capernaum, and he even testified that "Foxes have holes and birds of the air have nests, but the son of man has nowhere to lay his head" (Luke 9:58). Paul traveled itinerantly and eked out a living by receiving support from, at the very least, the Philippian church and by tentmaking where and when appropriate. In each of these instances, these men were serving the Lord and under his hand of blessing, but that hand did not manifest itself in abundance.

Even in the Old Testament this idea of the "blessed life," as emphasized by prosperity teachers, is misunderstood. Certainly physical and financial prosperity were included at times in the blessing of God, but they did not sum up his blessing nor were they necessary to it. Biblical scholar and moderate charismatic Gordon Fee touches on these Old Testament blessing and prosperity texts:

But what is often overlooked in such texts is that they are invariably tied to the concepts of God's righteousness and justice. It is only as one is righteous—i.e., walks in accordance with God's Law—that one is promised the blessing of abundance and family. But to be righteous

---

9. Francis Chan, *Crazy Love*; Richard Stearns, *The Hole in Our Gospel*; David Platt, *Radical*.

meant especially that one cared for or pleaded the cause of the poor and the oppressed.

Such a concern is so thoroughgoing in the Old Testament that it is found in its every strata and expression: Law, Narrative, Poetry, Wisdom, Prophet.[10]

The blessing of God is tied to virtue and obedience, not to rights. Additionally, this blessed life demands attention to the very thing that the prosperity gospel tends to ignore: the plight of the poor.

In the New Testament, the economy of the blessed life is put on its head in one sense. The way Jesus talks about things, it is the rich that need to worry, but the poor who will find God at their elbow assisting them. The kingdom of God is offered to poor people in the Sermon on the Mount. They can be blessed in their poverty. The rich need to look out because their wealth is seen by Jesus as a distraction from being able to focus on the more weighty matters of the kingdom. They get consumed with greed (cf. Luke 12:13–21) and with comfort (cf. Luke 6:24). They are exhorted to get rid of this material distraction lest they forfeit their soul by it (cf. Matt. 19:16–30). Thus in the New Testament, possessions are seen as more of a bane than a boon.

Of course, the Bible does tell us that "Every good gift and every perfect gift is from above, coming down from the Father of lights with whom there is no variation or shadow due to change" (Jas. 1:17). But to load those gifts with material pleasures and money pouches is to specify beyond the text and to miss the sense of what blessing in the kingdom life primarily entails.

Second, *possessions tell a compelling narrative about the identity of the possessor.* What we have or do not have does not have the authority to dictate our self-worth. "The rich and the poor meet together; the Lord is the maker of them all" (Prov. 22:2). Our worth is a concept bound up in the event of the eternal Son sacrificing himself on our behalf. It is declared by the creative and redemptive words of the Word. What we have by way of possessions tell little about our identity, despite almost every attempt of modern marketing to infiltrate our self-perception and create dissatisfaction. However, what we do with possessions and how we feel about them actually tell quite a bit about who we really are.

Inanimate objects take on the powers of life and death in the hands of animated persons. A knife is just a knife. It can cut vegetables to

---

10. Fee, *The Disease of the Health and Wealth Gospels*, 517.

provide dinner for homeless immigrants, or it can be used to take the life of those same people. It all depends how a person as a possessor relates to it as a possession. This connection is at the heart of developing a practical theology of possessions. How I use what I have says something about who I see myself to be in God's world. Money, like a knife, can be used to hurt or to heal. It can be used to give hope or to spew hatred.

The best theological treatment of possessions comes from the pen of Luke Timothy Johnson. It is now in its second edition and should be required reading for anyone concerned with the philosophical and theological nature of possessions—which should be anyone leading a local church. Johnson builds a theology of possessions by establishing that our life is a gift and not something we possess. In that sense we can say "we are alive," not "we have a life." He clearly demonstrates that the misuse of possessions leads to idolatry as its fundamental error. He also shows the significance of possessions as opportunities to impact the world. Perhaps the statement that best summarizes his thought comes in the middle of the book, where he states:

> Possessions are not good or evil in themselves; they derive significance from the way they extend our bodies in the world and thereby symbolize and affect our response to reality. There is a very close connection, therefore, between self-disposition and the disposition of possessions.[11]

In other words, we say a lot about ourselves by the way we handle our stuff. Possessions are not just tools removed from our identity. They say something about that which lies at the core of our being. In many ways, the "real us" comes out in how we view possessions and how we hold possessions.

The personal value that possessions have is an important area of introspection for each of us. In an effort to guide our thinking about our assets, Johnson introduces the valuable term "eschatological detachment." He does so as he reflects on Paul's only use of the term for possessions, found in 1 Corinthians 13:3:

> ... there he is contrasting some heroic donation of possessions to genuine love: "If I give away all that I have, and if I deliver my body to be burned, but have not love, I gain nothing." A more distinctively Pauline touch is found in 1 Corinthians 7:30–31, where Paul says that one of the consequences of living in a

---

11. Johnson, *Sharing Possessions*, 73.

period of eschatological tension is that "those who buy [should act] as though they had no goods, and those who deal with the world as though they had no dealings with it. For the form of this world is passing away." The point of this, of course, is not that Christians are to stop buying or selling, but that in doing so they should not allow the measure of this world to be their measure; they should have an *eschatological detachment*. Paul does not encourage his churches to withdraw from society and form closed, intentional communities. The Christian church is not an alternative social structure, but a way of living in freedom within the world.[12]

The future hope of God's kingdom fully consummated should stir us to resist the allure of temporal treasure. We should find a detachment from the world because we have a robust eschatological hope. Paul once told the Colossians that the mystery he was called to unveil was Christ in them, which was "the hope of glory." That hope is intended to shape our present ties to this world. Christ's presence in our lives is to be a regular reminder of the victory of God that gave us eternal life, which officially severed our reliance for our identity and our destiny on anything this corruptible sphere has to offer.

Third, *possessions are a vital currency in the ethic of God's kingdom*. It is plain old greed that wars against the use of this currency. We are, at bottom, a greedy culture. Our problem isn't capitalism as an economic philosophy, our problem isn't socialism per se despite its failings, our problem isn't big business, it isn't "the 1 percent," or the 99 percent, for that matter. Our problem is the human heart. The human heart recoils at the thought of deferred gratification and it finds ways to sanctify the most carnal urges imaginable. As a pastor, I have been stunned to hear people tell me that they have prayed about leaving their spouse and have peace about it. They have prayed about leaving a perfectly good local fellowship and are convinced that God is in it. We will put divine frosting over the most miserable cakes of self-indulgence. I am convinced that this is what some (not all) in the prosperity camp have done. Greed has a new name: "blessing." Self-indulgence has been consecrated as "claiming a promise." Opulence is now "the favor of God." But no matter how many semantic gymnastic moves people attempt, the heart behind it all remains. You can claim all the promises you want, but if your illocution is encumbered by greed, it is repulsive to God.

12. Ibid., 100.

How should possessions be used in the kingdom of God? The short answer is that we should use them as direct vehicles of blessing. I use the term "direct" because we cannot let greed sneak its way into a trumped-up narrative of blessing others. Benny Hinn and Kenneth Copeland might argue that their private jets keep them rested in travel so they can be an even greater blessing to others. But this is special pleading. Such creative excuses for affluence ought to be rejected as a *prima facie* absurdity. Instead, possessions should be used to enhance the opportunity for people to see the glory of God in the face of Christ. They should be used to eliminate distractions by providing necessary food, clothing, shelter, and education, rather than used as distractions by eliciting a lust for more.

When the apostle Paul went before the Jerusalem counsel at the outset of his missionary journeys, they only required one thing of him: that he care for the poor (cf. Gal. 2:10). They could have asked anything of him, but the heart of the mother church in Jerusalem was that the poor be cared for both because of the intrinsic worth of humanity, and because the proclamation of the gospel did not need the distraction commensurate with physical deprivation. In this sense, utilizing resources for the sake of others fits with both common grace and special grace.

Practically speaking, at the level of the local church we need to teach a clear theology of possessions. We need to show people from the text that what you do with what you have says something profound about who you are. We need to study a proper use and view of our resources in more casual discussion formats like small groups and gender-based discipleship. We need to be active in local and global social-mission work. Perhaps creating a task force in the local church, assigned with the job of generating a report of the local community's largest socioeconomic needs and entering into conversation with them about how the church might go about addressing those issues, would be a great step in the right direction. Perhaps partnering with one small third-world community and sharing possessions, social resources, and spiritual ministry in an effort to draw them into the fullness of kingdom life would be a great enterprise. The truth is one local church can't change the world, but they might be able to change a small community. The important thing at the end of the day is that we clearly see that our possessions create responsibility, and our job as leaders and lay people is to consider carefully how we execute on it in concrete fashion for the glory of God.

## The Truth about Power

I believe in the power of God. I believe that miracles happen today. I believe that supernatural things happen ... even in North America! In one respect this is one of my greatest personal laments about prosperity doctrine. It takes advantage of a good impulse in creatures who long to see the power and majesty of their God put on display and loads that expectation with the wrong content.

Years ago I remember watching two exposés of alleged faith-healer Benny Hinn. The most disturbing part of the reports involved seeing what the viewers of Hinn's crusades and meetings don't see on his television broadcasts. The reports I watched showed segments of the audience filled with handicapped individuals in wheelchairs who, with the help of a their caretakers, followed Hinn from city to city, waiting in desperation for this "man of God" to bestow on them a healing. One of the reports exposing him was a 1999 HBO documentary called *A Question of Miracles: Faith Healing*. It shared, among other stories, about a couple with a handicapped child who were looking to Hinn to heal their son. At one of the crusades he was granted a healing. However, as time passed, that healing failed to manifest itself. As a result they were told by Hinn's organization to give more money in faith. They sent an additional $2,000 only to have their son die several months later.

Such preposterous accounts enrage us and leave us with an awful taste in our mouths for these charlatans. But there is a danger here that unsuspectingly undercuts one of the most glorious things about God that we can experience ... the realization of his power. Witnessing such atrocities creates such cynicism that many cede to Hinn and men like him the authority to dictate to us that God cannot show up in potency because surely God cannot be in the circus theses men have created. We become guilty of letting our cynicism swing the pendulum all the way in the other direction. This reaction only swaps one blatant error about God for a more subtle but equally wrong one. The pendulum swings from a God who does theatrical maneuvers on demand to a God who has been manhandled by naturalism. One can be coaxed out of the cave at will by the power of the ringmaster, and the other slumbers away in hibernation. We are not free to exchange one misunderstanding for another. Nor are we free to create a logically fallacious slippery-slope argument in an effort to stay away from danger. We must get our beliefs about God right.

Since one of our main windows into God is through the activities of the person of the Son, it is important that we see what Jesus thought about the normalcy of God's power expressed in human life. There are six theological truths about Jesus that must be considered in this regard:

1. Jesus did miracles.
2. Jesus was fully, 100 percent, God.
3. Jesus frequently did miracles through the power of the third person of the Trinity, the Holy Spirit.
4. Jesus told his followers that they would do the things that they saw him doing.
5. Jesus told his followers that they would do greater things than they saw him doing.
6. Jesus sent the same Holy Spirit through whose power he chose to work into the world to invade the lives of believers.

Few people reading this book would dispute statements one and two. If someone rejects them they would be classified by historic definition as a heretic. Statement three is often not thought about enough. Typically people assume that Jesus did his miracles via divine fiat. Since he is God, while on earth he did miracles to prove his deity, and he did so by exercising his power directly. Certainly his works were intended to vindicate his words. And undoubtedly he could, and at times did, access his divine authority and power directly. However, to assume that this was always and even normally the case seems to go too far.

Here we need to stop and do some deeper thinking about the Trinity. I also would strongly suggest that at the local-church level we do some crucial teaching about the Trinity as well. I shepherd and teach in the hub of the Mormon Belt and know just how vital it is for lay people to be able to grasp and explain this foundational doctrine.

The classic definition of the doctrine of the Trinity is best phrased this way:

> God is one essence, eternally existing in three co-equal persons, each of whom performs subordinating functions.

This definition recognizes that God is one in being and that, as one, he has eternally subsisted as three distinct but mutually related and mutually beneficial persons. It also states that these persons are not ontologically superior or inferior to one another, but they do have distinct roles that function, at times, in a hierarchical fashion.

The study of the relational workings of the three persons of the Trinity is known as the doctrine of the "economic Trinity." This aspect of trinitarian theology is of chief concern in thinking about the power of God and what it might mean for our lives today. On earth Jesus had all the prerogatives of deity, and yet we see the text repeatedly stating that the Holy Spirit was active in his life and ministry. Why would this even be necessary? There are two clear answers. First, this is simply the way that the Trinity is. This aspect of the mutually active and mutual indwelling properties of the "economic Trinity" is known as perichoresis. The intimacy and unity of God is expressed, in part, in the mutual, abiding presence and interests of the three distinct persons with one another. Second, Jesus intended to model for us what a human who fully relies on the Holy Spirit is capable of. Wolfhart Pannenburg notes, "The Spirit was earlier given to the Son permanently and without measure so as to equip him for his work."[13] That God intended Jesus to be a model for us in this respect seems without doubt when we look at John's portrayal of Christ in particular.

Statements four through six above become clear when we get to John 14–16. In John 14 Jesus entered into dialogue with his disciples. He told them that he would be preparing an eternal dwelling for them. He told them that he was exclusively the way to eternal relationship with God. He informed them that he put the character of the Father on display before them. And he introduced the fact that he would be sending the divine presence of the Holy Spirit to assist them throughout their journey. In the middle of this chapter comes a startling proclamation from the lips of Jesus. He declared:

> Truly, truly I say to you, whoever believes in me will also do the works that I do; and greater works than these will he do, because I am going to the Father. Whatever you ask in my name, this I will do, that the Father may be glorified in the Son. If you ask me anything in my name I will do it" (John 14:12–14).

The preceding context to this statement emphasizes the doctrine of perichoresis as Jesus responds to Philip's desire to see the Father by saying:

---

13. Pannenburg, *Systematic Theology*, Vol. 1, 321.

*feasting on the rations of a simple savior* 233

Do you not believe that I am in the Father and the Father is in me? The words that I say to you I do not speak on my own authority, but the Father who dwells in me does his works. Believe me that I am in the Father and the Father is in me. Or believe on account of the works themselves" (John 14:10–11).

In the succeeding context to Jesus' bold proclamation that believers will do both the works that he did and even greater works, Christ introduces his disciples to the abiding resource of the Holy Spirit. This Spirit functions as another comforter like unto Jesus himself. The introduction of the Holy Spirit here, and the consequent explanations of the Spirit's varied work throughout portions of the rest of chapters 14–16, show us that he strategically introduced this resource at the point of a perichoretic explanation and a prophetic proclamation of future power. This order is no accident. Jesus was letting the disciples know that the kingdom life is one where God shows up in power through the work of his Spirit in the lives of his people.

No one knew this experience better than Jesus. Just look at the following verses from Luke's Gospel illustrating this perichoretic relationship between the Son and the Spirit:

> And the Holy Spirit descended on him in bodily form, like a dove; and a voice came from heaven, "You are my beloved Son; with you I am well pleased" (Luke 3:22).
>
> And Jesus, full of the Holy Spirit, returned from the Jordan and was led by the Spirit in the wilderness (Luke 4:1).
>
> And Jesus returned in the power of the Spirit to Galilee, and a report about him went out through all the surrounding country (Luke 4:14).
>
> And the scroll of the prophet Isaiah was given to him. He unrolled the scroll and found the place where it was written, "The Spirit of the Lord is upon me, because he has anointed me to proclaim good news to the poor. He has sent me to proclaim liberty to the captives and recovering of sight to the blind, to set at liberty those who are oppressed, to proclaim the year of the Lord's favor." And he rolled up the scroll and gave it back to the attendant and sat down. And the eyes of all in the synagogue were fixed on him. And he began to say to them, "Today this Scripture has been fulfilled in your hearing" (Luke 4:17–21).
>
> On one of those days, as he was teaching, Pharisees and teachers of the law were sitting there, who had come from every village

of Galilee and Judea and from Jerusalem. And the power of the Lord was with him to heal (Luke 5:17). [Note: This power was likely with him via the Spirit, based on Luke's consistent perichoretic language.]

In that same hour he rejoiced in the Holy Spirit and said, "I thank you, Father, Lord of heaven and earth, that you have hidden these things from the wise and understanding and revealed them to little children; yes, Father, for such was your gracious will" (Luke 10:21).

In John it seems clear that Jesus was telling his disciples that they could expect that those who believed on him would walk in a parallel power to his via the Holy Spirit. To reject this idea or to downplay it is to not do full justice to Jesus' words. The things that the disciples saw him do that they too could anticipate trafficking in were clearly miraculous acts. And this is set, by the words of Christ, as the opportunity (even expectation) for all believers because of the gift of the Holy Spirit.

Now, this idea makes every card-carrying cessatonist nervous. It feels like we can't talk about power without being part of the circus that is much of the modern-day charismatic movement. But to react to this is to let an abuse define a use. This is not wise and ends up turning theological propositions into sociological reactions.

The problem with advocates of Gourmet Jesus isn't that they believe God heals. It isn't that they believe human instruments might play a part in the process of healing. It is that they think it can be claimed because it was already paid for in the atonement, and that they have the power to call upon healing and monetary prosperity because of their rights as children of God. The power of God does not come to us because we claim a right or because we play by the guaranteed rules of particular spiritual laws. No, instead God's power works through his people because they depend upon him, run to him because of their organic impotence, and rest in his sovereign choice to act or not. But rest assured, God's power is available through the indwelling ministry of his Holy Spirit. And as we avail ourselves in humility to him, he may choose to work through us in miraculous and wondrous ways. The myth of cessationism (the idea that some gifts of the Holy Spirit were for the establishment of the church but ceased with either the maturation of the church or the instantiation of the written revelation of Scripture) is that what God did has changed his fundamental manner of empowering humans. But this flies in the face of historical and contemporary data, the text of the New Testament epistles, and the narrative of the book of Acts—not to mention that a cessationist would have to conclude God's plan for the believers mentioned in John 14:13 does not refer to all believers, but this does not fit the language of the verse nor its context at all.

So at the local-church level how do we embrace the power of God without giving into a theology that has God on demand, or one that has no boundaries and no warrant to keep individual subjective experience from turning the local church into a circus? Let me suggest some steps. First, the leadership of the church and the people need to settle in their minds that the starting point for all theology and ministry philosophy is the text and not personal experience. Too often practical ministry and even theology is mitigated by bad experiences, too many experiences, or not enough experiences. In the end, the power of God at work in the local church is a textual question before it is ever an existential question.

Second, preach through 1 Corinthians. I personally found it incredible in my own journey of looking into the power of God to force my hand as a pastor to study what the apostle says to the local church about issues of gifting and power. Preaching expositionally through the book allowed me to guard my preconceptions, be sure that my interpretation was contextual to the broad scope of the letter, and to make sure my presentation was sensitive to the context of local-church ministry.

Third, read credible theologians and shepherds who have considered the deep implications of this area of theology. A few recommendations would be:

- *Kingdom Triangle,* by J. P. Moreland. It is a sharp book that demonstrates the church's need for the life of the mind, the spiritual formation of the soul, and the experience of the Holy Spirit's power.
- *Convergence: The Journey of a Charismatic Calvinist,* by Sam Storms. Sam is a pastor/scholar who has spent years studying these issues and is very sensitive to the issues of the local church.
- *The Beginner's Guide to Spiritual Gifts,* also by Sam Storms. This is a great primer on a full but balanced view of the spiritual gifts. It provides some good theological and exegetical arguments for its position.
- *Showing the Spirit: A Theological Exposition of 1 Corinthians 12–14,* by D. A. Carson. This book is characteristic of the careful exegetical work typical of Carson. He is detailed and thorough in his exegesis. I think it is the best available study of this passage. No one working

through 1 Corinthians or these theological issues in general can afford to ignore this book.

Fourth, begin to pray over people in your church for healing by creating a context for church leadership to do so. This is an easy and non-threatening way to begin seeking God to show up in sovereign power in the lives of people in your church. At the church I pastor in Utah we began to do this. The first time we did, we prayed for a little eight-year-old girl to be healed of a condition that had produced warts all over her body. She had them everywhere and her condition had been this way for years. No natural medicinal approaches had been able to deal with the condition. Her father, a man of deep faith, brought her to the elders to pray for healing. We all laid hands on her and prayed. One week later she woke her father up in the morning, exclaiming, "Daddy, my warts are gone! My warts are gone!" He checked over her whole body and then called me, excited to share what had happened. I am ashamed to say, I was in disbelief. What I didn't know at the time was that before my friend brought his daughter for prayer, he looked at his wife and said, "God is going to heal our daughter because he wants to show Pastor Bryan something." That was prophetic to say the least!

Fifth, keep order but take risks. This is the hardest part. Paul made clear in 1 Corinthians 14 that order in the public service was important. No one benefits if subjective impressions and ideas dictate what happens in corporate worship. Having said that, it would benefit the local church significantly if we actually expected God to move among us. My friend J. P. Moreland makes a great statement in *Kingdom Triangle* that I have utilized repeatedly in my ministry. He personally testifies, "Each year, I ask myself this question: how much of my ministry last year required the existence of the Christian God to explain it? How much would have happened if God did not exist?"[14] I have taken this idea and in my own ministry turned it into a question that I ask men on an annual discipleship growth plan that I have them fill out as they look forward to the coming year. It goes: "What will you accomplish this year that will require God to show up in some extraordinary way for it to materialize?" As local-church leaders, we need to help our people think about God the way he presents himself to us in the Bible rather than both the way our naturalistic culture does and the way our reactions to theological abuse push us.

14. Moreland, *Kingdom Triangle*, 135.

## The Most Elusive Virtue in Our Culture

The best book I have ever read outside of the Bible was first published in 1648. I recall reading this for the first time and being absolutely assaulted by it. It is titled *The Rare Jewel of Christian Contentment*. It was written by a Puritan named Jeremiah Burroughs. If contentment was rare in his day, I wonder what he would say if he could have seen today's culture in the West. When I read him, I feel blasted by a crisp arctic air that comes unpolluted into my lungs and at once assails me, refreshes me, and leaves me wanting more. In classic Puritans style, Burroughs loads his cannon with Scripture and systematically blows apart every shred of discontentment and self-entitlement we are predisposed to hold onto. He does so in thirteen chapters by basically setting out contentment, showing us that Jesus taught it, extolling how wonderful it is, condemning grumbling and discontentment, and finally telling us how to get it. It is the one book aside from the Bible that our culture needs more than any other.

Think of it. Marriages split up because of discontentment. Midlife crises hit individuals and families because of discontentment. Financial crimes are committed because of discontentment. Pornography reigns as a billion-dollar business because of human discontentment. Abandonment issues emerge because of discontentment. In fact, it is difficult to conceive of morally aberrant behavior that is not, one way or another, rooted in discontentment. But rarely do we identify it as the root cause. So we give aspirin to the cancer patients by giving them relational fixes, mechanisms born from Skinnerian behavioral psychology, and therapy sessions to forge action plans and safeguards for indulgence. None of these are inherently bad. Cancer patients need painkillers. But they do not actually cut to the heart of many of the problems that plague us. However, I think Burroughs does.

His treatise is too loaded to comment very specifically on it in a manner that would do it any justice. You just have to read it. Let me say it again . . . you just *have* to read it! But to whet your appetite and to let you sample it, here are a few important highlights of his thesis. He, as a wordsmith, defines contentment this way:

> Christian contentment is that sweet, inward, quiet, gracious frame of spirit which freely submits to and delights in God's wise and fatherly disposal in every condition.[15]

---

15. Burroughs, *The Rare Jewel of Christian Contentment*, 19.

He then moves systematically through nine facets of this definition and explains each in detail. By the end of the first chapter you will have spent more time thinking strategically and deeply about contentment than you likely have your entire life.

Burroughs shows the inadequacy of "stuff" to satisfy the heart of man. He hauntingly exposes the fact that objects cannot fill the void of discontentment at the center of so much human life:

> Godliness teaches us this mystery, [N]ot to be satisfied with all the world for our portion, and yet to be content with the meanest condition in which we are... Mark, here lies the mystery of it, a little in the world will content a Christian for his passage, but all the world, and ten thousand times more, will not content a Christian for his portion.[16]

What he means in the distinction between "passage" and "portion" is important. He is saying that a little by way of money and possessions will content the follower of Christ and suffice for his earthly journey, but all the money and possessions in the world will not bring real contentment in terms of satisfaction, joy, or meaning into his life because that is fulfilled by Christ alone.

We empirically know this to be true. More is never enough. And it is this impulse that Gourmet Jesus indulges. It is this clientele that orders his delicacies. We must be on our guard as people committed to protecting and nurturing the flock of God. Our cultural bent toward greed is apparent, and we must be vigilant to hold it at bay. In my opinion a slow, thoughtful, and prayerful study of Burroughs's book would be great medicine for a church riddled with the disease of avarice.

I will let the apostle Paul have the final say on this matter:

> But godliness with contentment is great gain, for we brought nothing into the world, and we cannot take anything out of the world. But if we have food and clothing, with these we will be content. But those who desire to be rich fall into temptation, into a snare, into many senseless and harmful desires that plunge people into ruin and destruction. For the love of money is a root of all kinds of evils. It is through this craving that some have wandered away from the faith and pierced themselves with many pangs (1 Tim. 6:6–10).

---

16. Ibid., 43.

9

# Homogenized Jesus

## The Christ of Evangelical Pop Culture

*Evangelicalism, now much absorbed by the arts and tricks of marketing, is simply not very serious anymore.*

DAVID WELLS

ON THE NIGHT STAND next to my bed sit three items that give rise to the chasm separating various sectors of present-day evangelicalism. Each serves as a unique reminder to me of what I want and don't want in the evangelicalism that colors my own life. Each speaks its own Christology to me, whispering of a Jesus to be rejected or embraced. Let me tell you about each item.

First, there sits a figurine of Jesus still in the package, albeit a bit damaged at the inquisitive hands of my youngest daughter. The package bears the title "Dashboard Jesus." He is designed to bounce around as you traverse the countryside, offering you "enlightenment on a spring." It seems to me that "Dashboard Jesus" sits in an uncomfortable land between silliness and blasphemy. He resides in a world where the worst thing possible to the identity of Christ takes place: trivialization. To trivialize Jesus is to make him pointless. It is to make him unnoticed. It is to make him too common. It is to make him irrelevant. And this is one of the great sins of passionate people today. In an effort to infuse Jesus into everything, they diffuse the potency of his person and the radical nature of his call. Brought into everything, Jesus ends up transforming nothing.

Second, there sits a framed collage made by a young woman who was in my youth group when I was a youth pastor during my days in seminary. She later served in the church that I planted and presently lead. She lived with our family for ten months and has seen our domestic life from as intimate a view as anyone I know. The framed collage has a quote on it from the famed missionary Jim Elliot, who gave his life along with four of his companions in an effort to bring the gospel to the unreached Auca Indians in Ecuador in 1956. The quote reads: *"Lord, make me a crisis man. Let me not be a mile-post on a single road, but make me a fork that men must turn one way or another in facing Christ in me."* Above the quote is a sign like one you would see on the side of the road, yellow with black arrows showing that you can only go forward in one of two splitting directions. This frame is powerful. It reminds me of just what I want my life to be like. It reminds me of the kind of person Jesus was and is. In another part of his journals, Elliot referred to Jesus as "The Great Short-Lived." Of course the irony of this title and Elliot's own martyrdom can hardly be missed. In his short life Jesus was a fork in the road to everyone who encountered him. He called people to sacrifice, to take up their cross and follow him, to choose the narrow road that leads to life, to shun the unattainable temptation to serve both God and the currency of the world, to build towers out of their lives at great cost, and to wash the filth off of the feet of travelers. This framed quote from a beloved family friend reminds me that the "Christ in me" that others must face needs to be the Jesus of the text, not the Jesus of triviality.

Finally, there sits on a lower shelf of the nightstand a picture. It is of me as an adult with a man I have known since childhood. He is not family, and he is about forty years older than me. He looks distinguished with a full mustache and grey hair neatly parted to the side. We are side by side as friends from different eras. His name is Harry, and I met him when I was a child and he was a volunteer with a ministry that was designed to help children at the church I attended learn the Bible. A lifelong bachelor, Harry had no children of his own. But every week he would come to listen to me recite verses. He would teach me the Bible. He was like a spiritual uncle, affirming what I learned at home and reinforcing the larger message of the Scripture to my young mind. Every birthday I still receive a card from Harry etched in the best penmanship I have ever seen. This picture reminds me that Jesus shows up in the faces of the faithful; that Jesus is not about commodification. He is about humility and community. He is about kindness shown to the least of these. And the picture of an aging but vibrant man with the one he touched with the marks of discipleship graces me with an indelible image of Jesus, the great molder and servant of men.

Dashboard Jesus, Jim Elliot, and Harry give me different visions of Jesus. The latter two are complementary. They serve to bring together passion and consistency. But Dashboard Jesus reminds me of much in Christianity that makes me sick to my stomach. How did we arrive at diffusing Jesus into so many parts that we diminish him?

## Homogenizing Jesus

When something is homogenous it is made similar to something else. In dairy production, homogenization is the process by which the fat globules in the cream get broken up into a small enough size that they will remain suspended in the milk and not separate from it and rise to the surface. If milk is not homogenized, then the cream separates and leaves skim milk on the bottom and cream on the top of the container. Homogenization then permits the molecules to intermix and remain as one substance. Keep in mind that without this process the natural course of events is for the substances to separate, clearly delineating two distinct entities.

So what then does it mean to say that Jesus has been homogenized? It means that he has been reduced and disseminated in the culture so the things that make him distinctive are no longer apparent. Now, these days, to look at Jesus and the culture spawned in his name and compare it to the culture at large is to see little distinction between the two. It is vital to note that this minimization has been purposeful on the part of the American church. Remember, homogenization is not a natural process. If Jesus was left as he presented himself and the culture at large was left to itself, there would be a natural distancing between the two. It is work to keep them together. I think it is a fair question to ask why the American church feels so compelled to keep Jesus tied to culture.

The answer to this question is found in the concept of "relevance." When we say something is "relevant," we mean that it relates to the issues of the present day in a manner and through a means that is socially applicable and acceptable. So to say that we are "making Jesus relevant" is to beg the question of whether or not he is *intrinsically* acceptable and applicable to the social mores of our culture. In the first two chapters we established that the Jesus of history and the Christ of faith are the same person. So the question must be asked: Is this Jesus who walked in first-century Palestine relevant to us in the twenty-first century, or must he be "made" so by our cultural translation efforts? And if he must, can we actually change the presentation of Jesus without marring the person of Jesus?

This is where things have gotten muddy. Good -efforts to win the lost and see the church grow don't always translate into benign methodologies. Not only do ideas have consequences, but the way we present those ideas also have consequences. We innately know this to be true. It is one of the reasons we package sensitive information carefully when we talk to people, because we want to set the table well for the information to be digested and discarded. Certainly packaging information isn't wrong and is literally impossible to avoid. Yet that doesn't mean that it is neutral or that it should not be critically analyzed to see if, a) it gets in the way of the content, and b) if it actually manipulates the content itself.

## Two Critical Concerns

Homogenized Jesus has created two serious issues for the church. Each has been an issue in its own right in the broader culture, but the church has followed suit and made them sufficient problems of its own.

The first is the attitude of *consumerism*. Worship services are experiences to be rated. In fact, you can just visit www.churchrater.com and do it yourself. If you are looking for a place to worship, just click on the church name in your state and browse through the reviews. It is an ecclesiastical Urbanspoon just for your tasty-Jesus palate. In fact, if you are a church leader, you can even schedule a church consultant to interact with you to make your local body more appealing to the senses of those outside consumers. When these customers come to the Sunday-morning event they can choose from a number of menu items. If you attend Saddleback Church you can go to the main service and take in typical worship music with a full band. If you want some rock and roll you can go to "Overdrive." If you want music and a venue that appeals to twenty- and thirty-somethings then you can go to "Fuse." But maybe you still pine for those old hymns of the faith . . . well, you can attend "Traditions" and get your Isaac Watts and Fanny Crosby on. These are just a few of your options each weekend.[1] Saddleback is hardly alone as a large church providing a menu of doxological options. At one level we could just brush such approaches off as filigree to get people to hear the real message. But this demeans worship, ignores the anthropocentric drive of consumerism, and implicitly communicates that God comes to us on our terms.

The second concern is *trivialization*. This may be the greatest travesty of present-day church life. Over the past forty years the Incarnate God, the second person of the Trinity, has been reduced to marketing slogans, advertising jingles, action figures, magnets, buttons, candy, bobble heads, diet books, bracelets, necklaces, spinning tops, t-shirts, vacation cruises, spanking paddles, video games, costumes, dolls, Scripture Cookies, Testamints, Bible Bars, bumper stickers, car emblems, candles, board games, stationery, pens, window decals, and license plate holders. Jesus sells. And the more we see his image plastered on every commercial product imaginable, the less our culture actually understands who he really is. When it comes to Jesus, familiarity does not breed contempt; it breeds something far more dangerous and far more threatening: indifference.

## An Uncritical Approach

My wife and I used to have friends in Texas who owned a parrot. I led a small group once at their home, and they would have to cover the birdcage with a sheet. If its vision wasn't blocked; the parrot would disrupt the meeting by calling out. Often it would call out its owner, my friend Mike's name . . . *"Miiiichaaeel . . . Miiiichaaeel . . . Miichaaeel!"* I recently read that parrots learn dialects. In the wild they pick them up from other birds, and then return the sounds by mimicking what they heard. Their imitation then is dialectically sensitive. They learn their calls from others, whether they are humans or other birds.

In a similar sense to a parrot, the church has unfortunately adopted its vernacular, its culture-speak, from whatever the prevailing aroma of its broader social context dictates. This parrot culture that comprises evangelicalism has left it without its own identifiable characteristics. If you don't want to upload your videos onto YouTube you can do so on GodTube. If you don't want to watch *Real Housewives of Orange County*

---

1. Saddleback Church, "The Venues."

you can always tune into a newer reality series, *Pastors of LA*, and see what church stars are up to. If you can't find your spouse on Match.com, try Christian Mingle. If you miss the Grammy Awards just make sure you catch the Dove Awards. There was a time when, if you couldn't cut it on *American Idol*, you might try your vocal cords out on *Gifted* on the Trinity Broadcasting Network, or work your way into the All American Gospel Youth Competition (complete with *American Idol* lookalike logo). If you gather with the family for an evening of fun, why play Monopoly, Pictionary, or Settlers of Catan when you could play Bibleopoly, Bible Pictionary, or Settlers of Canaan? It seems that the Christian marketing motto has become, "Whatever you do, we can do worse!"

Evangelicalism's uncritical adoption of mass cultural motifs creates a perception of the kingdom of God that is uncreative and maladaptive. Ironically, these are the two things it is trying desperately to avoid and these are two things that Jesus could never have been accused of. It makes little sense for Christianity, with its history of risk, persecution, and cultural transformation, to now subject itself as a little brother to the operating principles of secularism. Why would we waste our time trying to be so acceptable that we end up looking like our society's less advantaged twin? Mike Erre notes in his book, *The Jesus of Suburbia*, "Two thousand years of church history should suggest that the movement of Jesus is most dangerous when it is opposed."[2] I agree. So how did we come to so uncritically paint our faces to look like everyone else in an effort to neutralize the opposition?

## The Process of Jesus' Homogenization

The young people of the 1960s were the children of the Greatest Generation who had fought in World War II and had witnessed the economic depression of the 1930s. They had seen domestic hardship and dealt with global chaos. When they settled in after WWII, they created largely responsible homes rooted in a sound work ethic guided by concrete values. These homes provided rhythm, insulation, and a certain restraint provided by social dogmatism and domestic structure. When this generation had children, an interesting phenomenon began to develop. The provision of security and structure permitted a sense of narcissism and a yearning for self-autonomy to build within the next generation. What

---

2. Erre, *The Jesus of Suburbia*, 13.

emerged was a reactionary cultural swell of license and liberation. If the late '50s and early '60s showed us *Leave It to Beaver*, the late '60s and early '70s exposed what the Beaver did when it was all left up to him.

Essentially, he opted for a life with little restraint. He opted for a communal identity that looked outside of the nuclear family. He strained for the top of Maslow's hierarchy, questing (often with the help of "herbal supplements") toward self-actualization. But the problem with the self-actualization of this generation lay in both the "self" that was being actualized and the vague notions of what actualization really looked like. They went out to find themselves and never did, so they tried again in the 1990s and called it a midlife crisis. In truth, we could adopt another term for this generation's rendition of self-actualization: *narcissism*.

Christopher Lasch's piercing social commentary *The Culture of Narcissism*, published in 1979, was at once an astute cultural analysis of the 1970s and a prophetic oracle of the spiral of self-absorption subsequent to his day. The narcissistic propensities of North American cultural life relates to the evangelical fascination with creating a parrot pop culture. The narcissistic ego longs for affirmation and acceptance. The demons of comparison fly free in any arena calling for personal accomplishment. We see others not as co-laborers but as competitors in the free marketplace of money and ideas, and how we perform dictates to us the narrative of our own self-worth. Over three decades ago, Lasch observed:

> In an age of diminishing expectations, the Protestant virtues no longer excite enthusiasm . . . Self-preservation has replaced self-improvement as the goal of earthly existence. In a lawless, violent and unpredictable society, in which the normal conditions of everyday life come to resemble those formerly confined to the underworld, men live by their wits . . . In earlier times the self-made man took pride in his judgment of character and probity; today he anxiously scans the faces of his fellows not so as to evaluate their credit but in order to gauge their susceptibility to his own blandishments. He practices the classic arts of seduction and with the same indifference to moral niceties, hoping to win your heart while picking your pocket.[3]

Comparison and manipulation are demons released from the pit of emotional insecurity, an issue that our culture has no shortage of.

The creation of a parrot culture, as an expression of our insecure longing for acceptance, has remained a value that has found expression

---

3. Lasch, *The Culture of Narcissism*, 53.

throughout the last four decades. Many may object to the assessment that our parrot culture is an expression of our longing for acceptance. They will argue that it is an effort to win people by creating minimal and unnecessary barriers. This is what they term as relevance. I am not attempting to question motives. I have no question that people in the mega-church movement, the "Purpose-Driven" model, or more culturally nimble postmodern/emergent models of local-church ministry philosophy long to see people come to know Christ. In fact, the sheer numbers of people attracted to these approaches become, for their proponents, a central vindication of their appropriateness. My argument in response would simply be that on the face of it, immediate results don't erase long-term effects, nor do they vindicate the rightness or wrongness of the philosophy. The parrot evangelical culture has a few driving concepts that have fueled its vessel for the past forty years. To understand the homogenizing of Jesus we must identify these because they actually form the pillars of what we know of as evangelical pop culture.

## The Chemicals of Homogenized Jesus

### Commodification and Cool

Our world is a conglomeration of consumables and the United States leads the world in consumption. Consumption is an essential part of life. Food is essential for survival. Air is necessary for life. We were designed by God as consumers. But we have now made an "ism" out of something entirely natural. Through consumerism, we have polluted the stream and made the water of God's goodness toxic. We sit at the table of his provision and glut ourselves in overindulgence. This excess is wrong in and of itself because it cheapens the gifts and the giver. But its most surreptitious consequence is how it leads us to commodify Christ, his gospel, and his church.

### The Conundrum of Cool

The commercialization of Jesus is pandemic in our culture. Through mass market to mass culture, Jesus has become entirely objectified. His image is everywhere from the glorious to the gaudy, from the solemn to the showy: Jesus moves product and is himself a product. His objectification in our culture makes him the kind of thing that can be owned by a constituency and the kind of thing that can be morphed by market appeal. Sometimes satire helps us see things for what they are.

A decade ago the animated show *King of the Hill* critiqued Christian culture's capitulation to market demands in an episode titled "Reborn to Be Wild" during season eight of the program. On the show, Bobby, Hank's teenage son, is moving toward rock-and-roll culture, and Hank is concerned. So he ends up getting Bobby connected to a local youth pastor who runs an outreach for kids by making Christianity cool. The youth reach out to Bobby, and he is immediately sucked in because, in his words, "They're cool and they're totally Christian." Bobby ends up experimenting with Christian kitsch and pop culture as he replaces his rock and roll music with Christian rock, dons a "Satan Sucks" t-shirt, and gets a cross earring, but Hank can't reconcile it with his background. At one point Hank laments to his drinking buddies, "When I was young you went to rock and roll concerts on Saturday nights and asked for forgiveness on Sunday. Now it's all mixed together." Hank doesn't understand Homogenized Jesus. In fact, in one of the most memorable lines of the show, he rebukes the youth pastor, who is also a Christian rock/grunge music singer, saying with pleading exasperation, "Can't you see you're not making Christianity better. You're just makin' rock and roll worse." It's funny—hilarious in fact—in part because it's true on multiple levels. But the most poignant part of the satire is the lesson at the end of the show when Hank takes Bobby home from the concert (called Messiah Fest). He takes Bobby into the garage and gets down a box with a bunch of Bobby's old toys and gadgets that Bobby once thought were cool but are now just thrown in the box. Bobby remembers how he used to love them but now has outgrown them and Hank talks about how stuff goes from being cool at one stage of life to being lame the next. At that point Hank looks up at his son and says, "I don't want the Lord to, you know, end up in this box."

Hank Hill put his finger on my fear for the Jesus of evangelical pop culture. I am afraid that he is going to end up going back into the box when he is no longer sexy and no longer hip. When he loses the "cool" factor, he will need to be reinvented, re-homogenized to fit a new culture since it is always changing. I am not denigrating the idea of speaking in appropriate ways to culture, but I am rejecting the idea that Jesus gets a facelift so he can look cool and speak the same language as the culture around him . . . like a parrot.

Theology and the gospel do not change. "Jesus Christ is same yesterday and today and forever" (Heb. 13:8). But culture constantly shifts. "Cool" changes like the wind. What's "in" is quickly out. And the church tries to keep pace. It tries to speak the language. It tries to be relevant. The church-growth movement has filled evangelicalism with conference after conference. We have entire magazines devoted to church marketing. We are resourced with people who devote their professional lives to keeping us up with the times and not lagging behind.

To put it plainly, consumers drive the market, consumers are consumed by trends, and trends define what's cool. So to be a church that markets to the needs or wants of consumers demands the wherewithal and focus to make "cool" a driving value. And this is why Hank Hill's observation is so spot-on. The tricks that a church pulls out of its marketing bag today will not work in five to ten years. The market will have shifted so if what is being marketed is a homogenous Jesus dressed up to look like the social trends of the day, then Jesus' relevance has a very short life cycle.

A fantastic cultural critique on what is wrong with the commercialization and faddish nature of the church and its attempts at market appeal is David Wells's book, *The Courage to Be Protestant*. Wells observes that our obsession with commercializing the church to the modern consumer has been entirely wrong-headed. For him (and I agree) it got the wrong results, was based on the wrong calculations, utilized the wrong analogy for its approach, and chose the wrong customer. Its recipients, the unchurched, are without the gospel and thus without a desire for theological truth and Spirit-directed life. Therefore, to speak their language in a marketing strategy will more often than not reduce Jesus, dilute theology, and make the life of the Spirit seem pedestrian. Wells writes:

> The truth is that no matter how proficiently we learn to "do" church for the Western, affluent, highly individualistic market, we are doomed to failure. Indeed, the more proficient we become, if that proficiency requires that we denude ourselves of theology, the more certainly we doom ourselves to failure. The method is inherently flawed. If it succeeds in replicating itself at all, it will only be replicating its own failure. That is what the marketers have failed to see.[4]

---

4. Wells, *The Courage to Be Protestant*, 47–48.

*homogenized Jesus* 249

In perhaps one of the more astute observations I have read in recent memory, he adds just a few pages later:

> Furthermore, what is to be gained if we are so intent in reaching out to the unchurched that we then unchurch the reached? Certainly what is happening today is that the reached of an earlier generation are being unchurched. So, not only is this approach generationally destructive but it is also trafficking in something of a fraud. The price of marketing is that the church hides its nature and biblical Christianity hide its face. So, what is there to learn in these churches? Why would anyone want to stay?[5]

I do not think this has to be the case with marketing, but unfortunately almost all of what passes for church marketing today fits his criticism.

"Cool" will always be in flux. Christology will never change. If the twain don't meet, the answer is not in editing the latter. The church can't always be cool and Christocentric. In fact, the desire to bring the two together seems flawed. Maybe if the church were consistent rather than cool, it would reflect a stability and security indicative of an unchanging gospel much needed by people weary of trying to be chic.

The Commodity of Conversion

When Jesus and his Bride are perceived as objects to consume and repackage, then theological components crucial to them get commodified. The church has done just this with conversion. It actually started back in American revivalism. Conversion went from a process orientation of growing into belief, as seen in the Puritans and the First Great Awakening, to a momentary infusion of belief or repentance in the Second Great Awakening. While theological Calvinism today stands as an heir to the heritage of Edwards, Whitefield, and others, our modes in evangelism and preaching owe more to the revivalist heritage of Finney, Moody, and Billy Sunday.

The way evangelicalism talks about conversion is so deeply embedded in its collective psyche that to question whether or not it is actually biblical seems treasonous. But this question must be asked. As it stands, our lexicon for conversion could use some help because it is not really all that biblical. We use phrases like "the sinner's prayer," "receiving Christ in to our lives," and "asking Jesus into our hearts." The middle of the three is the only one with even a shred of biblical language (cf. John 1:12). The other two have nothing in the text to connect to for affirmation at all. Conversion as

---

5. Ibid., 55.

a punctiliar transaction is as much gospel in evangelicalism as the gospel itself. Conversion as a measurable is rooted in almost all church-growth and church-planting literature. Conversion as a concrete moment to point back to at times of personal doubt is psychological gold to Christian sanity. Conversion as a ticket to heaven is its greatest marketable reality.

In many sectors of evangelical pop culture, getting people "converted" is the process known as evangelism. The ideological children of Second Great Awakening revivalism have canonized prayer as the means of ensuring conversion. If someone wants to come to faith, they are told to pray something like:

> Lord Jesus, I want you to come in and take over my life right now. I am a sinner. I have been trusting in myself and my own good works. But now I place my trust in you. I accept you as my own personal Savior. I believe you died for me. I receive you as Lord and Master of my life. Help me to turn from my sins and to follow you. I accept the free gift of eternal life. I am not worthy of it but I thank you for it. Amen.[6]

There are many versions of this prayer, but they all essentially say and hope to accomplish the same thing. In full disclosure: I have led many people in this prayer over the course of my ministry. I have spoken in revivalist contexts where I was encouraged to call people down front for this very purpose. I have trained people to close the deal with this kind of a prayer. I no longer think getting them to pray this prayer is the goal of evangelism.

I will leave my prescription for this problem to the next chapter. For now, a good summary of evangelicalism's enthusiasm for an evangelism immersed in what I would term "prayerful regeneration" comes from Gordon Smith when he writes:

> The revivalist heritage has left many contemporary Christians with the belief that conversions are the fruit of the right practices or techniques. By learning these techniques, one can become a "soul winner;" with the right methods, one could learn how to "lead people to Christ." Some Christians have taught simple formulas in a one-size-fits-all approach to evangelism: ask the right questions, lead people through a series of simple statements, guide them through a timely prayer and one can state with confidence that these persons have become Christian believers.[7]

6. Kennedy, *Evangelism Explosion*, 50–51.
7. Smith, *Transforming Conversion*, 12.

Conversion is packaged in a form that is readily acceptable, extracts fairly little from someone, and is easily measurable. Church planters can report to the higher-ups about their "conversion growth rate." Crusade evangelists can issue supporters statistics on how many people gave their lives to Christ during the week of meetings. Heads are bowed, hands are counted, and hearts are changed . . . or so it is thought.

## Privatization

This commercialization and commodification of Christ, the church, and conversion leads right into another driving concept behind Homogenized Jesus: *privatization*. If Jesus is my "personal" Savior, then I relate to him primarily in a private and personal relationship. Privatization of religious experience is definitely not exclusively an evangelical phenomenon. In fact, this ability to make religious experience private is what often makes individuals feel impervious to theological critique. This privatization of religious experience is the residue of gnosticism. It is the product of weighing mystical encounter above other facets of religious life and giving it a final say in the relationship between God and man. The liberal can hold on to it. The fundamentalist can hold on to it. The postmodernist can hold on to it. It transcends theological systems. Who can possibly speak into the subjective reality of one's private religious experience with any misgivings? When combined with the western value of personal autonomy, it becomes a type of unassailable religious trump card.

It is no historical accident that Joseph Smith and the Mormons arose out of the similar chaotic, religious milieu as Charles Finney. The atmosphere surrounding the Second Great Awakening was rife with a hunger for personal religious experience. No religious movement more values it as a trump card than the Mormons. For them, religious, personal, inner, spiritual experience is quite literally the be all and end all. Logic stops where it begins. Their emergence out of a dissatisfaction with what was left from the Great Awakening of Edwards and Whitefield tells us about more than just their story. It tells us about the religious sociology of a generation. They were but one group that came out of that time abandoning orthodoxy. Those who made up the Second Great Awakening stayed in the bubble of orthodoxy, and brought personal religious experience right to the center of it as it hadn't been since the mystics of the medieval period. The difference being that the culture of the nineteenth century (even more so the twentieth and today) already possessed the value of personal autonomy. In the medieval period, religious life and forms held people into a liturgical and communal apparatus that wouldn't permit personal experience to be unmoored from the larger movement of the church. Those forms were on their way out in a land like America, born from revolution, thriving as a place of opportunity, filled with camp meetings and pioneers.

So today evangelicalism is heir to the autonomous throne, holding firmly the scepter of personal experience. This emphasis on individual personal life has led the church away from proactive shepherding and into the realm of reactive therapy. Once Christianity gets cut away from its necessary connection to corporate life and historical continuity with the past, it runs the risk of communicating to the broader world that Jesus is just a personal coping mechanism. Michael Horton notes, "To the extent that churches in America today feel compelled to accommodate their message and methods to these dominant forms of spirituality, they lend credence to the thesis that Christianity is not news based on historical events but just another form of therapy."[8] This makes evangelicalism vulnerable to more than just cultural fads. It exposes it to the claims of the irreligious that Christ and Christian theology are just ideas we use to get by in a harsh world.

This unwitting result of the privatization of Christian life is detrimental to our witness. By feeding the monster of personal autonomy, Jesus becomes homogenized to the core values of our broader culture. Thus if Oprah wants God in her own form and Chopra wants God in his own form, then Joe and Sally in the Bible Belt can also have God in Christ just how they want him: their own personal, privatized Jesus.

## Compartmentalization

The natural next step from privatization is compartmentalization. If Jesus is available to the inner life on our terms, and that inner life has very little accountability to either the broader scope of Christian consensus or historic Christian thought, then we are free to invite him into some areas and keep him out of others. I remember growing up in church and being instructed with the classic template for personal priorities on the acrostic JOY: Jesus, Others, You. The other day, my middle daughter

---

8. Horton, *Christless Christianity*, 180.

came home from a Christian camp and shared with me the same acrostic. Thirty years removed, Christian culture spits out the same formula. It is not an overreaction to say that this is surreptitiously toxic. We are bred in our homes and taught in our educational system to be linear thinkers. It is part of western cultural logic. So to teach a young person that their priority checklist in life goes: 1) Jesus 2) Others 3) You, is to make Christ an item to be dealt with and then moved past. This linear prioritization is seen in the brazen compartmentalization our church culture commits regarding Christ and his principles.

This evangelical proclivity is one of the main reasons for the truth found in the repeated postmodern assertion that the church is filled with hypocrites. There are several key areas where this hypocritical dragon rears its head.

## Sexuality

Sex sells and apparently the church has noticed. I recall watching a Christian Contemporary Music (CCM) video of a female artist some time ago, and I was stunned at the sexuality oozing from the video. The singer's coquettish glances coupled with the amorous aroma of the video made me wonder what exactly the artist was trying to accomplish. It is not unusual to go into a Sunday-morning evangelical worship service and find sexuality percolating up on stage in the manner of dress and demeanor. To some this may sound puritanically prudish, but rest assured, the world takes notice of our presentation. In his tour de force book *Why the Rest Hates the West*, historian Meic Pearse observes:

> The "liberation" of sex from the constraints of traditional morality has, then, been a rerun of the "liberation" of humanity from God: at the very moment of being absolutized, it has thereby been trivialized and rendered worthless. Having been desacralized, it becomes a mere object like any other and, instead of being a guarantor of our specialness, leaves us once more isolated and alone.[9]

Unfortunately, the church's indiscriminate embrace of broader culture has made indecorous dress and behavior acceptable. But shouldn't we ask if this would happen with Jesus at the center? If Christ can get checked off the priority list, then he does not need to be involved with

9. Pearse, *Why the Rest Hates the West*, 136.

our presentation of ourselves. What actually ends up on display are not just bodies but insecurities of the soul yet to be brought under the lordship of Jesus. If a person's identity is in Christ, then they are not looking for the attention such an appearance elicits.

## Media

To blame the "media" has become a cop-out for accepting personal responsibility. Yes, our culture hits us with an onslaught of propaganda. Yes, temptation lurks around every corner and sits at our fingertips. But making a scapegoat of the media is getting old. Christians are individually responsible for what they consume, and complaining about secular culture being secular is like griping because the sun feels hot. It is acting according to its properties. The problem is that we are too indiscriminate as evangelicals concerning both what we take in and why we take it in.

Film is a great example of this lack of discrimination. Christian men will watch PG-13 comedic films that have scantily clad women and suggestive dialogue. Christian women will watch PG-13 films with young, virile, shirtless male vampires. In fact, they will even go in groups of church friends and call it fellowship. Is this the fault of secular media moguls, making millions, whose value system is consistent with partial nudity and sexual vampires; or, of Christian people who tell their kids to stay sexually pure while bifurcating their visual allegiance? The truth is self-apparent.

There is a way for evangelicals to interact with media and a way not to. Most of our evangelical pop culture is writing a playbook in how not to. Media like music, film, television, art, and literature all tell us stories about the self-concepts of culture. The Christian's first job, then, is not to be a mindless consumer of media but to be a judicious analyst of cultural messages. The goal for the Christian is not slaking his thirst for entertainment (although that may, at times, be just fine), but surveying areas where the kingdom of the world can be captured by a greater, more glorious meta-narrative.

But media for the modern evangelical becomes a point of distraction from life rather than an object of learning, growth, and engagement. We actually recede into media forms to disengage from real life. This type of technological recreation has no connection to re-creation at all. Mark Powley is right when he says, "The truly high-definition things in your life are the things that surround you right now. Whatever you're sitting on. Whatever your view is. Whoever you're with. TV, film, and the Internet can only ever approximate this."[10] Media as distraction from life in the name of recreation has so obsessed our Christian culture that our indiscriminate dalliances now serve as centerpieces and rallying points for Christian fellowship.

## Money

In the chapters regarding Gourmet Jesus, I have already discussed our obsession with materialism. I won't belabor or recycle that here. However, as it relates to evangelical pop culture's copycat enterprise, the issue of monetary allocation is a live one. As a seminary student years ago, I had a friend and fellow seminary student who was attending a North Dallas mega-church. It was a pace-setting church in the Southern Baptist realm of evangelical Christianity. One day he received from them a solicitation for financial giving. They wanted to install a fountain in front of the church and were seeking to raise $250,000 for it from their constituents. What can we say to an evangelicalism that will pay a quarter of a million dollars to watch water cycle through pipes and spout in the air while people in Haiti dip buckets into garbage- and sludge-ridden rivers? God help us! A wise man once said, "Where your treasure is, there your heart will be also."[11] You may have heard of him. He was a very non-homogenized Jesus.

## Celebrity

American religion scholar Stephen Prothero once wrote,

> The Jesus movement, the mega-church phenomena, and the CCM industry share more than historical connections. They also share a coterie of Christian critics. According to detractors, the Jesus movement was theologically shallow, mega-churches pander to therapeutic culture, and CCM is about entertainment not evangelism. The core complaint seems to be that all these folks have adapted too much to American culture. Rather than making America more Christian, the Jesus People, the

---

10. Powley, *Consumer Detox*, 122.
11. Matt. 6:21.

mega-churches, and the CCM industry have tried to make Christianity more American. The have molded Jesus to the world instead of molding the world to Jesus.[12]

Nothing evinces accuracy of these criticisms more than the phenomena of Christian "celebrity." Americans made a celebrity out of Jesus through movies, plays, and music throughout much of the middle portion of the twentieth century. Liberalism lifted Jesus up as a moral hero and the media concurred and supported it. Evangelicalism, it seems, took things one step farther. It replaced the moral celebrity of Jesus with the celebrity of his representatives. Since Jesus is more than a moral hero, he rightfully could not be reduced to that state—so who would be left to take his place in the spotlight of celebrity culture but his representatives.

CCM, possibly more than any other single representative form of the evangelical ethos, has contributed to the celebrity copycat culture we now have in the church. Prothero mentioned that critics charge CCM as being "about entertainment, not evangelism." This is difficult to dispute. Could you imagine having an annual awards show that costs thousands of dollars to put on and televise that was for awards in evangelism? "And the award for best evangelist in a crusade goes to . . . Billy Graham . . . this is Billy's thirty-fifth evangelistic Dove award!" It seems pretty clear from profit margins to marketing that celebrity is the name of the game.

In the third year of our church plant, we joined with another church that was only a little over a year older than ours. To add excitement to our event, we thought it would be interesting to bring in a CCM artist for a concert to kick things off. So we found one and began talks with his management representatives. For anonymity's sake I will just call him "The Celebrity." As I read through the contract we were to sign to bring The Celebrity out to our venue, I noticed some disturbing expectations. Here is the actual wording of item number thirty-two on the tour rider portion of the contract:

32) Catering (Fifteen People)

Lunch: A well balanced lunch consisting of a salad, fresh fruit and sandwiches. Feel free to have some creativity with lunch. Deli trays get old every day! Hot sandwiches and soup are a great treat!

Dinner: Our standard entourage for this type of engagement will not exceed fifteen persons, please include this number along with your

---

12. Prothero, *American Jesus*, 153.

*homogenized jesus* 257

local crew to determine dinner requirements. Please discuss meal plans with the Tour Manager during the advance. A choice of two hot entrees, salads, vegetables, bread, and beverage should be planned. Please maintain healthy food choices. Please no pizza, lasagna, fried foods, or other fatty dishes.

    a. Backstage: Our requirements are very simple. Please provide the following:

        i. Forty Eight (48) 16oz. bottles of non-carbonated spring water

        ii. Twelve (12) assorted fruit juices

        iii. Six bottles Pellegrino or Perrier bottled water

        iv. Fresh-ground hot coffee & decaf, with Half & Half, two-percent milk, and assorted sweeteners

        v. Assorted herbal tea service & decaf, with hot water, assorted teas, lemon, and honey

        vi. Plate of fresh fruit to include: apples, bananas, oranges, seedless white grapes, etc.

        vii. Mixed nuts (salted) and chips and salsa

        viii. Napkins, cold cups, coffee cups, and with a container with clean ice

        ix. Please, no candy, potato chips, chocolate or junk food of any kind

Bus Food: Specifics will be advanced with tour manager. Generally pizza, wings, or hot sandwiches will be ordered from a local place.

    b. Bus Stock: Please provide the following items for the bus. These items should be available at the end of the night.

        i. Twenty pounds ice

        ii. Twenty-four bottles of water

        iii. Diet Coke

        iv. Cranberry juice

        v. One-half gallon one-percent milk

        vi. Assorted cereal

        vii. Assorted fresh fruit

        viii. Assorted bagels w/cream cheese and butter

Assorted fruit juices? Pellegrino or Perrier? Herbal tea service with lemon and honey? Of course this and a number of other amenities were necessary in addition to the bargain flat rate of $7,500 for the two-hour show (which, compared to other artists I looked into, really was a bargain). Here was my question and comments at the time regarding this portion of the rider in an e-mail back to the management company:

> What is the deal with the backstage food requirements? Are we contractually obligated to provide Perrier, salsa and mixed nuts? I am not opposed to specifications. We will provide refreshments and necessary meals; however, this seems ridiculous. We want to bring [The Celebrity] and his band in, and we will treat them well and provide for their needs. We are planning our first Bible conference as two church plants that have a combined history of less than seven years laboring in the most unevangelized corridor in America. I have to be honest, the nature of the backstage food requirements makes me wonder if we are bringing in someone to help us worship or an American star.

Needless to say, we did not have The Celebrity come. I only share this anecdote because it best illustrates what happens in churches all over America. The cult of Christian celebrity is embarrassment to the kingdom of God, and continued proponents of evangelical pop-culture are to blame for this.

In 1997, Christian recording artist Steve Camp wrote *107 Theses* as a call to bring reformation to his CCM colleagues. It is quite an insightful document. He laments, among other things, the celebrity culture, but what stood out to me was that he devoted eleven of the 107 theses to the fact that those performing this "ministry" of CCM had a mandate to be held accountable by the local church. How refreshing! But apparently his words have either largely gone unheeded or church leaders have failed to do their job to deal with this embarrassing earmark of our parrot culture.

## Petrification

Wood gets petrified when mineral substances fill in the cracks and crevices that time and elements have worn way. When wood is petrified, it takes on the appearance of its original state but is now textured a bit differently and hardened over by the mineral compounds. Homogenized Jesus petrifies culture. Jesus seeps in the openings and replicates what the culture looks like and the whole thing gets hardened over. To the naked eye it looks just like the original culture, but when you touch and lift it the difference starts to become noticeable.

From bookstore chains to radio stations to paraphernalia, Jesus is filling in the cracks, and evangelical culture seems to hope that the world won't even notice. That way, people can be taken by Christ a bit unawares. The transition is then made easier into church life. The mega-church model has staked its entire missiology on this idea.

Churches petrify secular culture by condescending to the customer. This happens by removing Christian symbolism, by making doctrine remedial or removing it altogether, and by making the atmosphere chipper and light or creating it to fit cultural edginess. Wells expresses the approach:

> The conventional wisdom is that seriousness is the death knell of successful churches. In an age of entertainment, such as our age is in the West, we have to be funny, engaging, likable, and light to succeed. So seriousness must be banished. Preserve the taste but cut the calories.[13]

Tasty Jesus is here, and he is the main course in the mega-church movement.

This cultural petrification is happening, whether we look at the Boomers and their missiology of mega-church, Generation X and its brand of emergent theology, or Millennials and their own organic hipster approach. Pick your generation representing present-day evangelical culture, and you will find repeated attempts to get Jesus in the gaps and make the transition as seamless and hiccup-free as possible from the kingdom of the world to the kingdom of God. But is this the call of the church, and is it the role of Christ in regard to culture?

## Conclusion

Homogenized Jesus is designed to look just like the culture at large. He is designed to be non-threatening. He is designed to be a tweak to life as people know it. He is intended to change us enough but not too much. He is fashioned to keep us comfortable by letting us keep cultural continuity between our pre-Jesus and post-Jesus days. For many, Homogenized Jesus comes as an accident of cultural captivity. But for others he is the fruit of a very clear missiological strategy. Has it worked? Are Christ and his church more "relevant?" I don't think so. That's why I have written

13. Wells, *The Courage to Be Protestant*, 28.

the next chapter. I like what Brett McCracken says: "Pastors who think they'll win over the cool kids by forming the church in the cool kids' pop-culture image are liable to find themselves even less relevant than when they started."[14]

The chemical concepts that have come together and homogenized Jesus to the world need to be broken up. Our next chapter is devoted to this. It serves as a response to this Christ. The goal is to get beyond mere critique and into real principles and pragmatics to help the culture see Jesus rightly.

---

14. McCracken, *Hipster Christianity*, 182.

10

## Resting in the Relevance of a Disparate Christ

*American evangelicals, it seems, have a hard time recognizing the comic caricature that they have become.*

STEPHEN J. NICHOLS

I WAS AT ONE of the most amazing church facilities I had ever seen in my life. It needed its own zip code. It was one of the most renowned churches in America. I was just visiting, taking in the Sunday-morning sights and sounds. Churchapalooza! The place was huge. I made my way into the main worship venue where the Senior Pastor was going to speak. He is a well-known man who has garnered great respect and much of it well deserved. I have appreciated a number of things about his ministry, his heart for people, his vision and clarity. God has used him without question. As he stood up to speak, he delivered a message that had a bit of angst as the church he pastors has taken its share of criticism from people all over. Every pastor knows the feeling to one degree or another. When you lead a church, some people love what you are doing and others don't. Taking criticism is just part of the job description. As the pastor shared, he spent a good amount of his time defending his church's record. He talked about what was happening at the church and how people were growing. This was all well and good until one stunning statement. It went like this: "I would have to say, I think we might have the most mature church in America." Wow! That was quite a claim. But how would he know? Well, he actually went on to tell us. His evidence for his conclusion came in a series of stats about the thousands of people in small groups, the thousands that had passed through this course and that course. The numbers were huge, no doubt, but how did he get from metrics to maturity? How did he get from classes to character? How did he get from stats to sanctification? I was stunned. Had we come to the place in America where you could graph the work of the Spirit?

As I listened, I felt like Professor Keating teaching poetry in *Dead Poets Society*. I wanted to rip out the tables of church metrics and graphs just like he had his students rip out Dr. J. Evans Pritchard's formulaic template for measuring the quality of great lyrical verse. I don't want to be harsh or judgmental to this respected man. He has done a lot for the kingdom. I just don't understand the obsession with reducing spiritual growth to math.

I planted the church that I pastor. I came from the Bible Belt of Texas to the Mormon Belt of Utah. It was both a cultural shock and an experience of another, slightly less hip, parrot culture. The Church of Jesus Christ of Latter-day Saints have their own bookstores, just like we evangelicals did in the Bible Belt. They have their own radio programs just like we did in the Bible Belt. They have their own movie production companies just like we did in the Bible Belt. They have their own business networks and professional connections just like we did in the Bible Belt. Their billboards dominate the landscape just like evangelical billboards in the Bible Belt. Church buildings dot every few blocks, not unlike the plethora of church buildings afforded various evangelical denominations in the Bible Belt. If the evangelical message to culture has been "Whatever you do, we can do worse!," Mormon culture seems to be saying, "Whatever you do, we can do *significantly* worse!" But seeing this parrot culture has caused me to reflect long and hard on the one we have created in evangelicalism. It has made me see what others outside evangelical culture must see, looking in from the outside. It has made me more acquainted with their alienation and with their repulsion.

What can the church do about Homogenized Jesus? The answer to that is the focus of this chapter. Before getting into particulars about the local church's role, a biblical study of Jesus and his relationship to culture is in order. Here I will look to the Gospel of John for guidance. Going to the text liberates us to God's wisdom on the matter. I echo D. A. Carson's thoughts on this:

To pursue with a passion the nourishing wholeness of biblical theology as the controlling matrix for our reflection on the relations between Christ and culture will, ironically, help us to be far more flexible than the inflexible grids that are often made to stand in the Bible's place. Scripture will mandate that we think holistically and subtly, wise and penetratingly under the Lordship of Christ—utterly dissatisfied with the anesthetic of the culture.[1]

## Christ and Cosmos

The biblical terms that come closest to reflecting what we mean when we talk about secular culture or ideology are terms like "world" and "age." In 2 Corinthians 4:4, Satan is characterized as the "god of this world." Here the term rendered in the ESV as "world" is the term *aion* in Greek, from which we get our English word "aeon," which means age. So when Paul refers to Satan as the "god of this *aion*," he means that Satan is the governor or caretaker of the ethos of the times. He is the steward of the mood of the day.

In addition to *aion* the other Greek term that frequently carries the same idea is *cosmos*. In English when we refer to the "cosmos" we are referring to our galaxy or maybe our world and the space around it. We refer to things as "cosmological," showing that they have to do with how the world operates. *Cosmos* is an important Greek term. It is used in various ways to speak about the physical world, humanity at large, sometimes it refers to a portion of either, but a very frequent use of the term is as a referent to fallen humanity and the ideas represented therein. It is the closest thing biblically we can get to speaking about secular culture. Perhaps a good definition of this use of the term would be to say that the "world" consists of the prevailing moods, ideas, images, depictions, ethics, perspectives, and expectations of society. That sounds a lot like the term "culture."

If this is what the world is, then the natural question is: Does the Bible show us how Jesus related to the world? Absolutely it does. No place is this more developed than in the Gospel of John. In fact, 42 percent of the uses of the term *cosmos* in the entire New Testament are found in John's portrayal of the life of Christ. So what does it teach us?

---

1. Carson, *Christ and Culture Revisited*, 227.

The place to start is with the prepositions. Prepositions locate nouns and so they tell us about the noun and how it functions regarding other terms in the sentence. In the case of *cosmos* Jesus comes "into" the world (John 10:36; 11:27; 16:28; 17:18). He takes up residence "in" it (John 1:10; 9:5). As a resident, he is the light "of" the world (John 8:12; 9:5), but he himself is not "of" the world (John 8:23; 17:14, 16); neither is his kingdom "of" the world (John 18:36). Those who follow him are also not "of" this world (John 15:19; 17:14, 16). In fact, those same followers are identified as having come "out of" the world (John 15:19; 17:6). For John, Christ and his followers are who they are in correspondence to the world. This is important because it tells us that our relationship to culture is not incidental to our identity but intrinsically tied to it.

## Contrasts

It will help us to look at some contrasts between Jesus and the world as presented by John. First, John contrasts the peace that Jesus provides with what the cosmos provides. "Peace I leave with you; my peace I give to you. Not as the world gives do I give to you. Let not your hearts be troubled, neither let them be afraid" (John 14:27). Also, Jesus declares in John 16:33, "I have said these things to you, that in me you may have peace. In the world you will have tribulation. But take heart; I have overcome the world."

Second, Jesus' knowledge of the God the Father is entirely antithetical to the world's experience of the Father. In Jesus' prayer in John 17, he says, "O righteous Father, even though the world does not know you, I know you, and these know that you have sent me" (John 17:25). Jesus' connectedness to his Father sets him apart from a world that is disconnected from the Father.

Third, the Spirit sent by Jesus comes bearing truth. The world is portrayed as something that cannot receive the truth or the Spirit who bears it. "And I will ask the Father, and he will give you another Helper, to be with you forever, even the Spirit of truth, whom the world cannot receive, because it neither sees him nor knows him. You know him, for he dwells with you and will be in you" (John 14:17). It is worth noting that while the world cannot receive the Spirit of truth, those who know Christ will know the Spirit of truth. Thus they are set apart from the world in terms of both their capacity to receive truth and their experience of it.

## Dispositions

Aside from these contrasts, the general disposition of the world toward Jesus and his followers is important. John writes that Jesus understood the world to hate him and his followers (John 15:18–19). Jesus says that the world will rejoice at his death and departure, while his followers would lament (John 16:20). The world hates Jesus because of his negative assessment of its works (John 7:7). Surely the world's rejection of Christ and what he came to offer is rooted in the fact that the world is under the rulership of Satan (John 14:30; 16:11),

But what does John say of Jesus' disposition and relationship to the world? While the world hates Jesus, he is said to "love the world" by seeking to rescue its members in compassion (John 3:16–18). He loves the world by acting as a light to the world to draw people out of darkness and into relationship with God (John 3:19–21). He loves the world enough that he came to it "to bear witness to the truth" (John 18:37). His mission of "truth-bearing" was not done in a covert manner. He was direct and very aboveboard. As Jesus himself declared, "I have spoken openly to the world. I have always taught in the synagogues and in the temple, where all the Jews come together. I have said nothing in secret" (John 18:20).

## Application

Christ's relation to the cosmos must form the basis for our relation to the cosmos, because our identity as believers is first and foremost an identity that is "in Christ." The fact that we exist "in Christ" forms the basis of Paul's concept of the believer, and acts as the ground for all of the benefits of the spiritual life of those who comprise the church. The fact that Jesus' relationship to the cosmos is the analogy for our relationship to the cosmos is made clear by one text in particular found in John's Gospel. It reads:

> I do not ask that you take them out of the world, but that you keep them from the evil one. They are not of the world, *just as I am not of the world*. Sanctify them in the truth; your word is truth. *As you sent me* into the world, *so I have sent them* into the world. And for their sake I consecrate myself, they also may be sanctified in truth (John 17:15–19). [emphasis added]

The parallels between Jesus and believers are clear. Jesus is not defined by the world and neither are we. Jesus was sent missionally into the center of the dark storm of fallen society—the world—by the Father and in the same way we are sent by Jesus to that same cultural storm. This doesn't yet give us all the particulars of our engagement, but it tells us that our identity and our mission in regard to the world resemble Jesus' identity and mission. What follow are some principles of orientation and engagement with culture that we glean from our mandate to reflect Jesus' engagement with the cosmos.

*Our engagement with the world is rooted in a communal identity.* In Jesus' high priestly prayer, he prayed that his followers would be used by his Father as a means to bring about belief in the world. To accomplish that, Jesus asked the Father to make believers united in reflection of the joyful love of trinitarian oneness. He prayed, "I do not ask for these only, but also for those who will believe in me through their word, that they may all be one, just as you, Father, are in me, and I in you, that they also may be in us, so that the world may believe that you have sent me" (John 17:20–21). This dual union of us together and us with God communicates a relational closeness that is intended to appeal to the world. The world is dog-eat-dog. It is a place of suspicion and cynicism. It is filled with relationships where everyone is waiting for the other shoe to fall. But the church is not to be like that. It is to be filled with unity born of mutual love and concern. It is to find its resourcing for this in the Trinity itself. This discontinuity, between how relationships in the world operate and how those in the church operate, forms an essential part of our engagement with the culture around us.

*We must not long for identification with the world.* Jesus' identity was not bound up with what the world thought of him. In fact, he was completely and entirely rejected by the ideologues of his day. As he looked forward to his death he told two of his disciples, Andrew and Philip, "Whoever loves his life loses it. And whoever hates his life in this world will keep it for eternal life" (John 12:25). If we are to despise our "life in this world," then we must reject the constant pull to let it define us. We must pull away from seeking its acceptance. But this is precisely the opposite impulse of the worshippers of Homogenized Jesus. They continually seek to make him as palatable as possible. Jesus is de-theologized. Jesus is made non-threatening. Jesus is so contextualized (read: watered-down) that he has no historical or timeless theological context of his own to speak of. Dick Staub rightly asserts that "Christians are called to be the light of the world not the lite of the world."[2] But the

---

2. Staub, *The Culturally Savvy Christian*, 41.

pop culture evangelical homogenizers of today have ignored Jesus' own posture in regard to the world and have become more concerned with Jesus' "cool" factor. As a result, Jesus gets perceived by secular culture as trivial instead of transformative.

The quest for cool ends up making the church look silly and, ironically, irrelevant. I really like Brett McCracken's advice to the church about all of this when he writes:

> The never-ending quest for cool is arduous and draining. I'm not sure you can ever learn cool, so my advice would be to stop trying so hard. What churches should be doing is engaging their communities and cultures and seeking to equip their congregations to express themselves in whatever way is truthful and authentic (in the non-clichéd sense of the word). No recipe or how-to formula will provide instructions on how to be a cool church that is appealing to fashionable young people, and I suspect that the harder you try, the harder it becomes to sustain such a community. No one stays hip for very long, after all—especially when the "hip" is never completely comfortable in its own skin in the first place.[3]

Does culture right now look at mainstream evangelicalism as though it has much of substance to offer it? It sure doesn't seem so. I agree with Staub when he says, "I've never heard cultural observers describe contemporary Christianity as a profoundly spiritual movement offering deep union with a transcendent God or as the basis for a spiritually inspired, intelligent, and aesthetically rich cultural renewal."[4] This is sad because, in an effort to so identify with culture, Jesus is not just getting "repackaged"; he is actually getting unloaded. Once all the "hip" is unwrapped, Jesus is nowhere to be found.

*Our fidelity to the Word of God will naturally create a disconnection with our culture.* This is simply inescapable. Again in his high priestly prayer, Jesus prayed, speaking of his followers, "I have given them your word, and the world has hated them because they are not of the world, just as I am not of the world" (John 17:14). The Word of God forms our canon of faith and life and consequently colors everything the church is called to do and be. We should not be rude or obnoxious toward culture with the Word of God. At that point we would actually be pitting the Spirit of God against the Word of God, and this is literally one of the last

---

3. McCracken, *Hispter Christianity*, 190.
4. Staub, *The Culturally Savvy Christian*, 43.

things a follower of Christ should ever do. But we can neither run the risk of making the text so genteel that we actually cloud its message nor shroud it in something more tasty. David Wells reflects on various biblical affirmations and states:

> On all these matters we have God's truth, and for the church to be shy about saying "We know... We know... We know," is an act of self-betrayal... Scripture... sees itself, and is seen as the self-disclosure of God that is therefore unlike anything else on earth. It is the truth. What it says corresponds to what happened in the world of which it speaks. It really does reflect what is in the human heart. It is the measure of reality. It is the standard by which we are to judge life's religions and philosophies, its programs and values, its hopes and its fears.[5]

The moment the church publicly establishes the Bible as the final rule of its ethic, the chasm between church and culture will be fixed and cannot be crossed fully unless one wittingly or unwittingly bends its ethic to the other. The culture can bend to the church in conversion or the church can bend to the culture in compromise, but one of them will have to give for there to be homogeneity. What we need are church leaders who will not bend Jesus to the culture and so homogenize him with it. Instead, in faithfulness to the Word of God, church leaders must be willing to be hated with Christ until either God's Spirit moves to convert those in the world to him, or he ultimately returns to declare that "the kingdom of the world has become the kingdom of our Lord and of his Christ" (Rev. 11:15).

*We are called to an ambassadorial relationship of rescuing love.* As I mentioned earlier, the missional sending of Jesus "into" the world by the Father forms the basis for our own mission to go "into" the world sent by the Son. We come offering the world something it does not have in the substance of the gospel. The key idea here, as it relates to John's picture of the world, is that we must go "into" it because we are not "of" it. To go on mission is to go to a place that is not home. To treat it as home is to confuse what is meant by both "mission" and "home." Ambassadors know from whence they come and they acquaint themselves to where they are going.

A slight alteration of attention is warranted now to consider some key principles for reaching out to the culture. Thus far, you might be

---

5. Wells, *The Courage to Be Protestant*, 80.

under the impression that I have capitulated to a fundamentalist approach to culture. Rest assured that is not the case. However, it is true that at this present time in our culture, our biggest issue of engagement is that we have not been alien enough. Yes, we want to be ambassadorial in regard to culture, but when it comes to the state of evangelical pop culture, the very reason for the rise of Homogenized Jesus is that the lines of distinction have not been drawn clearly enough. Therefore it is impossible to respond appropriately to this Jesus without emphasizing that the prevailing culture and the church must have a strategic discontinuity fostered by believers.

But this alien identity does not mean there is no context for connecting with the culture. Our mission philosophy cannot be an engagement by disengagement, any more than it can be an engagement by wholesale identification. It now seems appropriate to tangentially consider what makes for a good ambassador to a world (culture) driven by antithetical notions of what constitutes a good life. This is precisely where we find ourselves, and so we need some principles to hold on to as a guide.

## An Ambassadorial Guidebook

*Embrace the neutrality of common grace.* In theology, a distinction is made between two categories of grace. The first is special grace, which consists of God's gracious work of redeeming the life of one of his elect. The second is common grace, which consists of blessings we have in common simply because we are God's creatures. In creation God endows people with common threads as common creatures in a shared world. Here are a few of the things that we share with others as part of God's common grace:

> *The image of God*—we each are created in God's image and endowed with glory and honor. This image includes our personhood, our common responsibility to govern and be stewards of the affairs of this world, and our inherent dignity.
>
> *The creation itself*—God made all things, and they testify of his majesty and character.
>
> *Sustenance for life*—God provides food and necessities for his creation irrespective of their beliefs regarding him.
>
> *Relationships*—God blesses believers and unbelievers with the opportunity to forge mutually beneficial relationships.

> *Morality*—While humanity is fallen, it does not mean that we are all as bad as we could be. God created humans as the kind of being that has an innate moral awareness. No doubt our tradition and experience play deep roles in forming our moral sense but, at bottom, there still remains a morality to be had.

The fact that we share these traits enables us to have a productive society despite our deep differences. It enables us to have points of necessary and fulfilling connection even though we may not have the same eternal citizenship. To ignore this connection is to miss an important and often overlooked aspect in Christian theology. Common grace is starting to get a bit more attention, but for a long time the church had very little to say about it. But common grace does more than make us able to be on the same page as human creatures, it enables us to find points of resonance with the world even if our inner lives are characterized by different things.

Two doctrines in Scripture work together to permit us as humans to find common ground: common grace and original sin. I like what Tim Keller wrote about this:

> The Biblical doctrine of the universal image of God, therefore, leads Christians to expect nonbelievers will be better than any of their mistaken beliefs could make them. The Biblical doctrine of universal sinfulness also leads Christians to expect believers will be worse in practice than their orthodox beliefs should make them. So there will be plenty of ground for respectful cooperation.[6]

This is good food for thought as it relates to social action. Can I partner with the Mormons in my area on issues of the sanctity of human life or in standing for a traditional view of marriage? Common grace would seem to say that this could be a locus of cultural resonance, a pocket of mutual concern. Because of the biblical doctrine of the image of God in man, it is safe to say that God gets honor when his image is cherished, whether it is by me or a Mormon. It doesn't mean he is honored to the same degree. Consider an analogy. If one of my daughters gives me a gift and another little girl in our church gives me the same gift, I will cherish them both but not to the same degree. The relationship that I have with my daughter makes the gift more cherished. But this in no way means that the gift from the little one who is not my daughter is scorned. God

---

6. Keller, *The Reason for God*, 19.

gets more glory from a morally appropriate lost person than from a morally depraved lost person. This doesn't mean he accepts him as a son. Sonship is an issue of special grace, but in a pluralistic society where the church will always (and should always) be in some level of discontinuity with the culture, common grace cannot afford to be ignored.

*Celebrate diversity in form without ignoring that even form has a function.* It is inappropriate for us to conclude that style is always neutral. It is also inappropriate for us to load style with morally determinative power. The same song can be sung in a variety of forms and still bring equally deep glory to God. The same song could also have dance put to it that could range from beautiful depictions of human movements to licentious and stimulating depictions. Form may be largely irrelevant in some scenarios. However, in others the form takes on a function that detracts from the content.

A couple of decades ago, churches were embroiled in what came to be known as the "Worship Wars" over styles of music. The whole discussion and debate often seemed merely reactionary. One side said "Form doesn't matter." The other side intimated that "Form always matters." It took too long for people to see that the truth was that form and style mattered less than the traditionalists thought they did and more than the non-traditionalists thought they did. So how did the church rectify the situation? Some churches converted to new styles of music and gave up hymnody altogether. Some churches compromised in a blended worship. Some churches remained connected to old forms. From a biblical and culture vantage point each of these three solutions, if they contained the right spirit among the parties concerned, seem to be perfectly acceptable. But some churches commodified. They took the approach that the best way was to please every ecclesiastical consumer by breaking up corporate worship into different venues, splitting generations apart so each could tickle their own doxological fancy in the name of Jesus.

This did more than "solve" a worship problem. It created an ecclesiological disaster that plagues evangelical culture years later. Now churches have multiple worship venues not driven by schedule or home location, but by what form of music a person likes. So families go to one church but Junior goes to the faux-Nirvana room, Mom and Dad go to the David Crowder lookalike venue, and Grandma heads to the oldie-but-goodie Isaac Watts room—each basking in the self-glory of a worship experience that has put their consumerism smack at the center and ruined any opportunity for Sunday worship to carry forward an element of multi-generational fellowship and faithfulness.

Do not misunderstand me. Diversification of form or style is not wrong. It becomes wrong when we ignore it and act like it doesn't matter. What if our worship service became diversified in its musical form on a regular basis? What if we just picked a style and stuck with it for all ages? It seems that either of these approaches would at least keep the consumer from consuming the musical part of worship.

Forms of appearance, forms of media, forms of music, forms of teaching, forms of writing, forms of buildings, forms of disciple-making, and forms of liturgy all will change given enough time. There are no canonized lists in these areas. The key for the church is to celebrate various forms, enjoy them for what they are, and evaluate them on their ability to retain the essence and flavor of a content-rich theology. T. M. Moore is spot-on when he suggests:

> Taste in culture matters will always leave room for individual expression and preference. However, mere taste, or undisciplined taste, taste that follows every merely personal whim, apart from any larger narrative, can be destructive of true culture, whether in the arts, language, making a family or pursuing a career. Such an approach to culture matters compromises the larger Christian calling to let our light so shine before men that they might see our good works and, acknowledging their intention and character, give glory and honor to God.[7]

An ambassador is flexible with taste/form/style insofar as it never distorts or diminishes content. In doing so, he lives out the calling to resemble Jesus as a light to the world and never lets it get needlessly and foolishly sacrificed.

*Exegete culture in order to have communicative excellence.* Jesus knew his audience as he spoke and tailored aspects of his message to them. The four evangelists all wrote to different audiences sharing specific details to create unique (albeit similar) theologically driven narratives of the life of Christ. Paul wrote letters to individuals and churches in very different situations and structured his message accordingly. The seven churches of Revelation were given very specific messages from Christ that connected to specific background issues at each location. This biblical model of communication must be adopted by the church. It is insufficient for the

---

7. Moore, *Culture Matters*, 54.

local church to stand solely on the merits of proclaiming truth without considering that communication is both multifaceted and bidirectional.

It is multifaceted in the sense that it contains more than words. It carries what I would call intangible adverbs. Words are shaped by postures, expressions, moods, textures, tones, and volumes. These intangibles change everything regarding communication. It is also bidirectional. It depends upon a receptor. That receptor possesses their own set of values, interpretive grids, personal make-up, traditions, experiences, modes of reasoning, wounds, and joys. So in a sense, communication is a multifaceted, bidirectional enterprise involving two multifaceted beings. Wow . . . that seems complicated. And it is. That is why the church must know the culture to which it speaks and how to speak to it in a manner that holds forth the truth with unflinching consistency, yet cradled in the sensitivity demanded by intangible adverbs.

But how do we know what the adverbs are supposed to be? How do we discern what kind of a context to frame the content in? The answer is by exegeting cultural forms and language. It is important for church leaders to know the cultural lingua franca of the day. What works of literature are shaping people's thoughts? What films are baptizing the imaginations of today? What music is smuggling in messages of hedonism and despair? What recreations are straining the commitments of work and home? These and more must be answered by those who want to do more than proclaim.

## Some Suggestions

If we are called to relate to culture effectively, then let me make a few practical suggestions for local-church leaders. Given some time, you can brainstorm an awful lot more than this list, but at least it might serve as a place to start:

1. Do a small group based on film analysis. The first week, watch the film together as a group and give them a study/discussion guide to think about the theological/philosophical/cultural issues in the film. Get together the next week and discuss it. This will serve two main purposes. First, it allows you to utilize popular cultural forms to teach rich biblical truth. Second, it lets you model for those in the group what it looks like to exegete culture. It trains them to be critical engagers rather than uncritical consumers.

2. Create a book club that reads through a book significant to the cultural ethos of the world in which you minister and discuss it once a month. Take a work of fiction or non-fiction and go after it. Can you imagine reading Richard Dawkins, Sam Harris, Eckhart Tolle, Deepak Chopra, Reza Aslan, or Dan Brown and discussing it with your group? You would be teaching them how to pick apart literature and emboldening them with the fact that Jesus stands over culture, waiting to transform it.

3. Have a debate night. This could be great for a youth group. Pick an important topic in the culture and assign sides to research and develop arguments for their camps. Set clear ground rules and discuss. A youth ministry doing this with parental involvement on the subject of same-sex attraction and marriage could be remarkable.

4. Create a "Pastor on Culture" video that goes out to the church once a week. If you have a laptop it is simple to record and send out. Discuss a cultural topic, theme, form, or anecdote and relate it to sound doctrine.

5. For pastors: Read what your people are reading. Watch what your people are watching. Listen to what your people are listening to. Of course the caveat is always personal holiness, but you need to be actively evaluating and engaging the content that they are.

6. Have varied styles of music show up "randomly" during worship services. You might think it will be a distraction, but it likely will awaken dead sensors and focus people on the worshipful task at hand.

## De-homogenizing Jesus

Deepening Christian Culture

*Depth of History*

Knowing the narrative of the past and acquainting ourselves with the theological and philosophical shoulders on which we stand is essential for us to have any depth to our Christian culture. People who shun the insight and experiences of the past condemn themselves to a shallow existence. In a recent book, Michael Svigel contends that this rejection of and ignorance to the past is at the heart of what he calls evangelicalism's midlife crisis. This is great imagery. A man in a midlife crisis acts adolescently. He is shallowly trying to reclaim the lost years like Uncle Rico in *Napoleon Dynamite* longing to go back to '82. A man in midlife crisis changes his dress, his language, and his stuff, all to regain a sense of "cool" that he hopes takes him away from the inevitability of aging and into a euphoria of youth reborn.

In midlife, a man tries to become rootless so he can glide away from meaningful and costly connections with others. Lasch, commenting on the narcissism of culture, incisively noted, "the usual defenses against the ravages of age—identification with ethical or artistic values beyond one's immediate interests, intellectual curiosity, the consoling emotional warmth derived from happy relationships in the past—can do nothing for the narcissist."[8] Evangelicalism as a movement finds itself in precisely the same situation. Its anti-intellectual, de-historicized, culturally myopic nature is killing it.

Some of Michael Svigel's comments on the evangelical midlife crisis are worth quoting:

> The classic creeds and confessions of the faith had once connected the Protestant emphasis on scriptural authority to the ancient church's emphasis on Christ and orthodox theology. However, for the most part, independent-minded evangelicalism exchanged the wisdom and learning of the ages for a naïve and historically inauthentic Bible-only Christianity that had little need for any other norm of doctrine than the so-called "plain reading of Scripture." In this entirely new approach to biblical theology, the individual student of Scripture—from the pulpit to the pew, from the lectern to the latrine—was now a self-ordained theologian. Not only did modern evangelicals hold to the sufficiency of Scripture, but they held more and more to the sufficiency of self—the competency of the individual Bible reader to accurately handle Scripture without the input of anybody else.[9]

Evangelicalism is historically disenfranchised by its own doing. Having cut the ropes that once moored us to shore, we have said to the historic Christian community that the high seas of a fallen world can be navigated just fine by us and our Bibles. This has nothing whatsoever to do with the sufficiency and authority of the Bible; it has to do with the overestimation of the self in an ego-intoxicated world.

---

8. Lasch, *The Culture of Narcissism*, 41.
9. Svigel, *Retro-Christianity*, 35.

I recall preaching once and having a woman object to my quoting the reflections of historical figures on the text. She thought this needless and unimportant. Unfortunately, she is not alone. What we need is a respect for both the breadth and depth of the past and an understanding of our own limitations. To reject and ignore the voice of church history is to ignore the voice of the Spirit echoing through its halls and to underestimate the capacities of great men of God. As one well-regarded theologian noted, "The problem in rejecting all church history and tradition is that the reflections of less gifted minds tend to be substituted for the wisdom of the spiritual and theological giants of the past."[10]

Practically speaking, it is the role of church leaders to connect the congregation to the past. It is their role to teach them that they do not stand as independent thinkers, but as solitary minds leaning on a long lineage of careful thought and rigorously discussed and defended conclusions. Preaching needs to include appeals to the historical community and an explanation of how doctrine has developed. We cannot expect people to appreciate what we do not, nor can they value what they do not know. Public adult preaching and teaching is not the only place for exposing our people to the historical church. We must begin with our children. Moms and dads need to know it so they can teach it at home. Children's ministry curriculum needs to create space for it. Youth ministry must connect to the past. If we do not do this, we heighten the tendency for our young people to sociologically embrace their parents' faith without seeing those same parents' credibility strengthened by a multitude of witnesses. We must get historical if we are to save the future.

*Depth of Knowledge*

In our day, information has become equivalent to knowledge. But this is grave error. Information paradoxically functions as both a prerequisite to knowledge and quite possibly its most strident enemy. The amount of information we receive in a day is mind-boggling. Never in history has it been greater. Yet our knowledge is superficial . . . if we can even get away with calling it "knowledge" at all. Knowledge has to do with interaction. It has to do with more than propositions. It is about rumination and experience.

---

10. Davis, *Foundations of Evangelical Theology*, 229.

Let me illustrate. Knowledge does not function like a traditional light switch that either is on or off. Instead, it functions more like a dimmer switch. It comes on and grows to differing degrees. If it is dim, we still say that the light is on—but its light is not what it could be if we slid the switch up a bit. So it is with knowledge. I don't either know something or not know it. Instead, I know things to differing degrees. This means that, contrary to Descartes, knowledge is not about certitude. For the philosophically minded, you will notice that my proposal is consistent with what is known as a modest foundationalism. Modest foundationalism says that we do not need certitude to call something knowledge. Instead, we need reasonability or proper evidence to warrant a particular conclusion. For example, I know my wife loves me, and that knowledge is 100 percent. I have literally no doubts after sixteen years of life together, witnessing her heart at its best and worst, and seeing the consistency between what she says and what she does. I have more than ample evidence to be certain. I am 90 percent confident that O. J. Simpson committed the murders he was accused of almost twenty years ago. Lots of evidence compels me, but Johnny Cochran showed that the glove didn't fit, so room was left for a doubt to niggle in.

Theologically, this perspective of knowledge as an issue of degrees is vital. It allows us to understand that knowledge grows as our interaction with something grows. My knowledge of the Spirit grows as my interaction with the Spirit grows, in much the same way as my relationship with my wife does. How would I know that God loves me? Well, for starters, he and I should talk more and spend more time together. I should read more about him—remember, information is a prerequisite for the cultivation of real knowledge. I should spend time with others who know him. I should see how he related to others in the past. All of this will help me grow in my knowledge of him and his love for me.

The problem in evangelicalism is that in its trendy, faddish acquiescence to pop culture, it doesn't sit in one place long enough to form real knowledge. It suffers from a type of corporate attention deficit disorder. Knowledge takes time, it demands plumbing the depth of subjects without coming up for air all that often. It necessitates cogitating, lingering, ruminating, and waiting. A great way to see where we are is to contrast our present depth of thought with the Puritans. The one thing that stands out about their writings is how deeply they thought about specific issues. Has anyone besides God himself thought more deeply about contentment than Jeremiah Burroughs? Seriously, we are too discontented thinking about our busyness to get busy thinking about contentment.

At the practical level, this means staying with something for more than a few moments. I don't think expository preaching is canonized or that "thou shalt preach expository" should be made the eleventh commandment. But it is a fantastic way to stay a prolonged time with a specific set of issues or historical situation, get to know it, and so teach people to do the same. Additionally, we take things like prayer and fasting (and any of the spiritual disciplines for that matter) and teach on them, but we don't sit together with them. What I mean is that we try to learn about them by studying them, instead of long periods of doing them in community. Gone are the days of the midweek prayer meeting. Gone are the calls to corporate fasting. Now prayer is a transition from worship music to message, and fasting means skipping lunch to give to the missionaries. How will the next generation even know . . . I mean *really* know to a high degree what these things are? Information is replacing knowledge and we can't afford what it will cost.

*Depth of Mission*

Evangelicals often use their resources to keep ministry away. Churches find it relatively easy to raise money for third-world missions but long to relocate their own church to the suburbs to keep their upper-middle-class constituency happy. There is nothing wrong with supporting children through child sponsorship, but it probably shouldn't resolve the tensions in our conscience with global poverty. The more we keep ourselves restricted to the daily life of ease and comfort, the shallower our well of experience gets for meeting the deep needs of people and facing some of the most difficult questions of our day.

If you never travel to the third world, you will likely never really have to ask yourself why God fills greedy American homes with pantries that overflow, but has Haitian children eating mud cakes. If evangelical overseas travel consists of Reformation tours and K-Love cruises with Third Day, then it's pretty easy to see why the church has been experientially thin. I am not suggesting that short- or long-term missions provide the only means of deepening the well of experience, but I am suggesting that the well only gets deepened by experiences that exact something from us. Evangelicals need sensate experience with the edges of human existence to know what grace looks like on those edges and to grow in a belief in God's ability to extend to them.

The good news is that this depth of missional experience seems to be getting deeper. Churches are more attuned to people actually experiencing the world outside of the bubble of suburban life. Human indignity is on the radar screen of the church in ways that it simply wasn't in the mid- to late twentieth century. Technology has made us more aware of both need and opportunity. We just have to be cautious that we do not use it as a tool for a modified engagement that ends in practical disengagement. Evangelicalism will be strengthened as we smell the stench of brokenness, as we hear, first hand, the pleas of the hungry, as we, like Jesus, touch the lame and the crippled.

Practically speaking, you can get your church involved with a number of organizations that connect local bodies to the global poor. Steer away from short-term mission vacations and enter into short-term trips that foster long-term relationships intent on evoking systematic change to specific cultural contexts. The world is not a smorgasbord of need for us to taste portions of in an effort to make us more globally rounded. Instead, we get deeper in our own culture by eating and drinking long and hard of the needs in another culture. That is what we should be after.

Locally, we can do this by turning groups and ministries outward and serving in regular rhythms people who have nothing to give back. Weekly loving people in a nursing home who will never add a dime to the church could be a good place to start. Sharing afternoons at social ministries and outreaches to give more than food and clothes by building lasting relationships in an effort to show people that El Roi sees them and wants to know them might be yet another place to begin. You know your culture. Exegete it and find out where the nerve of need lies and minister to it. In doing so through a long-term commitment, your people will find it difficult to stay in the bubble of evangelical kitsch.

## The Ambiguities of Conversion

Simply put, the gospel can be best defined as:

> The good news that eternal life in God's kingdom can be had solely by believing 1) that God the Father sent God the Son to die in our place to satisfy his justice due to our sin against him,

and, 2) that the Son rose again to secure a new kind of life for us in that kingdom under his eternal kingship.

You will notice immediately that two important ideas are present in this definition. The gospel is grounded in the substitutionary work of Jesus and intrinsically tied to our entry into God's kingdom. Jesus talks about the gospel as the gospel of the kingdom[11] These two ideas come together and tell us what is most basic about the gospel. We need forgiveness, and forgiveness grants a new life under a new ruler.

If this is the case, evangelical pop culture and its commoditization of the gospel has been guilty of not telling the gospel truth about the gospel itself. To invite someone to experience the forgiveness of sins, with no expectation of that ushering them into kingdom life, is like inviting someone to your door and not letting them in. It creates a type of decisionism where magic mantras are invoked and sinner's prayers are prayed by sinners because, if they are, then assurance of eternal life can be had. But the gospel is about more than Polar Express tickets getting punched with the word "believe" so the bearer can see a celestial Santa Claus. The Bible only clearly defines eternal life in one passage, and in it Jesus says, "And this is eternal life, that they know you, the only true God, and Jesus Christ whom you have sent" (John 17:3). How interesting it is that eternal life is framed in the language of "knowledge." But as I referenced above, this knowledge is much more than information, it is an interactive relationship. Dallas Willard says that we know something "when we are representing it (thinking about it, speaking of it, treating it) as it actually is, on an appropriate basis of thought and experience."[12] Knowledge necessitates interplay between the knower and the object to be known. Eternal life then is knowing God via the transaction of Jesus death and the consequent translation into life under a new King in a new kingdom. To separate the two (kingdom and cross) would be like separating a gate from a kingdom or a doorway from a house. I would be left to invite someone to a doorway with nowhere to stay or to invite them to a house with no way to get in. The figure below illustrates the errors of decisionism on the one hand, and works-based moralism on the other.

---

11. The Synoptic Gospels are filled with this language: Matt. 4:17, 23; 9:35; 10:7; 13:19; 24:14; Mark 1:15; Luke 4:43; 8:1; 9:2, 60; 16:16.

12. Willard, *Knowing Christ Today*, 15.

*resting in the relevance of a disparate christ* 281

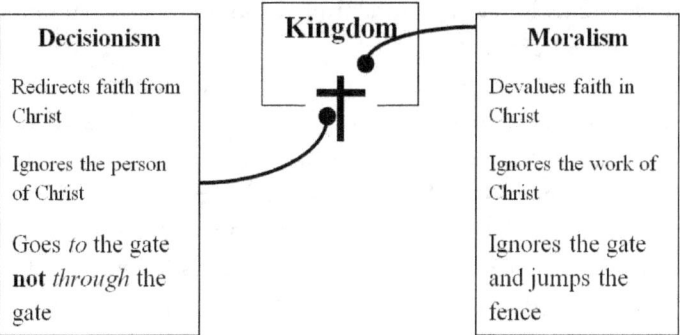

To steer us away from making conversion an object to consume demands some clear definitions. I am distilling some of the teaching of Dallas Willard here, as well as my own understanding of these concepts. Willard's books *The Divine Conspiracy* and *Knowing Christ Today* are of particular help regarding this issue of conversion.

Three terms need to be defined and then related to one another: truth, belief, and commitment. *Truth* simply defined is correspondence to reality. When what I am thinking about matches up with what is, in fact, the case in reality, then we call the relationship between the two (my thought and the object of my thought) true. For example, if a wall is brown, and I think "the wall is brown" then the relationship between my thought and the color of the wall is called truth.

The second term, *belief*, is best defined as a disposition to act. If I believe something I am ready to act *as if* it is true. My belief does not make it true. Truth is a statement about what connects to reality. I could hold false beliefs. For example, if I believed that God did not exist, that would be a false belief. It also would be an indication that I was ready to act as if God did not exist. But my belief that he does not exist in no wise means that he does not, in point of fact, exist.

Third is the term *commitment*. If I commit to something, then I am going to act *as if* I believe it. My commitment does not mean that I really believe it. I can easily commit to things that I do not really believe. I could commit to going on a diet with my wife because I love her but have no belief that the diet will actually work.

The "as if" terminology is crucial here. My beliefs don't make anything true. My commitment does not make me believe it. Now, there is no question that if I really believe something, I will in actual practice be committed to it; such is the nature and power of belief. But I cannot work backward. Belief is not the natural fruit of commitment. Commitment is the natural fruit of belief.

Now let's take these terms into the subject of conversion. I remember traveling to Puerto Rico on my first mission trip. I prayed with the first person I ever had to "to ask Jesus into his heart." His name was Nicholas and he lived on the US naval base there. I have no idea whatever happened to him, but he did pray the sinner's prayer with me. One of my fellow team members had his own evangelistic approach. He took one young boy aside and as part of his pitch he walked him over to the stove and turned on one of the burners. As the flames leapt up from the burner, he told the boy that this is what hell would be like . . . *forever!* Well, needless to say, if that is your approach with children under ten years of age, you are likely to have a pretty high "conversion growth rate." Scare tactics, sinner's prayers, carrots on sticks, promises of good life, tickets to eternal bliss—all of them can get us to commit, but none of them can make us believe.

The dastardly danger of creating conversion as a packaged product is that we will end up trusting the product and not the person. Most of evangelical Christianity readily shuns the idea that one must be baptized in water to be "saved." This is known as baptismal regeneration. But unsuspectingly the last 150 years of American evangelical theology has produced the notion of "prayerful regeneration." Now it is not a matter of getting dunked; it is a matter of saying prayers.

But this is unbiblical. From God's point of view, salvation of the human soul is punctiliar. God saves man; man does not save himself. In that sense, who is "in" and who is "out" is a reality known only to God. But here, evangelicalism's obsession has led us to marry our mission to quantification and confuse categories. Conversion is not a punctiliar process because conversion is the grace-endowed and grace-enabled response of man to God's gift of salvation. Do not misunderstand me. Salvation and in one sense conversion are both God all the way down, but conversion has to do with more than being "saved." Conversion has to do with drawing, deliberating, questioning, exploring, learning, relating, and, yes, believing. But at what point the human heart tips the scales of real belief is a point often known only to God. Our attempts to package it and quantify it and make it measurable are commodifying it for a consumerist church that has no level of comfort with Paul's blatantly ambiguous language about the souls of men and women.

Paul says things like "examine yourself to see if you are in the faith" (2 Cor. 13:5). He sees a mandate to discipline himself as he says, "lest after preaching to others I myself should be disqualified." He seems perfectly comfortable living in the land of ambiguity. Gordon Smith writes:

> Some, indeed many, people are on their way; they are seekers or inquirers. It may not be clear for quite some time whether they are "in" or "out." In the meantime, we live with ambiguity, comfortably so, knowing that a whole range of religious experiences cannot be counted or measured or controlled.[13]

I think if someone asked Paul his "conversion growth rate" his response would have been something like, "How in hades should I know?!"

Practically speaking, evangelicals church leaders must stop trying to package conversion into an unbiblical formula. When the Philippian jailer asked Paul and Silas what he needed to do to be saved, Paul never went for the sinner's prayer. He simply said, "Believe in the Lord Jesus and you will be saved" (Acts 16:31). We must stop counting heads and stop marking notches on our ministry belts. We must communicate the gospel of substitution and kingdom clearly and call people to repentant faith without adding to the Bible an artificial hoop. There is nothing wrong with a stake at the head of the trail but there is everything is wrong if it gets mistaken for the trail itself. We must teach a clear, practical theology of salvation and conversion. We must get comfortable with people coming to faith and not feel like we have to quantify whether they are already there or not.

## A Jesus for the Whole Self

In the last chapter, I shared that evangelical pop culture has privatized the spiritual life and compartmentalized it. Both are serious errors. Privatization severely hampers the accountability necessary for individuals to live in community, to be held to a common standard, and to move forward missionally as a church. If Jesus and I are the only ones who set the rules for our relationship, it is very possible for me to make Jesus overly agreeable to my personal agenda. When Jesus is primarily viewed as my

---

13. Smith, *Transforming Conversion*, 17.

personal savior, it becomes easy to compartmentalize him into areas of lordship.

Evangelicalism's compartmentalization of Christ may be its single greatest deterrent to reaching the culture. Without rehashing the issues highlighted in the previous chapter, let me just propose a local-church response to each.

### Sexuality

The church must lead in propriety while remaining vocal about sexuality. Sex is one of the most important things in human life. It is God's gift and the height of celebrated marital intimacy. It needs to be celebrated more in the church but without condescending to the infantilized language and adolescent humor of pop culture. It is to be treasured not trashed. Prudish notions of a Victorian Christianity remain at the helm of fundamentalism, but have no place in a church that celebrates a Christ of freedom. Illicit notions of an edgy, loose-lipped, and loose-hipped Christianity make light of the freedom of the gospel and damage the countercultural ethic of Jesus.

To heal the church's reputation in sexuality, we must tackle the health of the family. It starts with homes committed to maintain biblical standards of virtue. Homes of virtue demand shepherds and church leaders willing to counsel insecurities, train domestic leaders, heal broken relationships, pray and weep with parents of wayward children, and teach children to honor the home. Healthy homes will ultimately yield a countercultural sexual ethic. There is no room for the church to create a parrot sexual culture. The culture we live in is too far gone. Our commitment to domestic order, protecting the hearts and bodies of the vulnerable, and standing morally against the sexual exploitation and atrocities of our day is vital for a local church looking to make Jesus really relevant to wounded people.

### Media

When it comes to media, the important word for an evangelical church leader to remember is "tool." Media is a tool. It tends to be a subpar form of entertainment but a dynamic form of information and engagement. Instead of always blaming the media and blaming forms of media, we need to realize that we are "kicking against the goads," to use a biblical metaphor. I have concerns about how media gets used, and the church needs to shepherd media. In fact, in local-church life, social-media sites are to shepherding what the Food Network is to diet programs. It could be a useful medium, but man is it hard to control.

However, griping about Internet, blogs, video, podcasting, Twitter, and even the dreaded Facebook is like someone in Orville Wright's day complaining about the airplane. You may not like it, but it isn't going anywhere except up. Media technology in one form or another will be with us as a communicative tool until Christ's return. There are several ways that media technology helps the church. Here are a few:

1. It creates pathways of communication for church leadership church-wide throughout the week.

2. It creates ways to share prayer needs very rapidly.

3. It establishes forums of encouragement when people are in the midst of difficulty.

4. It permits inner-church communication that takes logistical components to a whole new level of efficiency.

5. It permits us to speak into one another's lives during and not just after the fact.

6. It creates a myriad of avenues for the gospel to go out.

7. It extends the reach of the local church outside its own locality.

8. It allows churches and individuals to take advantage of substantive ministry of the Word that would otherwise be unavailable.

9. It allows for live theological, philosophical, spiritual, and cultural discourse to take place despite lack of local proximity.

I like what John Mark Reynolds says: "Christendom needs preserved discourse within a living community."[14] This is what media technology provides.

The local church can use media to critically think about what the broader culture is saying. It can use media to accentuate community. It is a poor replacement for community and should never be seen as such but don't throw the baby out with the bathwater. Fundamentalism tends to view media with suspicion as an enemy. Evangelical pop culture tends to

14. Reynolds, *The New Media Frontier*, 39.

use it indiscriminately. What we need to do is see it as a tool to move the kingdom forward. If it is primarily a distraction, then it will be misused and abused.

## Money

I would encourage the reader to consider much of what was said in chapter 8 in response to Gourmet Jesus. The evangelical church's poor allocation of money is embarrassing to believers and grievous to God. We can't be naïve. Buildings cost money. Staff get salaries. Programs need resourcing. But we have to be reasonable. Why isn't it apparent that campaigns calling for elaborate, modernized cathedrals and fountains and airplanes and elaborate studios and aquariums might not be the best use of God's resources? Church budgets need to reflect biblical theology.

## Celebrity

The answer to Homogenized Celebrity Jesus is very simple: stop feeding him. Celebrity is the result of cultural popularity. Popularity emerges from mutual assent by individuals to consume something or be consumed with it. Perhaps Christian celebrity would decline if evangelical consumerism declined. It is probably fair to say that "consumerism is the most potent competitor to a Christian worldview in our culture."[15] The key phrase is "most potent." The power of wanting more makes us exalt "Christian" products and "Christian" people to heights that end up subverting the Christian gospel. The answer is not rocket science. We just need to stop ridiculous consumption and creaturely exaltation. Not to beat a dead horse, but here is one more swing . . . when we plan vacations to connect with Christian celebrities or call in to win trips from Christian radio or dial in to be the fifth caller to get a backstage pass to meet our Christian Bon Jovi, we have likely gone into absurdity. If we stop feeding the monster he may just go away.

15. Wilkes and Sanford, *Hidden Worldviews*, 60.

## Conclusion

Jesus loves the world. Jesus died for the world. Jesus came to the world, but the world rejected him. The world rejected Jesus' followers too. Jesus prayed for his followers, that they would be united for mission while they remained in the world. Jesus and his relationship to the world set the analogy for our relationship to the world. It is clearly one of alienation and ambassadorship. These are not in opposition but function as complementary roles of pilgrim people.

As Christ's temporary representatives, one of the worst things we can do is to make the One we represent frivolous and inconsequential. To trivialize Jesus is to make him irrelevant. In its midlife crisis of identity, evangelicalism has created a parrot culture to try and win the cool kids. Unfortunately, it has not only been ineffectual; it has been an abject disaster. Now much of evangelicalism is hardly recognizable by historical standards of ecclesiology.

When Jesus gets homogenized with other disparate elements, he becomes difficult to pick out. When he becomes a commodity for consumption, the Christ whose potency can transform culture gets labeled and put on the shelf for those in the market for a Tasty Jesus. May it never be!

# Epilogue

THERE IS AN ORGANIC Jesus. There is a real Christ. He is from eternity and was planted in the soil of human history. He grew like a fruit tree in the rendzina soil of Israel. Who he was stood out like a sore thumb. Fruit trees are pretty easy to identify, just look at what they produce. The problem wasn't unmasking his identity; it was accepting it. Not everyone wants an organic Jesus. He has been polluted by ideological chemicals for millennia. Some have stripped him of his potency by polluting him with the pesticide of naturalism, others with the residue of materialism. Some have showered him with protectant sprays of legalism and rigidity. Some have set free the worms of triviality to eat away at his fruit. Others have tried to cut him down in the name of relevance and social acceptance. However, it is time to reject all of these toxins and attempts to undercut him, and let Jesus be the Christ, and the Christ be Jesus.

I once heard that the accomplished theologian Karl Barth was asked what the greatest theological thought that ever crossed his mind was. He thought and replied: "Jesus loves me! this I know, for the Bible tells me so." His answer was pure art. You cannot sum up the heart of the grand meta-narrative with more beauty and simplicity and precision. But, if your "Jesus" is wrong, then the statement turns from beauty to ashes. The statement itself goes from being creedal to cruel. It becomes a harbinger of death. If you think your de-deified, moralistic Cream Puff Jesus loves you, then you are without hope. If you think your bluenose, exacting No Carb Jesus loves you, then you will forever be pining for that love to be real and felt. If you think your deregulated, vacillating Smorgasbord Jesus loves you, then he has left you with nowhere to stand. If you think your rapacious, subservient Gourmet Jesus loves you, then you will mistake the gift for the Giver. If you think your shallow, puerile Homogenized

Jesus loves you, then you will lose your grip on Christ in the cultural carnival. No Jesus critiqued in this book can love you as the organic Jesus of history, who is not laden with the cultural and philosophical sediment of self-intoxicated minds.

As church leaders, our call is to check our own representations of Jesus. It is to sift through our own presuppositions and see them for what they are. It is to teach our people to do the same. It is not to interpret Jesus afresh. It is not to be christologically innovative. It is simply to pay attention to the winds of history and the timeless rhythms of biblical revelation and reflect who Christ was, is, and always will be. The Christ of history exists to change the hearts of men and women and transform culture by the sheer dynamism of his gospel.

In one sense he is altogether unsavory. He comes not in the package of our predilections, but in a manner all his own. Jesus has loved me deeply and, at times, cut me sharply. He has healed my wounds and, at times, pulled slivers from my soul without much, if any, anesthetic. He has made me soar on heights of grandeur and, at times, made me sail through shadowy swamps. But unrelentingly and unfalteringly he has always, always been with me.

This unsavory Savior must be presented to the world, taught to the church, and ingested into our souls. In the western world we stand on the precipice of losing our theological moorings. It is time for the church to rise and bless the One who bought them and spread his unmitigated fame with doctrinal clarity, dispositional grace, and personal conviction.

# Bibliography

## Books

Allison, Gregg R. *Historical Theology*. Grand Rapids: Zondervan, 2011.
Barker, Dan. *Godless*. Berkeley, CA: Ulysses, 2008.
Bauckham, Richard. *Jesus and the Eyewitnesses*. Grand Rapids: Eerdmans, 2006.
Baxter, Richard, *The Reformed Pastor*. Reprint. Carlisle, PA: The Banner of Truth Trust, 2007.
Beale, David O. *In Pursuit of Purity*. Greenville, SC: Unusual Publications, 1986.
Belcher, Jim. *Deep Church*. Downers Grove, IL: InterVarsity, 2009.
Bell, Rob. *Velvet Elvis*. Grand Rapids: Zondervan, 2005.
Bock, Darrell. *The Missing Gospels*. Nashville: Thomas Nelson, 2006.
Borg, Marcus, and N. T. Wright. *The Meaning of Jesus: Two Visions*. New York: HarperSanFrancisco, 1999.
Bovell, Carlos R. *Inerrancy and the Spiritual Formation of Younger Evangelicals*. Eugene, OR: Wipf and Stock, 2007.
Bowman, Robert, Jr. *The Word-Faith Controversy*. Grand Rapids: Baker, 2001.
———. and J. Ed Komoszewski, *Putting Jesus in His Place*. Grand Rapids: Kregel, 2007.
Burroughs, Jeremiah. *The Rare Jewel of Christian Contentment*. Reprint, Carlisle, PA: Banner of Truth Trust, 1992.
Caputo, John D. *What Would Jesus Deconstruct*. Grand Rapids: Baker, 2007.
Carroll, John. *The Wreck of Western Culture: Humanism Revisited*. Wilmington, DE: ISI Books, 2008.
Carson, D. A. *Becoming Conversant with the Emerging Church*. Grand Rapids: Zondervan, 2005.
———. *Christ and Culture Revisited*. Grand Rapids: Eerdmans, 2008.
Clement. *The First Epistle of Clement to the Corinthians*. Edited by Alexander Roberts and James Donaldson. Ante-Nicene Fathers. Vol. 1, Peabody, MA: Hendrickson, 2004
Copeland, Kenneth. *How You Call It Is How It Will Be*. Fort Worth: Kenneth Copeland Publications, 2010. Kindle edition.
———. *The Laws of Prosperity*. Fort Worth: Kenneth Copeland Publications, 1974. Kindle edition.
Cross, Whitney. *The Burned-over District: The Social and Intellectual History of Enthusiastic Religion in Western New York, 1800–1850*. Ithaca, NY: Cornell University Press, 1981.

## bibliography

Dalhouse, Mark Taylor. *An Island in the Lake of Fire*. Athens, GA: The University of Georgia Press, 1996.
Davis, John Jefferson. *Foundations of Evangelical Theology*. Grand Rapids: Baker, 1984.
Demaus, Robert. *William Tyndale: A Biography*, Edited by Richard Lovett. London: Religious Tract Society, 1886.
Dollar, George W. *A History of Fundamentalism in America*. Greenville, SC: Bob Jones University Press, 1973.
Eddy, Mary Baker. *Science and Health with Key to the Scriptures*. Boston: The First Church of Christ, Scientist: 1994.
Edwards, James. *Is Jesus the Only Savior?*. Grand Rapids: Eerdmanns, 2005.
Ehrman, Bart. *Misquoting Jesus*. New York: HarperCollins, 2005.
Erre, Mike. *The Jesus of Suburbia*. Nashville: W Publishing Group, 2006.
Evans, Christopher, *Liberalism Without Illusions*. Waco, TX: Baylor University Press, 2010.
Fee, Gordon D. *The Disease of the Health and Wealth Gospels*, 2nd ed. Vancouver: Regent College Publishing, 2006. Kindle edition.
———. *1 and 2 Timothy, Titus*. New International Biblical Commentary. Peabody, MA: Hendrickson, 1988.
Foxe, John. *The Acts and Monuments*, Edited by Stephen Reed Cattley, Vol. 5. Reprint. London: R. B. Seeley and W. Burnside, 1838.
Funk, Robert. W. "The Once and Future Jesus." In *The Once and Future Jesus*. 5–25. Santa Rosa, CA: Polebridge, 2000.
———. and the Jesus Seminar. *The Gospel of Jesus: According to the Jesus Seminar*. Santa Rosa, CA: Polebridge, 1999.
———. Roy W. Hoover, and The Jesus Seminar. *The Five Gospels: What Did Jesus Really Say?*. New York: HarperCollins, 1993.
Getz, Gene. *Building Up One Another*. Colorado Springs: David C. Cook, 2002.
———. *Love One Another*. Colorado Springs: David C. Cook, 2002.
Greene, Colin. *Christology in Cultural Perspective*. 2nd ed. Grand Rapids: Eerdmans, 2004.
Grenz, Stanley J. and John R. Franke, *Beyond Foundationalism*. Louisville: John Knox, 2001.
———. and Roger E. Olson. *Who Needs Theology?*. Downers Grove, IL: InterVarsity, 1996.
Hagin, Kenneth. *How God Taught Me about Prosperity*. Broken Arrow, OK: Kenneth Hagin
Ministries Inc, 1985. Kindle edition.
———. *In Him*. Broken Arrow, OK: Kenneth Hagin Ministries Inc, 1975. Kindle edition.
Hannah, John. *An Uncommon Union: Dallas Theological Seminary and American Evangelicalism*. Grand Rapids: Zondervan, 2009.
Harrell, David Edwin. *Oral Roberts: An American Life*. Bloomington: Indiana University Press, 1985.
Harris, Harriet. *Fundamentalism and Evangelicals*. New York: Oxford University Press, 1998.
Henry, Carl F. H. *The Uneasy Conscience of Modern Fundamentalism*. Grand Rapids: Eerdmans, 1947.
Horton, Michael. *Christless Christianity*. Grand Rapids, Baker, 2008.

Irenaeus, *Against Heresies*. Edited by Alexander Roberts and James Donaldson. Ante-Nicene Fathers. Vol. 1, Peabody, MA: Hendrickson, 2004.
Jenkins, Philip. *The New Faces of Christianity: Believing the Bible in the Global South*. New York: Oxford, University Press, 2006. Kindle edition.
Johnson, Luke Timothy. *Sharing Possessions*. 2nd ed. Grand Rapids: Eerdmans, 2011.
Jones, Tony. *The New Christians*. San Francisco: Jossey-Bass, 2008.
Justin Martyr. *Dialogue with Trypho*. Edited by Alexander Roberts and James Donaldson. Ante-Nicene Fathers. Vol. 1, Peabody, MA: Hendrickson, 2004.
Keller, Timothy. *The Reason for God*. New York: Dutton, 2008.
Kennedy, D. James. *Evangelism Explosion*. Carol Stream, IL: Tyndale House, 1996.
Kenyon, E. W. *Claiming Our Rights*. Hopefaithprayer.com. No pages. Online: http://hopefaithprayer.com/books/Claiming%20Our%20Rights%20%20EW%20Kenyon.pdf.
———. *A New Type of Christianity*. Amazon Digital Services Inc., 2010. Kindle edition.
Kruger, Baxter C. *Jesus and the Undoing of Adam*. Jackson, MS: Perichoresis Inc., 2003.
Lasch, Christopher. *The Culture of Narcissism*. New York: W. W. Norton and Company, 1979 Norton Paperback, 1991.
Leith, John. ed. *Creeds of the Churches*. 3rd ed. Louisville: John Knox, 1982.
Lewis, C. S. *The Four Loves*, Grand Rapids: Family Christian Press, 1998.
———. *Mere Christianity*. New York: HarperSanFrancisco, 2001.
———. *The Screwtape Letters*. Reprint, New York: HarperCollins, 2001.
Livingston, James C. *Modern Christian Thought: The Enlightenment and the Nineteenth Century*. Minneapolis: Fortress, 2006.
Lyotard, Jean Francois. *The Postmodern Condition: A Report on Knowledge*. Translated by Geoff Bennington and Brian Massumi, Manchester: Manchester University Press, 1984.
Machen, J. Gresham. *Christianity and Liberalism*. Grand Rapids: Eerdmans, 1923.
Manning, Brennan. *The Wisdom of Tenderness*. New York: HarperCollins, 2002.
Marsden, George M. *Fundamentalism and American Culture*, 2nd ed. New York: Oxford University Press, 2006.
Marty, Martin, and R. Scott Appleby. *The Glory and the Power*. Boston: Beacon, 1992.
McConnell, D. R. *A Different Gospel*. Peabody, MA: Hendrickson, 1995.
McCracken, Brett. *Hipster Christianity*. Grand Rapids: Baker, 2010.
McLaren, Brian. *Everything Must Change*. Nashville: Thomas Nelson, 2007.
———. *A Generous Orthodoxy*. Grand Rapids: Zondervan, 2004. Kindle edition.
———. *A New Kind of Christianity*. New York: HarperCollins, 2010.
———. *The Secret Message of Jesus*. Nashville: W Publishing, 2006.
McMinn, Don. *The 11th Commandment: Experiencing the One Anothers of Scripture*. Irving, TX: 6Acts Press, 2000.
Meyer, Joyce. *Change Your Words, Change Your Life*. New York: Faith Words, 2012.
Meyers, Robin. *Saving Jesus from the Church*. New York: HarperOne, 2009.
Moltmann, Jürgen. *History and the Triune God*. Translated by John Bowden. New York: Crossroad, 1992.
Moore, T. M. *Culture Matters*. Grand Rapids: Brazos, 2007.
Moreland, J. P. *Kingdom Triangle*. Grand Rapids: Zondervan, 2007.
———. and William Lane Craig, *Philosophical Foundations for a Christian Worldview*. Downers Grove, IL: InterVarsity, 2003.

Moritz, Fred. *Be Ye Holy: The Call to Christian Separation*. Greenville, SC: BJU Press, 1994.
Nichols, Stephen J. *Jesus Made in America*. Downers Grove, IL: InterVarsity, 2008.
Nietzsche, Friedrich. *Ecce Homo*. Waxkeep Publishing, 2013. Kindle edition.
Osteen, Joel. *I Declare: 31 Promises to Speak Over Your Life*. New York: Faith Words, 2012.
———. *It's Your Time*. New York: Free Press, 2009.
Pagitt, Doug, and Tony Jones, ed. *An Emergent Manifesto of Hope*. Grand Rapids: Baker, 2007.
Pannenburg, Wolfhart. *Systematic Theology*. Vols. 1 and 2, Translated by Geoffrey Bromiley. Reprint. Grand Rapids: Eerdmanns, 2001.
Pearcey, Nancy R., and Charles B.Thaxton, *The Soul of Science*. Wheaton, IL: Crossway, 1994.
Pearse, Meic. *Why the Rest Hates the West*. Downers Grove, IL: InterVarsity, 2004.
Pelikan, Jaroslav. *The Christian Tradition*: The Emergence of the Catholic Tradition. Chicago: The University of Chicago Press, 1971.
Piper, John. *Desiring God*. Colorado Springs: Multnomah, 2003.
Powley, Mark. *Consumer Detox*. Grand Rapids: Zondervan, 2010.
Prothero, Stephen. *American Jesus*. New York: Farrar, Straus, and Giroux, 2004. Kindle edition.
Ryrie, Charles C. *Ryrie's Practical Guide to Communicating Bible Doctrine*, Nashville: Broadman and Holman, 2005.
Schweitzer, Albert. *The Quest of the Historical Jesus*. Mineola, NY: Dover, 2005.
Simpson, A. B. *The Christ in the Bible Commentary*, Vol. 4. Camp Hill, PA: Christian Publications, 1993.
Sittser, Gerald L. *Love One Another: Becoming the Church Jesus Longs For*. Downers Grove, IL: InterVarsity, 2008.
Sjogren, Bob, and Gerald Robinson. *Cat and Dog Theology*. Rev. Ed. Colorado Springs: Biblica, 2005. Kindle edition
Solomon, Robert C. and Kathleen M. Higgins. *A Short History of Philosophy*. New York: Oxford University Press, 1996.
Spong, John Shelby. *Why Christianity Must Change or Die*. New York: HarperCollins, 1999.
Smith, Gordon T. *Transforming Conversion*. Grand Rapids: Baker, 2010.
Smith, James K. A. *Who's Afraid of Postmodernism*. Grand Rapids: Baker, 2006.
Staub, Dick. *The Culturally Savvy Christian*. San Francisco: John Wiley and Sons, 2007.
Svigel, Michael. *Retro-Christianity*. Wheaton, IL: Crossway, 2012.
Tertullian. *On the Resurrection of the Flesh*. Edited by Alexander Roberts and James Donaldson. Ante-Nicene Fathers. Vol. 1, Peabody, MA: Hendrickson, 2004.
Veith, Gene Edward Jr. *Postmodern Times*. Wheaton, IL: Crossway, 1994.
Webb, William J. *Slaves, Women and Homosexuals*. Downers Grove, IL: InterVarsity, 2001.
Wells, David. *Above All Earthly Pow'rs*. Grand Rapids: Eerdmans, 2005.
———. *The Courage to Be Protestant*. Grand Rapids: Eerdmans, 2008.
Wilkens, Steve, and Alan G. Padgett. *Faith and Reason in the 19th Century*, Vol 2 of *Christianity and Western Thought: A History of Philosophies Ideas and Movements*. Downers Grove, IL: InterVarsity, 2000.

bibliography    295

———. and Mark L. Sanford. *Hidden Worldviews*. Downers Grove, IL: InterVarsity, 2009.
Willard, Dallas. *Knowing Christ Today*. New York: HarperOne, 2009.
Wright, N.T. *The Resurrection of the Son of God*. Minneapolis: Fortress, 2003.
Young, William Paul. *The Shack*. Los Angeles: Windblown Media, 2007.

## Other Material

Arnold, Matthew. "Dover Beach." Victorianweb.org. April 3, 2002. No pages. Online: http://www.victorianweb.org/authors/arnold/writings/doverbeach.html.
Beilby, James K., and Paul Rhodes Eddy. "The Quest for the Historical Jesus." In *The Historical Jesus: Five Views*, edited by James K. Beilby and Paul Rhodes Eddy, 9–54. Downers Grove, IL: InterVarsity, 2009.
Blake, Daniel. "Statistics Suggest Anglican Church of Canada in Huge Decline." Christianitytoday.com. February 13, 2006. No pages. Online: http://www.christianitytoday.com/article/statistics.suggest.anglican.church.of.canada.in.huge.decline/5307.htm.
Billy Graham Center. "Crusade Timeline," Wheaton.edu. 2005. No pages. Online: http://www2.wheaton.edu/bgc/archives/exhibits/NYC57/28timeline.htm.
Bleifuss, Joel. "A Politically Correct Lexicon." inthesetimes.com. February 21, 2007. No pages. Online: http://inthesetimes.com/article/3027/a_politically_correct_lexicon.
Blomberg, Craig L. "Where Do We Start Studying Jesus." In *Jesus Under Fire*, edited by Michael J. Wilkins and J. P. Moreland, 17–50. Grand Rapids: Zondervan, 1995.
Bureau of Economic Analysis. "Widespread Growth Across States in 2011," June 5, 2012. No pages. Online: http://www.bea.gov/newsreleases/regional/gdp_state/2012/pdf/gsp0612.pdf.
Canham, Matt. "Census: Share of Utah's Mormon Residents Holds Steady." Salt Lake Tribune. April 17, 2012. http://www.sltrib.com/sltrib/home3/53909710-200/population-lds-county-utah.html.csp.
Carey, Greg. "Rob Bell Endorses Marriage Equality," Huffingtonpost.com. March 18, 2013 No pages. Online: http://www.huffingtonpost.com/greg-carey/rob-bell-comes-gay-marriage_b_2898394.html.
Christculturenews. "10 Largest Churches in America." Christculturenews.com. June 5, 2012. No pages. Online: http://www.christculturenews.com/10-largest-churches-in-america/.
Church, Forrest. "The Gospel According to Thomas Jefferson." In *The Jefferson Bible*, Thomas Jefferson, 1–31. Boston: Beacon, 1989.
Copeland, Gloria. "Seeing the Unseen." kcm.org. http://www.kcm.org/real-help/article/seeing-unseen.
Driscoll, Mark. "Navigating the Emerging Church Highway," Equip.org, June 10, 2009 http://www.equip.org/articles/navigating-the-emerging-church-highway/.
Evans, Rachel Held. "Why Millennials Are Leaving the Church," CNN.com. July 27, 2013. No pages. Online: http://religion.blogs.cnn.com/2013/07/27/why-millennials-are-leaving-the-church/?hpt=hp_c4.

The Faculty of the School of Religion. "Biblical Separation." bju.edu. No Pages. Online: http://www.bju.edu/academics/college-and-schools/seminary/preachers-corner/publications/separation/.

Girard, René. 1984. "Dionysus Versus the Crucified," *MLN* 99, no. 4: 816–35. *MLA International Bibliography, EBSCOhost*.

Goldberg, Joshua. "Decline in U.S. Mainline Denominations Continues." Christianitytoday. com. February 15, 2010. No pages. Online: http://www.christianitytoday.com/article /decline.in.us.mainline.denominations.continues/25305.htm.

Hart, D.G. "When is a Fundamentalist a Modernist? J. Gresham Machen, Cultural Modernism, and Conservative Protestantism." *Journal of the American Academy of Religion* 65, (1997) no. 3: 605–33. Online: *Academic Search Premier, EBSCOhost*.

Hladky, Kathleen. 2012. "I Double-Dog Dare you in Jesus' Name! Claiming Christian Wealth and the American Prosperity Gospel." *Religion Compass* 6, no. 1: 82–96. *Academic Search Premier, EBSCOhost*.

International Monetary Fund. World Economic Outlook, October 2012. 250 pages. Online: http://www.imf.org/external/pubs/ft/weo/2012/02/pdf/text.pdf.

Jimenez, Fanny. "Social Envy – Study Finds Facebook Causes Depression and Isolation. Worldcrunch.com. January 27, 2013. No pages. Online: http://www.worldcrunch. com/culture-society/social-envy-study-finds-facebook-causes-depression-and-isolation/zuckerberg-social-network-health-depression-fb/c3s10718/.

Kenneth Copeland Ministries. "About KCM." kcm.org. No pages. Online: http://www. kcm. org/about/index.php?p=where_we_are.

Larsen, David L. "The Gospel of Greed Versus the Gospel of the Grace of God." In *The Gospel and Contemporary Perspectives*. edited by Douglas Moo, 72–79. Grand Rapids, Kregel: 1997.

Leonard, Heather, "This is What an Average User Does on Facebook." Businessinsider. com, March 6, 2013. No pages. Online: http://www.businessinsider.com/what-does-an-average-facebook-user-do-2013–13.

The Library of Congress. "List of Sub-Saharan African Countries." November 15, 2010. No pages. Online: http://www.loc.gov/rr/amed/guide/afr-countrylist.html.

Marsden, George M. "Edward J. Carnell." In *Makers of Christian Theology in America*. edited by Mark G. Toulouse and James O. Duke, 484–88. Nashville: Abingdon, 1997.

Mayes, Preston. "Fundamentalism and Social Involvement." *Maranatha Baptist Theological Journal*, 2.1. No pages. Online: http://more.mbbc.edu/journal/volumetwo/Fundamentalism-and-social-involvement/

McBride, William L. "Existentialism." In *The Cambridge Dictionary of Philosophy*, edited by Robert Audi 2nd ed., New York: Cambridge University Press, 1999.

McGee, Matt. "By the Numbers Twitter Vs. Facebook Vs. Google Buzz." Searchengineland. com. February, 23, 2010. No pages. Online: http://searchengineland. com/by-the-numbers-twitter-vs-facebook-vs-google-buzz-36709.

Mencken, H. L. "Dr. Fundamentalis." In *Crossed Fingers*, Gary North, Appendix A. Tyler, TX: Institute for Christian Economics,1996. No pages. Online: http://www. garynorth.com /freebooks/docs/a_pdfs/gncf.pdf.

Oon, Zhihao. 2008. "A Critical Presentation of the Life and Work of Franz Anton Mesmer MD and Its Influence on the Development of Hypnosis." *European Journal Of Clinical Hypnosis* 8, no. 1: 32–40. *Academic Search Premier, EBSCOhost*.

Pingdom. "Internet 2010 in Numbers." Pingdom.com. January, 12, 2011. No pages. Online: http://royal.pingdom.com/2011/01/12/internet-2010-in-numbers/.
Post, John F. "Naturalism." In *The Cambridge Dictionary of Philosophy*, 2nd ed., 2006.
Reisinger, Don. "6.1 Trillion Text Messages to be Sent in 2010." Cnet.com. October 19, 2010. No pages. Online: http://news.cnet.com/8301-13506_3-20020101-17.html.
Reynolds, John Mark. "The New Media: First Thoughts." *The New Media Frontier*. Edited by John Mark Reynolds and Roger Overton, 21–39. Wheaton, IL: Crossway, 2008.
Saddleback Church. "The Venues." No pages. Online: http://www.saddleback.com/flash/venues.html.
Scalia, Antonin. Interviewed by Leslie Stahl. *60 Minutes*. CBS, September 14, 2008.
Steffan, Melissa. "Brian McLaren Leads Commitment Ceremony at Son's Same-Sex Wedding," Christianitytoday.com. September 24, 2012. No pages. Online: http://www.christianitytoday.com/gleanings/2012/september/brian-mclaren-leads-commitment-ceremony-at-sons-same-sex.html.
Stefansson, Vilhjalmur. "Adventures in Diet, Part 1." Harpers Monthly Magazine (Novermber 1935). No pages. Online: http://www.biblelife.org/stefansson1.htm.
Thompson, Keith. *Word of Faith Teachers: Origins and Errors of Their Teaching*. Online documentary. November 8, 2012. http://frontlineapologetics.com/category/prosperity-gospel/.
Van Biema, David, and Jeff Chu, "Does God Want You to be Rich?," Time.com. September 10, 2006, 8 pages. Online: http://www.time.com/time/magazine/article/0,9171,1533448-7,00.html.
Van Loon, Michelle. "In Defense of Church Hoppers." Christianity Today, January 28, 2013 page 2. Online: http://www.christianitytoday.com/women/2013/january/in-defense-of-church-hoppers.html
Van Pelt, Jennifer, "Is Facebook Depression For Real?." Socialworktoday.com. No pages. Online: http://www.socialworktoday.com/archive/exc_080811.shtml.
Wallace, Dan. "My Take on Inerrancy." Bible.org. August 10, 2006. No Pages. Online: http://bible.org/article/my-take-inerrancy.
Willard, Dallas. "Knowledge of Christ in Today's World" (audio). Lecture series.

www.ingramcontent.com/pod-product-compliance
Lightning Source LLC
Chambersburg PA
CBHW070233230426
43664CB00014B/2293